Change in Schools

SUNY Series in Educational Leadership

Daniel Duke, editor

Change in Schools

Facilitating the Process

Gene E. Hall
and
Shirley M. Hord

State University of New York Press

Figure 16 in this volume is from *Implementation Checklist* of the GINN READING
PROGRAM, © Copyright 1984 by Ginn and Company. Used with permission.

Published by
State University of New York Press, Albany

For information, address State University of New York
Press, State University Plaza, Albany, N.Y., 12246

Library of Congress Cataloging in Publication Data

Hall, Gene E., 1941–
   Change in schools.

   (SUNY series in educational leadership)
   Bibliography: p. 365
   Includes index.
   1. School improvement programs—United States.
2. Curriculum change—United States.   3. School
superintendents and principals—United States—Attitudes.
I. Hord, Shirley M.   II. Title.   III. Series.
LB2822.82.H35   1986   371.2'07   86–5714
ISBN 0-88706-346-2
ISBN 0-88706-347-0 (pbk.)

10 9 8 7 6 5 4 3 2

Contents

Preface

In 1971 and 1972 when Dick Wallace, Bill Dossett, and Gene Hall started talking about a "different" change model, one that emphasized the personal side of change, there was little expectation that the proposed concepts would ever be systematically studied or result in useful applications. The group's first assumption, that change was a process not an event, was not in vogue in those days, when delivering a "teacher proof" box of new curricula was accepted as the way to produce immediate change. The second assumption, that the point of view of the individual is a vital consideration in changing an institution, was seen as heresy in terms of the dominant change model of the time. Now, both these assumptions are regularly stated as important and obvious by researchers, practitioners, and policymakers.

We and our colleagues have been fortunate to have the opportunity to pursue this line of thinking by studying the special opportunities offered by practitioners who knew more about change than we did. With them, we have been grounded in the dust and mud of the change process. We have observed and listened, and with our colleagues, we have attempted to make sense out of change in schools and colleges as it is experienced by its participants. From time to time, we have been able to make conceptual and operational breakthroughs. Our ideas and techniques have caught on and have proven to be useful for practice, research, and policy. The goal of this book is to describe these findings, their implications, and the conceptual framework they fit into.

Our work has been organized around a perspective known as the Concerns Based Adoption Model or CBAM (pronounced "see bam"). The concepts and procedures in this model make sense to practitioners and policymakers, for they provide ways to label change process phenomena, to take positive action in facilitating change, and to predict effects. To do these tasks requires a sophisticated understanding of the change process and how it is experienced by participants.

The human side of change is so important to this participant perspective that the key concept in the model's name is *concerns*. The concerns of change process participants are very real, thus attention to this personal side of change is important. It is not just a matter of being humane, it is central to successful progress in change. For new technologies and innovations to be used effectively, the users must become confident and competent in their use. The diagnostic techniques, intervention procedures, and procedures for monitoring the change process are the focus of this book. They provide the tools that change facilitators can learn to use and that will increase these individuals' effectiveness in helping participants gain confidence and competence.

The CBAM concepts and procedures provide ways of thinking about, communicating about, and doing something about change; we have valued our roles in the research team that has studied these ideas. We hope that you, the reader, will find them interesting, informative, thought provoking and applicable to your situation, whether as practitioner, researcher, or policymaker.

Acknowledgments

The concepts and study findings represented in this book are the results of extensive work, discussion, and, on occasion, intense debate among past and present members of the Texas-based CBAM staff. It is hard to think of these experiences we have had as work, for they have been stimulating opportunities for growth. Our colleagues at the Research and Development Center for Teacher Education who have engaged with us in the development of these ideas and who have significantly contributed are: Oliver Bown, Bill Dossett, Frances Fuller, Archie George, Marcia Goldstein Toprak, Teresa Griffin, Susan Heck, Leslie Huling-Austin, Susan Loucks-Horsely, Beulah Newlove, Bill Rutherford, Suzie Stiegelbauer, Joe Vaughan, Dick Wallace, and Pat Zigarmi.

We would also like to recognize fellow researchers who have contributed their ideas and study findings and the scores of practitioners who have allowed us to learn from them and their experiences—a very long list of friends and colleagues. Of particular importance to us and this work have been the special contributions of the following: Robin Matthews, Marge Melle, Jeff Northfield, Harold Pratt, John Thurber, Rudolf van den Berg, and Roland Vandenberghe.

Finally, we express our immense gratitude and abundant thanks to Janet McCord and Antoinette Rhodes, word processor wizards and colleagues extraordinaire, who labored long, hard, and untiringly to prepare this manuscript for publication. No other persons could have taken our scribbles and scrawls and made sense of them.

Chapter 1

The Concerns-Based Approach: An Overview

Principal
What a year! What a relief that summer is here and students and staff are gone. We really came a long way with the new schoolwide math program. I'm especially pleased that I was able to work with the "reluctant" seventh-grade team and help them gain the confidence to come along with the program—quite an accomplishment. Yes, quite an accomplishment!

High School Science Teacher
How would I ever have made it with this inquiry science curriculum if our principal hadn't come by regularly bringing equipment, helping me understand the lessons, and even teaching with me!

Elementary School Teacher
You wouldn't believe what I observed the principal doing! From information she collected from her teachers she made plans and got the first-grade parents involved in helping the teachers. The parents get the program materials ready so the teachers can use them with the pupils. This idea by the principal was folowed by another idea involving the school's permanent substitute who helps teachers in the same area. This principal is developing a whole range of creative activities to support the use of the new language arts materials by the teachers.

Throughout our years of research and experience, we have never seen a situation in which the principal was not a significant factor in the efforts of schools to improve. We do not mean to suggest that in all cases the principals were positively effective; but

1

rather, regardless of what they did, it directly affected the process of change and improvement in their schools. We also have observed that both men and women can be effective, as well as less effective, principals and that there are definite patterns to the behaviors and techniques that the more and less effective principals use in their change facilitator role. We further believe that, with guidance and training, many principals can become more effective in facilitating change. There are research-based tools and techniques that can help principals and other change facilitators reach this goal. The techniques are based upon the concepts and findings of the research we and our colleagues have done.

The premise that principals can make a positive difference is not taken lightly. Only after extensive observation and research have we come to this position. In our studies, we have observed and interviewed thousands of teachers and hundreds of principals. In addition, we have worked closely with college and university faculty, staff developers, central office administrators, and key personnel in intermediate units, state education agencies, and federal agencies. Throughout all these experiences, we have observed differences in how principals spend their time, how they approach the work of being a change facilitator, and how they set priorities. Clearly, these differences have effects on teachers and on their classroom practices. The specifics on how principals exert this influence have been clarified gradually. We can now identify and describe an array of techniques that principals can use to affect directly the concerns of teachers, classroom practices, and ultimately student achievement.

In this book, we will summarize the findings from fourteen years of research and observation. The research has been done in elementary schools, high schools, and in schools and colleges of education. The focus will be upon identifying and describing the tools, techniques, and approaches individuals can use to be more effective as change facilitators.

Although much of our emphasis will apply to principals, we believe the propositions and concepts set forth here are equally applicable to others concerned about and interested in becoming more successful change facilitators. These "others" can be assistant principals, department chairpersons, lead teachers, or grade-level chairpersons at the school level. At the district level, curriculum coordinators or consultants, subject specialists, staff developers, and district office administrators can use this information. All these persons and others such as staff members in intermediate units and regional laboratories and National Diffusion Network facilitators, can be change facilitators, and this book is addressed to all of them.

This book offers two sets of potentially useful information. The first set, which has already been referred to, includes the concepts and procedures anyone can use to facilitate change. The second, particularly important set also has to do with understanding the dynamics of the change process, but when individual teachers are the unit of analysis, when the innovation(s) is the unit of analysis, when interventions are the units of analysis, or when the school is the unit of analysis. To be most effective in facilitating change, principals in the schools and persons in the district offices and elsewhere must understand the dynamics of the change process as it occurs *within* schools. The change process can be perceived quite differently by outsiders and participants. Bridging this gap is an essential first step for effective change facilitators.

Earlier, we referred to principals as "change facilitators." This definition arose because one focus of our research has been on that part of the principal's role having to do with facilitating school improvement and implementing educational innovations. Admittedly, there are many more responsibilities of and roles played by school principals; however, a key role is that of change facilitator for their campuses. What they do, how they do it, when they do it, and to whom they do it make major differences. Principals know that what they do can make a difference. Teachers, policymakers, and researchers also know principals can bring about change. There is an extensive body of literature that points out the importance of the relationship between what principals do and what happens in schools; yet, identifying the concrete concepts and techniques practicing principals use daily has been difficult. Only in the last ten to fifteen years have research-based procedures been sufficiently well documented and described to enable development of concrete recommendations on how to become more effective.

Our present ideas on how principals and others can become

more effective change facilitators is the subject of this book, and we begin in this chapter by briefly describing the concepts and tools we have developed, as well as by introducing the key assumptions that underly our research and conceptual framework. In the remaining chapters, the concepts, research findings, and examples are described in more detail. At certain points, the research we and our colleagues have done is related to the research of others. In this way, readers will gain a new repertoire of resources with which to examine their own change facilitating behaviors, their plans, and the ways they view the change process as it unfolds for teachers, students, central office personnel, and others. We believe readers can become more effective as a result of this examination and through appropriate use of the tools and concepts herein described; however, it will require practice, further training, and coaching to gain maximum benefits.

The Purpose of This Book

Principals have been one of the focuses of recent research on school effectiveness. Principals have also been a center of attention in the concerns being expressed about the decrease in children's reading ability and in their scores on standardized achievement tests. Increasingly, the principal is being held accountable for the performance of students. The argument goes this way: if students are to have the greatest possible cognitive and affective gains, the schools will need to do the best possible instructional job. The most significant way to improve schools is through improving the instructional performance of teachers. Changing a teacher's practices and improving instruction is the bottom line, but teachers need assistance to change and develop. Who provides the leadership that facilitates teachers' improvement? There are several persons who can conceivably help teachers, but the most obvious individual is the principal. Not only is the principal legally responsible for what happens in a school, but the principal is in a special position. The principal is on-site, is knowledgeable about and in touch with the setting and context, is at the center of communication lines, controls resources, and has the power base to make a difference. Principals are seen as equivalent to managers in industry, and they are accountable for the productivity of their unit. Since there is a lot of truth to this argument, we decided to focus primarily on the change facilitator role of the principal. As we mentioned in the preceding pages, however, the concepts about which we are talking are generic and are powerful tools for use by others.

The concepts and results of our research are based on a particular approach we refer to as the *concerns-based approach*. This approach comes from a conceptual framework known as the Concerns-Based Adoption Model (CBAM), originally proposed in 1973 (Hall, Wallace, and Dossett). One particularly important precondition in the concerns-based approach is that the effective change facilitator understand how his or her clients (e.g., teachers) perceive change and adjust what he or she does accordingly. In too many cases in the past, it appeared that change facilitators based their interventions (i.e., what they did) on their own needs and time lines rather than on their clients' needs and change progress. As the first step, the concerns-based perspective places utmost importance upon understanding the clients.

For schools to improve, teachers must change. For teachers to change, there must be appropriate and promising practices and procedures (i.e., innovations) that they develop or adopt and, when necessary, adapt. Student achievement and other desired outcomes are enhanced when teachers improve their practices and use more effective instructional resources. Thus, the first order of business for school principals and other change facilitators is to understand the practices of teachers and their concerns about changing.

We believe that addressing and facilitating change can be done in humane and understanding ways. One of the strengths of the concerns-based approach is that it emphasizes, first of all, understanding teacher attitudes and skills so that support activities, such as staff development, coaching, provision of materials, and so on, can be directly related to what teachers perceive they need. Historically, teachers have all too often been provided with workshops, materials, and other resources based on the needs of others rather than on an understanding of teachers' needs.

Basically, we believe principals are responsible for their

schools' continual efforts to improve. For progress to occur, they must provide leadership in the school improvement process. They must work closely with teachers and have a well-developed picture of what is going on in the classrooms and across the school. They should understand the characteristics of the innovations being implemented and be able to anticipate some of the problems that might arise. However, other change facilitators can also play key roles, and we certainly believe principals cannot facilitate change alone. As will be pointed out in chapter 9, one result of our research has been the identification of a key second change facilitator/consigliere, who plays a very significant and complementary role to the principal's. Thus, another very important emphasis in this book is on creating and maintaining a concerns-based *change facilitating team.*

This book is written for those who wish to become more effective change facilitators. To this end, we have placed heavy emphasis on describing concepts and tools from our research that can be used in practice. More effective change facilitators understand the change process and its dynamics and are able to analyze school improvement efforts systematically. We will describe concepts and present the results of research, introducing references and other resources that can be used to develop skills and perspectives.

In one book, it is not possible to relate all the possible techniques and procedures or to prepare the reader to take on all situations. We believe, however, that careful students of the concerns-based approach will learn enough about the concepts and techniques to begin testing them in appropriate settings. The person who wishes to become skilled in using these concepts will need to study further. Further information can be obtained by accessing the references and resources identified in the book and through contacting one or more of the certified trainers listed in Appendix A. With practice and reflection, change facilitators can become more effective, and, consequently, efforts to change will be more successful.

Let us now set the stage with some background about our work and its underlying assumptions, with an overview of key concepts, and with some suggestions about the implications.

Background of the Concerns-Based Approach

The ideas for the Concerns-Based Adoption Model and for the tools and techniques that have been developed emerged out of the research and practice opportunities we and our colleagues have engaged in since the early 1970s. During this time, the value of many of the innovations that had been introduced in schools was questioned. It became increasingly apparent that the post hoc evaluations of the many educational innovations were only half correct. Evaluators were right to report "no significant differences" related to the innovations, but incorrect to conclude that the innovations were at fault; rather, we believe that the process of implementing these innovations had gone awry or was not fully addressed. Consequently, the innovations were frequently not fully implemented and, therefore, not fairly tested.

This situation led us to observe more closely the experiences of teachers and college professors as they adopted and implemented educational innovations. Seemingly, there was more to change than simply delivering the innovation "box" to the classroom door; rather, a *process* was involved. We hypothesized that there was a set of developmental stages and levels teachers and others moved through as they became increasingly sophisticated and skilled in using new programs and procedures. From our field observations and studies, we documented examples and began to describe these stages and levels, thereby contributing to the Concerns-Based Adoption Model. Subsequently, we observed and documented what various change facilitators, including school principals, were doing to address and attend to the different stages and levels teachers were experiencing. Through this work and related studies of others, a large and comprehensive research base has been developed.

We have chosen our words carefully when interpreting our data and discussing the findings with practitioners, policymakers, and researchers. We have also clarified many of the assumptions underlying our approach. Some of the concepts we use are defined here in special ways, as part of explicating the Concerns-Based Adoption Model (CBAM). Other terms are used as general labels for phenomena. In each case, we offer our definition for the term or concept, and we use examples to illustrate our usages. We hope readers will be able to relate their particular experiences to our descriptions and thus derive more meaning from them. By using the same language to describe research findings and practice, it will be possible to link the abstractions with the "real world," thereby bringing both into clearer focus. But first, our assumptions.

Assumptions/Perspective

There are several important assumptions and assertions that underlie the CBAM work. Some of them are presented here, and additional assumptions will be outlined as they become relevant.

1. UNDERSTANDING THE POINT OF VIEW OF THE PARTICIPANTS IN THE CHANGE PROCESS IS CRITICAL. There is a personal side to change that is frequently ignored. As has been emphasized already, we believe that, for change to be successful, the perceptions of the clients (e.g., teachers) must be understood by themselves and by the change facilitators. Without understanding where the clients "are," only through chance will the interventions made by change facilitators address the needs of innovation users and nonusers. One reason that change processes are not successful and that many worthwhile actions meant to support change are rejected by the participants is that interventions are not made at appropriate times, places, or in ways perceived by the clients as relevant. How many times do we need to hear teachers say, "Oh, now I understand what she was trying to say last year. It sure didn't make sense then," before we begin to take seriously their perceptions as a key part of the diagnosis? In chapter 3 we will be describing, as one diagnostic component, ways in which change facilitators can assess and interpret client "concerns." By understanding concerns, change facilitators can be more certain that their interventions are relevant to the needs perceived by their clients.

2. CHANGE IS A PROCESS, NOT AN EVENT. This assumption was first articulated by us in 1972, and it is still critical to our understanding of change. Until very recently, change facilitators, policymakers, and researchers tended to view change as an event. Policymakers would announce that a change was to occur on a particular date. The innovation would be delivered to the school,

and it was assumed teachers used it. It was also assumed that the teachers used the innovation appropriately. Summative evaluations were concluded during the first year of use. Subsequently, the innovation was judged a success or failure, and the next "fix" was selected for adoption. More recently, it has become clear, especially through CBAM research, that there is a process involved in implementing educational innovations and that this process requires time. Furthermore, there are phases and steps in the process that can be used to plan and pace change.

3. IT IS POSSIBLE TO ANTICIPATE MUCH THAT WILL OCCUR DURING A CHANGE PROCESS. We are often amused when change facilitators are surprised by some occurrence we could "see" coming. We believe it is possible for change facilitators to anticipate much that will occur during any change process. There are many predictable events and happenings. The most likely reactions to typical interventions and the emergence of particular needs can be anticipated. As a consequence, many aspects of the change process can be planned. By planning for the likely, the effective facilitator is better able to handle unanticipated occurrences and to utilize more effectively his or her limited time and resources.

4. INNOVATIONS COME IN ALL SIZES AND SHAPES. The term *innovation* is used in this book to represent the program or process being implemented. It does not necessarily represent something major, new, large, or dramatically different. An innovation can be something introduced several years earlier or something not expected to arrive for several years to come. Further, innovations can be either *product* innovations, such as new textbooks or curriculum materials, or they can be *process* innovations, such as different approaches to discipline, counseling techniques, or instructional procedures. The reader should keep in mind that for most of the discussion in this book, we will assume the innovation has positive attributes and is appropriate for the setting. At several points, we will decribe what happens when "bad" or inappropriate innovations are introduced.

5. INNOVATION AND IMPLEMENTATION ARE TWO SIDES OF THE CHANGE PROCESS COIN. In all cases, regardless of the type of change, in addition to the steps and procedures employed for developing the innovation, there is a parallel set of steps and procedures for its implementation. More has been written about the procedures to be

used in developing educational innovations than about how to implement them. Innovation development plans rarely take into account the complementary set of steps necessary to ensure that the innovation is used. In more successful change efforts, we have observed that there is a parallel set of policies and procedures that address implementation and the change process is viewed as consisting of innovation development plus implementation.

6. TO CHANGE SOMETHING, SOMEONE HAS TO CHANGE FIRST.. The ultimate effectiveness of an innovation depends on whether teachers and others change to incorporate the new practice. Thus, attention must be given to individuals and their nonuse/use of the new practice. Once an understanding of the individual has been developed, there are ways to aggregate individual data and examine the change process for an entire school or district. The first step, however, is to develop a picture of how each staff member, as an individual, experiences the change process. Only then is it appropriate to aggregate the individuals and plan the change process for all involved staff.

7. EVERYONE CAN BE A CHANGE FACILITATOR. All too frequently, responsibility for facilitating change is assigned to one person, such as the school principal, and everyone else assumes the job is done. Everyone in a school can be a change facilitator, however, including teachers. Parents, textbook sales representatives, intermediate unit staff, and sometimes even students make interventions intended to help teachers use innovations. Change facilitation for an organization is not a task that can be assigned to one person and then forgotten. Ultimately, change facilitation is a combination of workshops, telephone calls, newsletters, conversations in the lounge, and tips—tasks that we all do. Change facilitation is a shared responsibility that, in the most successful schools, involves everyone at one time or another.

These assumptions are parameters that guide the concerns-based approach. As the reader will see, they become cornerstones for the concepts, tools, and procedures that will be developed in more detail in later chapters. Essentially, we are advocating that change is a process for and by people. It has its technical side and its human side. It starts and ends with individuals, who in combination make our schools effective. The concerns-based approach offers a research-verified way for us to think about, plan for, monitor, and facilitate change, a way that takes into account the assumptions described above. There is, of course, more to change than can be represented in any single framework or model; however, here we can share some of the concepts that help by providing handholds and milestones useful in developing movement and charting progress. The concepts of the CBAM offered in the remainder of this book have been shown to have this utility.

Overview of CBAM Concepts

Since the Concerns-Based Adoption Model (CBAM) represents the conceptual framework for the research and theory to be described, it is important for the reader to start developing a picture of the essential elements of the model. A graphic representation of the model is included as figure 1. Clearly, no framework can capture all the complexity of the change process, but it should organize the phenomena and provide some keys. The keys in the CBAM model are labeled in figure 1 and represent the major elements—the subject of our research.

Note the Change Facilitator (CF) in the framework. Change facilitators can be principals, teachers, district personnel, intermediate and higher education personnel, and others who, for brief or extended periods, assist various individuals and groups in developing the competence and confidence needed to use a particular innovation. We have deliberately chosen the term facilitator rather than the more traditional term, change agent, since we believe facilitation is, indeed, the task about which we are talking. The term agent suggests a power-invested, one-way, coercive/manipulative approach to change that from our research and experience, appears to be unreasonable and impossible. The facilitator's job is to facilitate, which means to assist others in ways relevant to their concerns so that they become more effective and skilled in using new programs and procedures.

The *change facilitator* is thus a key in the CBAM model. The change facilitator can be a line administrator, such as a school principal; however, he or she can also be a member of the staff, such as a teacher or central office curriculum coordinator. Each

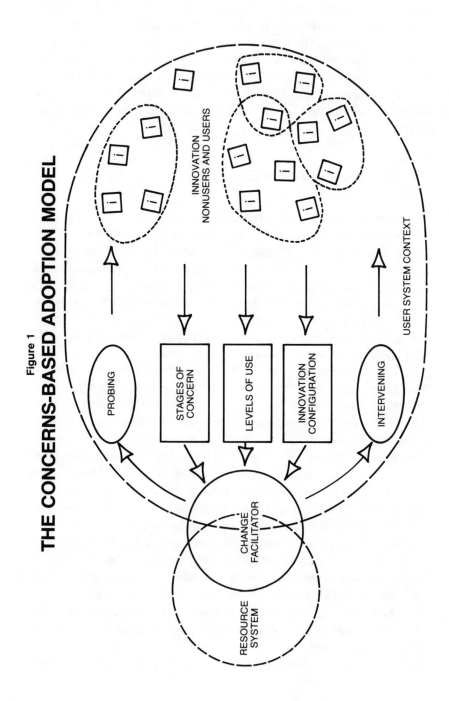

Figure 1

THE CONCERNS-BASED ADOPTION MODEL

person's place in the organizational chart clearly makes a difference in what he or she can and cannot do; yet, all effective facilitators respond and deliver their actions in similar ways, based on the needs of their teachers at any particular time. In other words, there are some generic competencies and skills change facilitators should have regardless of their placement within the organization.

Change facilitators have a *resource system* they can utilize. A principal in a large suburban or urban district, for example, has access not only to his or her own professional library, but perhaps also to an assistant principal, other teachers, and various resources of the central office, including staff developers and curriculum coordinators. In combination, these resources can be quite powerful. The dilemma for the change facilitator, though, is to determine which resources to use, when to use them, and how to use them. Making such decisions requires an ongoing concerns-based diagnosis.

In the CBAM model, change facilitators are responsible for using informal and systematic ways to *probe* individuals and groups to understand them. Three dimensions have been identified and verified through research for accomplishing this diagnosis: *Stages of Concern (SoC), Levels of Use (LoU),* and *Innovation Configurations (IC).* With these three sets of diagnostic data in mind, the change facilitator is informed enough to provide *interventions*—actions that affect and facilitate teachers' use of new programs or practices.

The three diagnostic dimensions, Stages of Concern, Levels of Use, and Innovation Configurations, represent key aspects of the change process as it is experienced by individual users. The Stages of Concern dimension addresses how teachers or others perceive an innovation and how they feel about it. Seven different Stages of Concern have been identified. These range from early "self" type concerns, which are more teacher focused, to "task" concerns, which address the logistics and scheduling arrangements with regard to the use of the innovation, and ultimately to "impact" kinds of concerns, which deal more with increasing the effectiveness of the innovation. Research has demonstrated that at different points in the change process, different Stages of Concern will be more intense. Thus, one key for the change facilitator

is to know whether a teacher has more intense self, task, or impact types of concerns. The implication is that the content as well
as the design of the facilitators' interventions will depend upon
which concerns are more and less intense.

Similar reasoning applies to the second diagnostic dimension,
Levels of Use of the innovation. Levels of Use addresses what a
teacher is doing or not doing in relation to the innovation. In the
past, use was considered to be a dichotomous variable; a teacher
either was or was not using the innovation. With understanding
of the Levels of Use dimension, the question becomes not one of
use or nonuse, but of what level of use?

Three different levels of *nonuse* have been identified. They
describe those who are taking "no action" to learn about an innovation to the person who has decided to use it. Five different
use levels have been determined. These begin with mechanical
use, where teachers are closely adhering to the user's manual and
attempting to adjust their behavior to take into account unanticipated events associated with inexperience in using the innovation. Ultimately, users will move on to routine and later, perhaps,
to refinement use, where they make adaptations in the use of the
innovation to increase its effectiveness and impact in their
classrooms. Levels of Use, or how teachers are using an innovation, is specific input for the facilitator in determining how to help
teachers become increasingly successful and effective in using the
innovation.

The third diagnostic dimension, Innovation Configurations,
addresses the innovation itself. This diagnostic dimension focuses
on describing the operational forms an innovation can take.
Teachers may adapt, or in some cases, mutate the innovation as
they become involved in its use. Through Innovation Configurations, it is possible to identify and describe the adaptations that
are in use and plan one's interventions in accordance with the actual operational form of an innovation in particular classrooms.

These three diagnostic dimensions, Stages of Concern, Levels
of Use, and Innovation Configurations, are independent concepts.
A person can be at any particular Stage of Concern and Level of
Use with any particular configuration of the innovation at any
given time. Therefore, the concerns-based change facilitator continually probes to assess the current state of teachers in each of

these dimensions. Diagnosis must be ongoing, and various procedures ranging from one-legged conferences to systematic questionnaires have been developed for meeting this goal. Each of the diagnostic dimensions and their assessment techniques is described in chapters 3, 4, and 5.

Another key to the change process in the CBAM is understanding the *interventions* that change facilitators make. The actions and events that influence teachers' use of an innovation are the basis for the change facilitator's efforts. Once a diagnostic profile is developed, something must be done. In our workshops and elsewhere, we have spent a lot of time insisting that change facilitators "do something." We have learned that action is one of the significant differences between more effective and less effective change facilitators. More effective change facilitators rarely miss an opportunity to do something. They watch for opportunities to take actions, even small ones, to foster and facilitate teachers' mastery of new programs and procedures. Understanding the different sizes and characteristics of interventions is important for change facilitators. Connecting interventions with each other and monitoring one's own intervention behaviors are also keys. As part of our research, we have developed a taxonomy for analyzing the interrelationships between interventions and for analyzing the internal parts of each intervention. Chapters 6 and 7 are devoted to describing Intervention Taxonomy and Anatomy of Interventions, and their use as analytic tools.

Context is also critical in understanding the change process. Different contexts place different constraints on what change facilitators can do and, at the same time, generate unique opportunities for facilitating change. Whether the change facilitator is a classroom teacher, assistant principal, central office coordinator, or whomever, they operate in a particular context. We do not believe that context in and of itself determines the success or failure of change efforts. Instead, change facilitators apparently differ in how skilled and effective they are in interpreting and using their context. More effective change facilitators seem able to identify opportunities in their contexts, while less effective change facilitators, in very similar contexts, perceive more constraints and therefore fewer opportunities to facilitate. We do not believe in being passive victims of context. The importance of context cannot be overlooked and will permeate our discussions.

Another key to the concerns-based perspective is represented in the arrows within the graphic representation presented in figure 1. If change is a process, not an event, then it is critical for the change facilitator to be *adaptive*; furthermore, they should be *systemic* in their thinking. The most powerful framework developed in recent years for analyzing change has been adaptive systems theory, with the related mathematical and practical applications derived from it (Bellman and Kalba 1958, 1959; Bellman 1961). In education, little has been done to introduce change facilitators and others to this way of thinking. According to the adaptive systems framework, change facilitators must continually adapt their behaviors based on new information about clients, contexts, and the effects of interventions on the individuals in the organization. By consistently gathering information about the state of the system, facilitators can adapt and adjust their behavior to be more relevant. As they make interventions, the system state changes, affecting individuals, groups, and their interrelationships. Thus, change facilitators must continue to assess the new system state and to use this data as the new diagnostic basis for making interventions. The effective change facilitator is constantly probing, adapting, intervening, monitoring, and listening to the client system. The effective change facilitator thinks *systemically* about how a change or alteration in one element of the system will affect other elements and subsets of the system. This ongoing, adaptive process is similar in many ways to how a biological organism adapts to its context or how human body systems shift and adapt depending on whether one has just eaten steak or candy. The CBAM model provides a set of concepts and tools to help change facilitators think and work in this same manner. Discussing ways to do this constant probing–adapting–intervening–probing–adapting–intervening is what this book is about. It is also about the people in the process, how to respond to their needs and perceptions and how to support their professional and personal growth, relative to the use of worthwhile innovations.

Implications

The concerns-based approach represents a unique way of looking at the change process. All too frequently innovations are "laid on" teachers or presented during an August "God bless you" workshop. The teachers are then left to struggle and discover through trial and error what the innovation is about and how to use it effectively. When a concerns-based approach is used, change facilitators work in concert with teachers to address their emerging and evolving needs. In this way, not only is change viewed as a process, but the personal side of change as experienced by teachers is taken into account.

From extensive research and research application results, we know that this approach can make a difference. It can make a difference with the recipients of change, most often teachers, and it makes a difference with students, the ultimate target of improvement efforts. Once innovation users are confident and competent in their use of the new practice, they can afford to be more concerned about how their work is influencing students.

Perhaps a noneducational illustration will help readers clarify the picture we are trying to develop. Let us use the simple innovation of driving a car. From Levels of Use data, we would be able to determine whether or not a person is a driver or not a driver. For example, the person at Level III Mechanical use, mentioned earlier, would be apt to step on the brake too hard, forget to push in the clutch, shift in disjointed ways, and focus entirely on the next ten yards of the road. By contrast, the person at Level IVa Routine use would be able to drive from one place to another by smoothly operating the clutch, anticipating the entire trip, and not focusing overly much on the next turn in the road. The nonuser would be doing absolutely nothing to learn about driving a car, and no behaviors would suggest the person had the abilities to drive a car.

Stages of Concern information would reveal how the driver feels about and perceives driving the car. Perhaps you can remember the "self" concerns you felt the first time you sat behind the wheel, engine off, and went through the motions, mentally regarding your competence and skill in driving and whether or not you could aim the car correctly. Self concerns are a very real and appropriate part of the change process. The change facilitators (in this case the driver education teacher and parents) will need to be reassuring and supportive when addressing self concerns. They will also probably want to spend more time addressing the task concerns dealing with details such as getting the car into gear and down the road.

Immediately, then, the change facilitator has two diagnostic dimensions to work with—Levels of Use (Do they drive?) and Stages of Concern (How do they feel about driving?). The third diagnostic dimension, Innovation Configurations, adds a very important piece of information—in this case, the kind of car being driven. There would be quite a difference in the approach to driver education depending on whether the innovation configuration is a Volkswagen Beetle, a Cadillac Seville, a Ferrari 308GT, or a Kenworth with 15-speed road ranger transmission. The driver education instructor needs to be adaptive in his/her coaching, based not only on the concerns and use patterns of the driver but also on the vehicle being driven.

The same procedure must be followed by the change facilitator in the educational environment. Attention should be given to teachers' concerns and levels of use, and on the configuration of the innovation they are using. How to accomplish all this and what these concepts really mean will be explained in detail in the remaining chapters.

One point of caution for the reader: Do not assume that you fully understand these various concepts from what you have read in this chapter. As a colleague of ours in New Mexico pointed out one time (and many others since), the concepts are "deceptively simple." Due to the labeling and to the fact that they implicitly make good sense, it is possible to talk about the concepts in rather superficial terms. For example, the car-driving analogy sounds straightforward. The same concepts can be used to develop a very complex description, however, as when teachers and others are involved in establishing an effective school or in implementing a major innovation bundle such as mainstreaming. There can be a great deal of subtlety and sophistication in the use of any one of the CBAM concepts. In combination, they provide a very powerful set of resources for the change facilitator, but the facilitator needs in-depth understanding and skills to use them well.

Another caution: The effective change facilitator always checks his or her diagnosis with clients before acting. It is one thing to describe a set of diagnostic concepts and intervention procedures; it is quite another to apply these ideas to real-life situations. The first thing to be done after developing a diagnostic profile is to use various procedures for checking whether or not the diagnostic profile is accurate and if the situation is still the same. This checking can be done in informal ways such as listening to what people are saying and doing.

For the change facilitator, study and practice with CBAM concepts will produce a set of tools and procedures that can be used to monitor the change process, diagnostic data to facilitate implementation, and planning concepts to show where and how activities should advance. Thus, the change facilitator can increase his or her effectiveness through using these processes and procedures. For the evaluator interested in monitoring the change process and for the theoretician or policymaker, these concepts and procedures can make a difference in how successfully change is planned and assessed. There should be something in this book for every reader interested in the change process.

The Rest of This Book

The remaining chapters of this book, with the exception of chapters 2, 10, and 11, are designed to introduce one of the basic dimensions making up the Concerns-Based Adoption Model. The book has been designed so that each chapter is read in sequence, beginning with chapter 1 and continuing through chapter 11. Additional references that may be useful to the reader in applying different concepts are cited in each chapter.

We concede that some readers will want to skip around. This can be done; however, the reader will lose some information and insight, since to some extent the chapters build from one to the next. In each chapter, key elements and concepts are described, and a combination of research findings, diagrams, and field examples are used to illustrate the concepts and procedures. In nearly all cases, easy-to-use clinical procedures are described.

Also available are research techniques that have the necessary reliability and validity characteristics for more rigorous assessment and monitoring purposes. The reader will know enough after each chapter to be just a little dangerous to themselves and others, for applying these ideas requires more than just reading. With practice, however, it is possible to become an effective concerns-based change facilitator; therefore, we hope the reader will be able to participate in training workshops or other forms of consultation after reading this book. Coaching and monitoring to see that the practice of these procedures is on target is important.

In chapter 2, the recent literature on change is reviewed. As was mentioned above, chapters 3, 4, and 5 are explorations of the three diagnostic dimensions of the Concerns-Based Adoption Model. In each chapter, a concept is described in detail, measurement procedures are introduced, and illustrations of the concept at work are provided.

Chapter 6 addresses the smallest unit of interventions, incident interventions. The importance of incident interventions is regularly underestimated by practitioners as well as by policymakers and researchers. We found in our studies that incident interventions were the key to the success or failure of change efforts. We feel so strongly about their importance that we have devoted an entire chapter to developing the reader's understanding of incident interventions.

In chapter 7, the levels of interventions and the development of an intervention game plan are explored. The incident interventions, although experienced apart, add up. In more effective and successful change efforts, these incident interventions aggregate in meaningful and collective ways so that the entire intervention game plan advances innovation use.

Chapter 8 addresses another part of the CBAM research by examining the *style* a facilitator uses. Although all change facilitator styles have not been examined, three contrasting styles have been the subject of study. The *responder, manager,* and *initiator* styles represent very different approaches school principals have used. There are clear and significant relationships between the change facilitator styles principals use and the resultant program implementation success by teachers. In this chapter, we examine the three styles, the behavioral indicators of the styles, and the implications of using the styles for effective change.

Chapter 9 emphasizes a very important finding. In our research on principals, we were surprised to discover that "principals don't do it alone!" In addition to the principal, in all our study sites we identified a second change facilitator or consigliere who played a very key role in facilitation. In fact, the consigliere and the principal seemed to work in complementary ways. In more effective schools, we found the consigliere and the principal making many more interventions together than in the less effective schools, and the relationship between them was more meaningful and substantive. In this chapter, the details of these analyses and the importance of the consigliere role are developed.

Chapter 10 illustrates how to put together all aspects of the concepts discussed. In this chapter, the diagnostic concepts, the assumptions about change, the adaptive systemic perspective, and the attention to the personal side of change are combined with illustrations and examples from research and practice. In this way, we hope the reader will develop a more complete picture, since in the previous chapters the units are rather isolated. In chapter 10, we bring the ideas back together with much more detail than was possible in the introductory chapter.

A final chapter discusses theoretical interrelationships of the diagnostic concepts and provides practical considerations about using the tools of the change process. The chapter concludes with suggestions for needed research and possible next steps.

Chapter 2

The Literature: Leadership For Change

The research is based on the assumption that meaningful change is a process that takes time (years) rather than being a singular event or decision point. (Hall and Rutherford 1976)

In sum, effective principals are able to define priorities focused on the central mission of the school and gain support for these priorities from all stakeholders. Their actions impinge on almost all aspects of the classroom and school that are likely to influence achievement of these priorities. They intervene directly and constantly to ensure that priorities are achieved. (Leithwood and Montgomery 1982)

Although thousands of empirical investigations of leaders have been conducted in the last 75 years, no clear and unequivocal understanding exists as to what distinguishes effective leaders from non-leaders and, perhaps more importantly, what distinguishes effective leaders from ineffective leaders. Multiple interpretations of leadership phenomena exist, each providing some insight into the role of leader but each remaining an incomplete and wholly inadequate explanation of complex relationships. Although behavioral scientists have granted few topical areas greater research attention, the results of these efforts remain a bewildering melange for even the most serious student of organizations. (Jago 1982).

For years the literature has expounded on the role of leadership, and currently popular journals have been touting the importance of the principal as the "instructional leader." But how exactly does leadership feature in school change? The answers to this question are varied. There are a number of conceptions about leadership in the literature, and there is a rich history of theory development and studies on this subject. The ultimate answer, however, seems to elude theorists and practitioners alike. The purpose of this chapter is to examine a sample of the relevant theories and study findings about leadership and explore their implications for school principals and others interested in leadership for change.

Three bodies of literature will be sampled. The first comes from the work done by industrial and organizational psychology, sociology, organizational management, and behavioral psychology comprising the leadership literature (see Bass 1981). The second body of literature is on change, knowledge utilization, school improvement, and dissemination. Third, studies in educational administration are explored for their contribution. In this brief chapter, it is only possible, of course, to consider a limited number of key writers and studies. The citations will provide a useful starting point, however, for those who want to learn more.

The Leadership Literature

The leadership literature has been categorized into four perspectives by Jago (1982). His organization is useful for the leadership literature "sampling" strategy of this chapter. The four perspectives focus on leadership traits, leadership styles, the interaction of the situation with the leader's traits, and last, the interaction of the situation with the leader's behaviors.

Leadership Traits

In the 1920s, many investigations were undertaken to identify those qualities associated with effective leaders (e.g., Bernard 1926; Tead 1929). Traits that were investigated ranged from physical ones, such as height and age, to capacity factors, such as intelligence and knowledge, and to personality factors, such as introversion-extroversion and dominance. Attention was also given to social factors such as cooperation or adaptability and performance factors such as initiative and dependability.

These studies did not result in strong and consistent findings. No particular individual trait or combination of traits was consistently found to be characteristic of effective leaders. One reason may have been the problem of selecting leaders who represented the proper combination of traits. The trait approach meant that leaders were born and selected, rather than developed or trained. This possibility was not well liked then and is still unpopular.

An interesting variation of the traits theory of leadership is attribution theory. Calder (1977) believes tht leadership is a disposition or trait that exists only as perceived by others. Thus, a study of leadership is not a study of what leaders do but a study of what goes on in the minds of leaders, observers, and followers that leads to the perception that certain behaviors and traits are associated with leadership.

Despite the lack of success of trait studies, the question of whether leaders are born or made is still being investigated (Patinka 1979).

Leadership Styles

From this perspective, researchers have attempted to discover factors that identify leadership styles or patterns of behavior. From this effort have come concepts such as consideration and initiating structure. Consideration is the degree to which leaders have sincere concerns for followers and express them by boosting others' self-esteem and expressing appreciation for their work. The idea of structure initiation describes the extent to which leaders structure their own and their followers' work to reach goals or complete work tasks. These concepts emerged out of the array of studies now known as the Ohio State Studies. For several decades, a series of researchers have focused on leadership behaviors and on particular instruments that were developed to measure concepts such as consideration and initiating structure. One of these instruments is the LBDQ or Leader Behavior Description Questionnaire (Halpin 1957), which is still used to study leadership behavior or style. Additional work by Halpin and Winer (1957), who were concerned about limiting leadership behavior to two constructs, resulted in the identification of four factors that accounted for the variance in school principals' behavior and provided insight into the relationships of leadership behavior, teacher response, and school climate. These factors were aloofness—formality and social distance—production emphasis (pushing for results); thrust (the hard work of the individual and task structure); and consideration (concern for followers' welfare and comfort).

Others have also expanded upon the two concepts of consideration and structure, and various frameworks have been developed for assessing and interpreting leadership. One widely used model was developed by Blake and Mouton (1964, 1976). Their "managerial grid" is used as an approach to training leaders. The Blake and Mouton expansion of the Ohio State model contains five leadership styles or behaviors, placed within a two-dimensional grid. One axis of the grid represents concern for people, and the other axis represents concern for production. A leader can be high or low on both axes, or high on one and low on the other; however, the authors insist there is only one best style irrespective of the environment or situation. To develop followers committed to task completion, and to develop trusting and respectful relationships with followers, a leader should rate high on both axes.

The Situation and Leader Traits

This line of investigation emphasizes the identification of clear, specific situational conditions or contingencies that appear to affect a leader's behavior. The basic premise is that under particular conditions certain traits will result in successful leadership. Fiedler's (1978) contingency model is an example of this perspective. The contingency model is based on two key elements. One is the motivational structure of the leader (a trait), and the other is situational control or "the degree to which the situation provides the leader with control and influence" (p. 62). The interaction between these two elements produces leadership behavior, according to Fiedler, and leadership effectiveness is determined by the extent to which a leader can change the situation to match his personality. In contrast to Blake and Mouton, Fiedler maintains that no one leadership style is best, that what is best depends on the situation. When the style of the leader and the situation are not compatible, Fiedler recommends that leaders be taught to change the situation. He believes that changing the situation is easier and more practical than changing the leader's style.

The Situation and Leader Behaviors

This perspective assumes that successful leadership is a function of behaviors, not traits, and that the interaction between behaviors and the situation is the key. According to this view, a successful leader understands the situation and adjusts his behaviors to it. Models have been developed that attempt to specify under what conditions certain leadership behaviors will be successful. For example, Jago points out that the effectiveness of consideration and initiating structure behavior may be dependent on follower needs and dependencies, follower ability, degree of task satisfaction, expectations of followers, and other factors (1982: 12). From this perspective, studying leadership behaviors without taking into account the situation would not make sense.

The bulk of leadership theory development during the past twenty to thirty years is based on the belief that successful leadership is situationally influenced (Fiedler 1967; House 1971; Vroom and Yetton 1973; Bass 1960; Hersey and Blanchard 1977; Tannenbaum and Schmidt 1958). The resultant research and training experiences reflect this perspective. For example, in the popular leadership training programs designed by Hersey and Blanchard (1977), leaders are instructed to use the "maturity" of the followers as a situational variable and then match their style/behaviors accordingly.

This description has highlighted some of the major differences in perspectives different theorists are advocating. Situational or contingency-based theorists advocate that leaders change their behavior/style when there are changes in the situation. Blake and Mouton advocate one style (high task, high relationship) for all situations. In summary, although there has been extensive study and theory development, what makes good leaders and what are the keys to their effectiveness are questions that still stir much debate and opinion. Although the answer has been elusive, the questions have become sharper, and we know more about the complexity of leadership functioning than ever before.

Implications of the Leadership Literature for Change Facilitators in Schools

When it comes to developing effective leadership, most theories either infer or state outright that the task can best be done by the leader changing his behavior or style to fit the situation. A notable exception to this position comes from Fiedler, who feels it is easier for leaders to change the situation. He does not say leaders cannot change, just that it is easier to change the situation to match the leader's style. Another exception has been the position advocated by Blake and Mouton (1964, 1976), who propose that there is one way of behaving that is best for all situations, that with high task and high relationship behaviors, the leader will have high production and high employee orientation. There appears to be virtually no literature disputing the idea that leaders can and do change their behaviors and styles rather easily.

Many of the leadership models consider the situation to be of critical importance to leader effectiveness, yet very little research or attention has been directed to systematically studying the situation. Questions, such as what factors constitute the situation, how they are known or measured, how many factors or which ones must change to effect a change in leadership behavior, and who or what creates and influences the situational factors, are in need of answers. With the exception of the well-documented synthesis and studies of James and Jones (James and Jones 1974; Jones, James, Bruni, Hornick, and Sells 1979), sufficient thought has not been given to defining situational variables, a necessary prior step to developing measures and conducting controlled studies.

There are several other problems that impair the task of directly applying the leadership literature to leaders in educational settings. In the first place, very little leadership research has been done in school settings or been focused on school leaders. To the extent that schools are like other organizations, this deficiency does not matter, but to the extent that they are different, it matters a great deal. One way schools are different is that measures of success are frequently derived from the performance of nonadult, nonemployed individuals, that is, students. Also, staff in schools have a great deal of autonomy in carrying out their responsibilities. There tends to be a great deal of work-related, horizontal communication, and the line workers (i.e., teachers) can have a great deal to say about how the school is run.

A second problem has to do with stability and change in organizations. In general, the leadership literature has not dealt with leadership during times of organizational instability, planned change, or upheaval, yet periods of change are more the norm than extended periods of equilibrium. Since schools tend to be changing and stable at the same time (i.e. new programs, same organization), drawing implications for school leaders from the leadership literature is doubly risky.

In spite of these problems, the leadership literature does offer some interesting information for school leaders. There is widespread belief in the literature that the situation is highly influential in determining the success of the leader, and the authorities tend to advocate that the leader change his behavior to match the situation. Fiedler, however, suggests that the leader change the situation. To accomplish this task, he offers some propositions that should be considered by school leaders.

Fiedler contends that in situations where leader control is high or relatively low, a task-motivated leader will perform best. In a moderate control situation, a relationship-oriented leader will be more successful. Thus, when introducing a change into the school organization, the school leader must first assess his control level within the organization as well as his own leadership motivation or orientation. If the two are compatible, the leader can proceed with the change process, but if there is variance between leader motivation and the situation, Fiedler would have leaders change the situation rather than changing themselves.

What does it mean to be a task-oriented or relationship-oriented leader? According to Fiedler, it means you are one or the other, not both at the same time. Task-oriented leaders focus their attentions first on accomplishing the change at hand, while the relations-motivated leader focuses first on the people (teachers) involved in and influenced by the change. The concepts of consideration and initiating structure articulated in the Ohio State leadership studies seem very similar to Fiedler's ideas on task and relations orientations. A "considerate" leader would seek to accomplish change by involving teachers as collaborators in the process and by encouraging innovation use through expressions of praise, appreciation, and respect. A leader who initiates structure will structure the work situation so that the teachers can accomplish the change. Unlike the contingency model, leaders can be high or low on both concepts; they are not on a continuum.

The attribution theory (Calder 1977) suggests that school leaders' successes (and failures) do not come solely from what they do but from what their followers (teachers) expect them to do and perceive they are doing. From this perspective, the principals and other change facilitators who are aware of teachers' perceptions of their efforts and of their own perceptions of others' behavior will probably be more successful.

Leadership research gives considerable attention to the relationship between style and leadership success or effectiveness. The studies have been done, however, without a consistent description or definition of the concept of style and without distinguishing style and behaviors. Yet the findings from the research have led to widespread acceptance of the position that there is little direct relationship between leadership style and leadership success, and some will argue that both are situationally mediated. A style that is successful in one school situation may not be so in another. Related to this idea is another widely accepted proposition—that leadership style is flexible and can be easily changed. A large body of reserch has focused on the flexibility or rigidity of leadership style (Hill 1973; Hill and Hughes 1974; Bass and Valenzi 1974; Jago and Vroom 1977; Hill and Schmitt 1977), again without defining the construct.

One outcome of our research has been the recommendation that clear and consistent distinctions be developed between what is style and what is behavior (Rutherford, Hord, Huling, and Hall 1983). Apparently, a critical weakness in much of the past leadership research and theory has been that these two very different concepts have been confused. If style is the gestalt of a leader's behavior, knowledge, concern, and tone, then it probably is not changed that easily. On the other hand, individual leadership behaviors change continuously. In the leadership literature, there are a large number of examples where authors have discussed style and measured behaviors, or discussed behaviors and measured traits, and so forth. Our research and experience leads us to believe that one's style is not changed easily; however, leaders can change their behaviors. We will return to this point in chapter 8 when we introduce the idea of change facilitator style.

Does the leadership literature offer anything positive regarding leadership styles? Indeed it does. In spite of its problems with undefined and unexplained terminology, there are a wealth of descriptors of style, such as those by Bass, Farrow, Valenzi, and Solomon (1975), Jago and Vroom (1977), and Tannenbaum and Schmidt (1958). Their classifications are more similar than dissimilar, strongly suggesting that there are some congruences in the elements or characteristics called styles. School leaders can use these characteristics to look at their own actions to determine if they are as they think they are and want to be.

The heuristic nature of the leadership literature is perhaps its most significant contribution. Many hypotheses relative to the relationship between style, behavior, situation, and leadership are suggested. Until these hypotheses are more carefully tested, it is not possible to know which style(s) and behaviors are best in which situation. A major part of the testing will be done by practitioners on the firing line, and with their guidance, research and theory will become clearer.

The Literature on Change

The literature on change does not directly address leadership. Instead, the change literature presents models of change, and in some of these, there are analyses of the role of the "change agent." From these models, one can infer how the school leader could facilitate change or school improvement. Some of the models have been selected for review in this section of the chapter. The models were picked because they are frequently cited and have particularly relevant implications for school principals and other change facilitators. Three models articulated by Havelock (1971, 1973a) will be briefly described, followed by a discussion of Organizational Development (OD). Then the linkage model is reported, in addition to findings from the Rand Change Agent Study. The Concerns-Based Adoption Model and our own research are described in subsequent chapters.

Havelock: Three Models

Havelock has an extensive track record of research and change model development. In an early analysis of the literature, Havelock (1971) described three different perspectives for understanding change, the Social Interaction Model, the Research, Development, and Diffusion Model and the Problem Solving Model.

SOCIAL INTERACTIONS MODELS. Endorsers of the various social interaction models assume that the change to be accomplished, or the innovation to be adopted, is already fully developed and ready for dissemination. The emphasis in this perspective is on understanding the change process in terms of a series of decision phases the individual adopter moves through and in relation to how an innovation is diffused throughout a social system. In general, five phases typically characterize the innovation adoption process. The initial phase entails developing an *awareness* of the innovation. This phase is followed by increased *interest* in and a search for more information about the innovation. The next phase is *evaluation*, when a decision is made to adopt the innovation, which is followed by *trial* and *adoption*. Of course, rejection could interrupt the process at any point. Though the process is primarily applied to individual adopters, it could be applied to groups or complete social systems.

The role of the facilitator or change agent in this perspective is more significant during the time the adopter is becoming aware of the innovation and seeking more information. Once the adoption decision is made, there is little need for the agent. Information flow and media sources are important in this model, where individuals within a specific social network seem to rely on each other rather than on less credible outsiders to learn about innovations. This description of the "natural" process of bringing about change downplays the possibility of individuals, such as a principal or others in the role of leader or change facilitator, influencing the process. The perspective heavily emphasizes adopter perceptions and characteristics and the dynamics of information diffusion about an innovation. Rogers and Shoemaker's *Communication of Innovations* (1971) is an excellent compendium of the research from this perspective.

RESEARCH, DEVELOPMENT, AND DIFFUSION (RD&D) MODEL. In Havelock's analysis, this perspective emphasizes the systematic and sequential nature of knowledge creation and utilization and is guided by the following five assumptions: (1) there is a rational sequence—research, development, packaging, dissemination—for evolving and applying a new practice; (2) there is large-scale, lengthy planning; (3) there is a division and coordination of labor directly related to the rational sequence and planning; (4) there is a passive but rational consumer who accepts and adopts the innovation; and (5) the expensive costs of development at the outset are acceptable because of the innovation's efficiency, quality, and suitability for mass dissemination and effective use.

The RD&D models conceive of change as an orderly, planned sequence beginning with problem identification, then finding or producing a solution, and finally diffusing the solution. The knowledge production is done mainly by researchers, followed by systematic development and dissemination. The adopter or receiver is seen more as a passive consumer in this perspective. The clearest delineation of the RD&D perspective has been presented by Guba and Clark (1976).

Some common strategies used with RD&D include the development of high performance products, which guarantee "user-proof" implementation, and information system building, which produces channels for diffusing information about innovations. The strategy of administered and legislated change, another RD&D strategy, assumes that a successful and beneficial innovation can be mandated into use. Nearly all efforts are concentrated in the research, development, and diffusion areas, with little attention being paid to helping the user implement the innovation once it has been delivered.

This perspective nicely describes the national curriculum development projects of the 1960s. The results of research were utilized in comprehensive development projects that resulted in "modern" materials and processes for use in the classroom. There was a definite direction to the activity, with research leading to development and then widespread dissemination. The products were even billed as being "teacher proof." It was assumed the programs were effective because they incorporated the most recent findings from research and theory and had been through systematic development and field testing. That most of these programs were never widely used illustrates the danger in not understanding more about the user end of the RD&D continuum. The problem-solver perspective, to be described next, does emphasize the user more.

PROBLEM-SOLVER MODEL. This third perspective on change is advocated by persons from the group dynamics/human relations tradition. Havelock outlined five positions advocated by the problem-solving perspective. The most important position is the consideration of user need, about which the leader or change agent should be primarily concerned. The second point is that diagnosing need is an integral part of the change process. Third, the leader or change facilitator is to be nondirective with users and is not to be perceived as an "expert" or advocate of a particular solution (i.e., innovation). Fourth, internal resources should be fully utilized. Finally, the strongest user commitment will come from self-initiated and self-applied innovations.

The problem-solver model, unlike the social interaction and RD&D models which consider the innovation adopter as the receiver and the target of the change process, involves the "adopter" throughout the process, collaboratively solving his/her problems. "Consultants" work as resources along with the receivers.

Several strategies are typically followed in the problem-solving models. It is expected that an internal, problem-solving capacity can be developed through collaboration with outside consultants, who provide training in innovation-free, "process" skills. The process involves all staff in team efforts to analyze the features of their problem(s) and generate alternative solutions. The outside consultant offers training in group process skills and assists in evaluation. These consultants do not advocate particular solutions or innovations. In the end, the clients must determine their own solution and proceed with implementing it.

Although the emphasis of the problem-solving model is on the "receivers" and their interactive and collaborative problem-solving activities, the presence of a consultant, who helps significantly in training, supporting, and assisting the client system develop problem-solving skills, is required. Obviously change consultants who work in this special way require special skills for relating and working with their clients. Havelock states that "the concept and role of the change agent is central to the formulation and implementation of [this] strategy" (1973b: 239). The most widespread model within the problem-solver perspective is called Organizational Development, briefly described next.

Organizational Development (OD)

One of the best known strategies for change, typifying the problem-solver approach, is called Organizational Development (OD). OD had its beginning in business settings, and in the late 1960s was adapted for use in schools. Although it was proposed as a strategy rather than a model or theory, it has the characteristics of other models in that it is based on a set of assumptions about change, is composed of a set of distinct components or dimensions, and has definite implications for how change should be accomplished. A key reference for OD applications in school settings is the work by Schmuck, Runkel, Arends, and Arends (1977).

A basic assumption of OD is that the nature of the group or organization is the source of many of the problems related to changing schools. "It is the dynamics of the group, not the skills of individual members, that is both the major source of problems and the primary determiner of the quality of solutions" (Schmuck et al. 1977: 3). Clearly, the focus of change for OD is the group(s), not the individual. OD views schools as systems of people working at tasks interdependently and eventually moving into collaboration with other sets of individuals as they move from one task to another. As for individuals, this model leaves ". . . the processes and structures within individuals to the individuals themselves, their ministers, and their psychiatrists" (Schmuck et al. 1977: 9).

A major objective of OD consultation is to bring about effective functioning of the various subsystems. Subsystems are amorphous entities comprised of people, supplies, space, and information; they perform the many functions that constitute an organization such as a school. The development of organizational adaptability is the ultimate goal of OD, and improving subsystem effectiveness and interpersonal skills are the core strategies for accomplishing that goal. The skills necessary for subsystem effectiveness are described by Schmuck et al. (1977) as seven interdependent capabilities: clarifying communication, establishing goals, uncovering and working with conflict, improving group procedures in meetings, solving problems, making decisions, and assessing changes.

Successful implementation of OD is dependent on a number of variables (Schmuck et al. 1977). There must be strong support from top management and from building principals. In particular, there should be acknowledgment by district personnel that the actual state of affairs in the target school is not ideal. It is especially important that the organization have enough time to be properly introduced to OD and how it works. One academic year including approximately 160 hours of direct OD work by staff would be an appropriate amount of time for the first year in a moderately large school, if its readiness level was appropriate.

During the period of introduction and implementation of OD, the guidance of trained and skilled OD consultants is required. Consultants are more likely to be helpful to the school, of course, if the school staff makes active use of them. For the change to be maintained, continuity of the school principal is important, and it is recomended that the principal stay with the school to take on the consultant role for at least a year after the outside consultant leaves. If schools do not build internal capacity and/or become dependent on external consultants, long-term institutionalization may not occur. In the ideal situation, the school staff does develop internal capacity to use OD skills and uses these skills to solve newly emerging problems. That the OD model can be implemented and sustained has been carefully documented (Fullan, Miles, and Taylor 1981); however, its ultimate goal is all too infrequently attained.

Linkage Model

Essentially, the linkage model is concerned with establishing "communication networks between sources of innovations and users via an intermediary facilitating role either in the form of a linking agent or a linkage agency" (Paul 1977: 26–27). The key function of the linking agent, then, whether the agent is internal or external to a school system, is to facilitate the work of persons involved in change or improvement activities. The objective is to help these persons acquire and use relevant ideas, products, and related sources. The linker increases the kind and amount of information that can be used for decision making.

Three factors distinguish linking agents from nonlinking agents. "First, linking agents direct their actions at the improvement of individual or institutional performance. Second, they use knowledge or knowledge-based products and services as key instruments of improvement. Thirdly, in order to connect those engaged in change with ideas, findings, descriptions of practices, training materials and other needed knowledge-based products, they must perform boundary-spanning roles" (Nash and Culbertson 1977: 2–3).

In education, where this approach has been applied extensively, the emphasis is on linking organizations, which can use new research and its products, with resource systems, which produce the new products. It is assumed that the users of new knowledge live in a system different from the creators of knowledge and that the systems are not effectively connected. Interaction must thus be achieved, and the most effective way to do this is with human linkers. The key task for the linking agent is to span the boundaries of the two systems to bring about closer collaboration.

The linkage models depend in a very focused way on the linking agent's knowledge of new products and on their abilities to persuade and help others use new resources. "The key function of the linking agent is to facilitate the work of persons involved in change and improvement activities. The objective is to help these persons to acquire and use relevant ideas, products and related sources" (Rutherford et al 1983: 58). Ten roles linking agents should assume have been suggested by Crandall (1977): as the product peddler, information linker, program facilitator, process enabler, provocateur/doer, resource arranger, information linker, technical assister, action researcher/data feedbacker, and educator/capacity builder. Successful linkers found in studies by Louis and Rosenblum (1981) are characterized by their initiative, the amount of time they spend on-site, the amount of training they provide to school personnel, and the variety of training tools they use. These characteristics provide strong messages about effective change facilitators. Whether they are called linkage agents or principals, the skills are what appear to be important.

The most comprehensive operational model of linkage is the National Diffusion Network (NDN). This U.S. Department of Education program has been very effective at linking teachers with recently developed educational programs. One of the keys to the success of the NDN has been the formalization of the linking agent roles. Each state has a State Facilitator (SF) who works with teachers and schools in that state. In many ways, the SF works as a problem-solver consultant, helping school staffs clarify their problems and needs. The SF can turn to a catalog, *Educational Programs That Work* (NDN 1980), that lists recently developed programs that have been through a national validation process. The process includes an evaluation of effects and a review by a federal committee, the Joint Dissemination Review Panel (JDRP).

Another strength of the NDN as a linkage model is the establishment of a second linking agent, the Developer Demonstrator (DD). DDs are the official representative for each program approved by the JDRP. DDs travel across the nation giving presentations about their program and assisting teachers in implementing them. The SFs "link" the DDs' innovations with a particular school's needs. Following completion of an "adoption agreement," the DD provides training and implementation assistance. In practical ways, the NDN personifies recent change models and demonstrates one rich combination of theory and practice.

The Rand Change Agent Study

The Rand Change Agent Study (1974) has been widely cited because of the implications this research has had for change in educational settings. The study took place between 1973 and 1977. It examined four federal "change agent programs" that were designed to give seed money to school districts for creating, introducing and spreading the use of innovative educational practices. The first phase of the study focused on initiation and implementation of the projects, and the second phase addressed incorporation and continuation of the project activity. This policy study was national in scope (the sample came from eighteen states) and included a large number of individual projects (N = 293). One explanation of the widespread awareness of this study was the publication of brief reports (approximately fifty pages) each year of the study. This reporting schedule was in sharp contrast to the more typical practice of delivering a single, large "final report." Another difference was that the Rand study investigated the implementation and institutionalization phases of the change process. This examination was done at a time when the importance of the implementation phase was just beginning to be recognized. Others were beginning to examine this critical phase at that time as well (Fullan and Pomfret 1977).

In brief, the results of the Rand Change Agent Study suggest that schools change as new practices gain support, are adapted to the local situation, and become integrated into the regular operation of the organization. The reports emphasized three stages in the change process: initiation, or securing support; implementation, based on change in the innovation and the school through a process of "mutual adaptation"; and incorporation or institutionalization, when changes become a permanent part of the system.

Implementation of successful projects in the Rand study were characterized by adaptive planning, or constant planning to adapt a change to the local setting. In addition, staff training was provided to meet the needs of local school personnel. Local material development or adapting materials to the needs of the local school was seen as a key process. Finally, a critical mass of innovators was determined for providing support for one another and for the innovation.

Implementation outcomes depended on internal factors: organizational climate, motivation of participants, implementation strategy used by the local leaders, and scope of the change. In terms of the organizational climate, the active support of the principal was very important. When teachers perceived that the principal liked a project and that the project had the principal's active support, the project fared very well. "In general, the more supportive the principal was perceived to be, the higher was the percentage of project goals achieved, the greater the improvement in student performance, and the more extensive the continuation of project methods and materials" (Rand Change Agent Study 1978: 31). The principal's major contribution was in giving moral support to the staff, critical to the continuation or institutionalization of the project.

One important responsibility for the facilitator recommended by this research is in staff development for the local school personnel. In addition, developing local, interinnovator support systems was seen as critical. The Rand study also suggested that change facilitators support local users in adapting the "change" to their particular setting and in adapting materials to match local needs. Questions of fidelity, the degree of match between the developers' model and the local adaptation, were not confronted. In part, this inattention could have been due to the nature of the federal grant, which encouraged local creativity. Two nagging questions that we will return to in chapter 6 are: To what extent should the facilitator encourage local users to adapt the innovation? and, How much mutation is allowable before the innovation is no longer reconizable?

In hindsight, the popularity in the 1970s of the little understood concept of mutual adaptation by the education community was probably a reaction to the "teacher proof" orientation of innovation developers in the 1960s. The widespread support for the locally developed programs of the NDN was probably a further step in the direction of allowing the local school to develop its own innovations. This cottage industry orientation is beginning to be questioned in the late 1980s, with the emphasis now on district and statewide decision making in all aspects of schooling.

The Change Literature and Change Facilitators in Schools

The models summarized by Havelock provide useful overviews and outlines but little specific detail about the behaviors to be used by change facilitators. In another publication, Havelock (1973b) examined more closely the characteristics of change agents. He suggests that an effective facilitator needs to have a "psychological wholeness." In his guide for training change agents, Havelock states that three elements of psychological wholeness are attitudes, knowledge, and skills. A desired attitude would be one of concern for others and a belief in one's power to help others, coupled with a strong sense of self-identity. Change agent knowledge should include a good knowledge of self, of others, and of the systems and subsystems being changed. Needed skills are described as the abilities to work harmoniously and collaboratively with others, to increase others' awareness of their potential, and to convey one's skills, knowledge, and values. These psychological factors stand only as propositions, however, for Havelock admits they have no empirical validation.

The different perspectives summarized by Havelock hint about the behaviors and skills of school change facilitators. For example, if a principal were to employ the social interaction model, he/she would bring a particular emphasis to the change facilitator role. The principal would introduce information about the change and ascertain whether teachers had sufficient information for deciding to adopt the change. The principal would also try to influence the most highly regarded teachers to adopt the change so that other peers would follow. He/she would emphasize communication lines and address teachers' perceptions of the innovation as they consider adoption.

The principal's actions in the RD&D model would probably be based from the perspective of the innovation consumer. The innovation would have been developed elsewhere and made available as a fully finished product, based on research and ready for adoption. The principal's day-to-day behaviors would probably be indistinguishable from his/her role when using the social interaction perspective. The RD&D perspective does not emphasize communications with or among potential adopters, nor does it state that there are adopter characteristics that can make a difference in change success. The assumption, then is that once the teacher has decided to adopt, no further assistance is needed for implementation.

With the problem-solver approach, there must be strong support from the school principal as the faculty and principal work with the OD consultant. All receive a great deal of process training in order to self-diagnose needs, make decisions about solutions, and implement the selected solutions. The consultant is expected to work in a nondirective, collaborative way with the faculty, and the principal must take on the consultant role after a time so that the school can develop its own internal, problem-solving capacity. The consultant does not represent any particular innovations (i.e., problem solutions); rather, it is assumed that the school staff will be able to seek specialized expertise when needed.

If the principal, a lead teacher, or other school facilitator is connected with or informed about new programs, processes, or ideas, the linkage model might be used for exercising instructional leadership. In this case, the facilitator would actively encourage the staff's involvement in change to improve practices. The facilitator would provide information about the innovation for decision making and provide training materials to support use of the change. The facilitator's effectiveness would be dependent on his/her knowledge of the sources of information about new products and on his/her ability to persuade and help teachers select and use the new ideas.

The Rand study's central message to principals and other facilitators is to be supportive. Further, the extent to which the principal approves a change and actively supports it directly affects the success in attaining change goals and the continuation of the change.

Although the literature associated with models of change says relatively little about leadership behaviors and styles, the literature that includes studies of the principal as a facilitator of change does provide more information. The next section, which looks at the literature on the principal, provides further clues to the change facilitator role the principal and other school facilitators might take on.

Studies of Principal Effectiveness

There is general consensus in the literature that the principal is the key to educational change in schools. Suggestions about the ways principals can make a difference can be found in the literature on educational administration, school change, and school effectiveness.

The Leadership Role of the Principal

One recurring theme in the principal literature is that the principal's primary responsibility is as the instructional leader. A large array of studies and proclamations convey that if educational programs for students are to improve, principals must take the lead in providing teachers with the instructional leadership they need and are entitled to as they strive to improve their practices. In their analysis, Cotton and Savard (1980) reviewed twenty-seven documents concerned with the principal's role as instructional leader. From these reports, they located only seven studies they judged to be both relevant and valid investigations of instructional leadership. Six of the studies focused on elementary schools, the other, on a secondary school. All seven studies found that the principal's instructional leadership had a significant influence on student achievement. The actual behaviors that contributed to effective instructional leadership were described by Cotton and Savard as (1) frequent observation and/or participation in classroom instruction; (2) communicating clearly to staff what is expected of them as facilitators of the instructional program; (3) making decisions about the instructional program; (4) coordinating the instructional program; (5) being actively involved in planning and evaluating the instructional program; and (6) having and communicating high standards/expectations for the instructional program.

Persell and Cookson (1982) reviewed more than seventy-five research studies and reports to address why some principals are more effective than others. They identified nine recurrent behaviors the more effective principals displayed (p. 22).

1. Demonstrating a commitment to academic goals
2. Creating a climate of high expectations
3. Functioning as an instructional leader
4. Being a forceful and dynamic leader
5. Consulting effectively with others
6. Creating order and discipline
7. Marshalling resources
8. Using time well
9. Evaluating results

A great dilemma of the principalship is how to attend to the management aspects of the school and also concentrate on being the school's key instructional leader, and discussion of this problem is very common in the literature. Fege (1980) takes the view that the success of the principal as an instructional leader is largely dependent on the ability of the principal to distinguish between the routines of management and the goals of instructional leadership and improvement. An interesting finding by Cotton and Savard (1980) supports this view, for they found that principals who are effective instructional leaders are also effective administrator/managers.

The studies, however, relay a mixed message about the realities of the principalship and the potential of principals to lead. Lipham (1981) and Corbet (1982) claim that leadership is the responsibility of the principal and cannot be left to others. Other researchers have found, though, that instructional leadership is not a central focus of the real-life practices of principals (Wolcott 1973; Sproull 1977, 1981; and Martin 1980). McNally (1974) noted that principals are not exercising to any considerable degree the instructional and program leadership function widely agreed to be their most important responsibility. Howell (1981) found that principals only spend approximately 14 percent of their time on activities related to curriculum such as scheduling students, coordinating course placement, supervising, and observing. His conclusion is that today's principals are not and cannot be "instructional leaders" in the conventional sense. Salley, McPherson, and Baehr (1979) contend that unless environmental characteristics, particularly those related to the organization of the school and school system, are changed, the principal will rarely be a change agent.

Other researchers, while acknowledging the principal's difficult situation, believe the answer to successful leadership lies in the principal's ability to make the best possible use of the available discretionary time and resources. Sarason (1971) found that principals do have considerable authority over how they use their time and resources, but differ in their knowledge and appreciation of its utility. He further contends that the degree of authority principals have depends very heavily upon the uses they are able and willing to make of decision-making opportunities. In a similar vein, Isherwood (1973) concluded from his observation of fifteen secondary school principals that opportunities for developing and exercising "informal authority" seem to exceed by far the formally designated powers and responsibilities of the principalship. Morris (1981) found from his research that there is much, rather than little, discretion available to the building administrator in education. He further concluded that there is much room at the school level for flexibility and adaptability in applying school system policy. Stewart (1982) claims that every job has demands and restraints but that within these constraints, leaders have many choices they can make. All in all, then, there is a compound message: The daily administrtive tasks can fill the principal role, but it is possible, at least for some, to be instructional leaders as well. In some cases, principals seem to lead in spite of the context.

The Principal as a Facilitator of Change

Another set of research studies has examined the principal's leadership role in relation to change. As early as 1951, in a review of research performed during the previous twelve years, the principal was identified as a key influence on the adaptability of a school and on the process of change (Ross 1951). Subsequent research has repeatedly singled out the unit manager as the key to educational change (Baldridge and Deal 1975; Rand Change Agent Study 1978; Brickell 1961; Miles 1971; Tye 1972; Fege 1980). Even more studies support the importance of the principal in school improvement efforts (Hall, Rutherford and Griffin 1982; Hord and Goldstein 1982; Rutter, Maughan, Mortimore and Ouston 1979; Rand Study 1978; Venezky and Winfield 1979; Hall, Hord, and Griffin 1980). In their synthesis of research on improving schools, Lieberman and Miller (1981: 583) summarize the studies when they state, "the principal is the critical person in making change happen."

A small body of research has begun to concentrate on what principals actually do in the process of facilitating change. Reinhard, Arends, Kutz, Lovell, and Wyant (1980) conducted a study funded by Teacher Corps to investigate principal behaviors that support or hinder externally funded change projects. In doing their research, the investigators divided the change process into four stages and looked at the principal's role in each stage. The four stages were (1) planning and initiation; (2) building a temporary operating system for the project; (3) developing and implementing; and (4) ending and institutionalizing. At each stage, they found specific contributions by the principal that were crucial to project success.

Crucial at the first stage—planning and initiation—was the principal's agreement with the project, his input into the project proposal, and the communication of his support and enthusiasm to others. At the second stage, successful projects had principals who took an active, positive role in the project, "sold" the project to the superintendent, and quickly provided all necessary material and personnel resources. During the stage of development and implementation, successful principals remained interested and ever ready to help solve any problems that might arise. It was during this period that principals in successful projects began to turn over operation of the project to other personnel. In the fourth stage, the critical behaviors for successful principals were a continuing commitment to the project and an ability to provide the resources needed for project continuation.

Thomas (1978) studied principals from more than sixty schools with alternative school programs and focused on how school principals managed the diverse educational programs in their schools. From this study, she identified three patterns or classifications of principal behavior related to facilitating the alternative program. The principals' actions were based on their role as either director, administrator, or facilitator. Thomas describes these roles as follows:

> Director—this principal makes the decisions in his school, both procedural and substantive. He will take a great interest in things affecting the classroom, such as curriculum, teaching techniques, and staff development and training, as well as those things affecting the school as a whole, such as scheduling and budgeting. Teachers in a school with this type of principal contribute to decisions affecting the classroom, but the principal retains final decision-making authority.

> Administrator—this principal tends to separate procedural decisions from substantive decisions. He will give teachers a large

measure of autonomy in their own classroom—over what they teach and how they teach—but will tend to make the decisions in areas that affect the school as a whole. He will perceive his functions as distinct from those of his faculty, and will tend to identify with district management rather than with his staff.

Facilitator—this principal perceives his role as one of support; his primary function will be to assist teachers in the performance of their duties. Unlike the administrator, however, this principal will be more concerned with process than procedures. Principals who exhibit this type of behavior often perceive themselves as colleagues of their faculty, and are most apt to involve their teachers in the decision-making process. (1978: 12–13)

Thomas concludes that although many factors affect implementation, the leadership of the principal appears to be one of the most important factors in the success or demise of an alternative program. Schools under the leadership of a directive or facilitative principal had greater success in implementing the alternative programs than did schools headed by an administrator-type principal. Furthermore, where strong leadership was lacking, the alternative programs tended to offer something different from what was originally intended, and teachers within the program tended to follow disparate classroom practices.

Leithwood, Ross, Montgomery, and Maynes (1978) studied twenty-seven principals regarding their influence on the curriculum decisions made by teachers. From their study they discovered four discrete types of principal behavior. Fifty percent (N = 13) of the principals were classified as *administrative leaders.* They were described as passive observers of the curriculum process who get directly involved only in case of an evident problem. With only one exception, these principals were not concerned about their lack of influence on the curriculum. Principals in a second category (N = 2) were termed *interpersonal leaders.* These principals were directly involved in the curriculum decisions, and this involvement was almost exclusively through interpersonal relationships with teachers, most frequently on a one-to-one basis. Their interactions included observations of teachers, with feedback and planning for the future, all for the purpose of getting teachers to make changes supported by the principal. Additionally, these principals used techniques and procedures to increase teachers' knowledge and skill in relation to the new program or methodology.

Three principals were classified as *formal leaders.* They relied on their legitimate authority to influence teachers by issuing direct instructions about curriculum decisions. These principals were rather specific about the objectives to be taught, materials to be used, evaluation procedures to be followed, and, in one case, teaching methods to be used.

The final classification was the *eclectic leader,* and there were eight principals who fit into this category. These principals influenced curriculum decisions by using a variety of strategies for supporting and directing teacher choice. Some of the strategies employed were: involving teachers in decision making, establishing priorities in consultation with staff and arranging the organizational structures to accommodate these priorities, forming and supporting teacher planning groups, encouraging teacher sharing as a means of influencing each other, establishing a work environment that encouraged teacher experimentation and initiative, and providing support for teachers in many ways.

An extensive study of the day-to-day interventions of nine elementary school principals involved in facilitating specific curriculum innovations was conducted by researchers at the Research and Development Center for Teacher Education (Hall, Hord, Huling, Rutherford, and Stiegelbauer 1983). The principals were identified by district administrators as portraying one of three hypothesized change facilitators: initiators, managers, or *responders* (Hall, Rutherford, and Griffin 1982; Hall and Rutherford 1983; Hall, Rutherford, Hord, and Huling-Austin 1984). How the principals interacted with their faculties in the school and with others outside the school is reported extensively in chapter 8.

In summary, the research on principals as change agents consistently reports that principals can make a difference and that there are some distinguishable ways in which they behave that determine their effectiveness.

Effective Principals

Recently, much of the principal research and literature has been based on the primary question, "What makes a school effective?" A related question then is, "What is an effective principal?" or, "What role does the principal play in school effectiveness and school improvement?"

In his study of schools for the urban poor, Edmonds (1979) identified several "indispensable" characteristics of effective schools. These characteristics included strong administrative leadership that places the acquisition of basic skills as the highest priority, and leadership that develops within the school a pervading belief that all students can and will attain expected levels of achievement.

Especially informative regarding principal leadership is a review prepared by Leithwood and Montgomery (1982) in which they identify two types of principals, "effective" and "typical." They found that the way in which principals address educational goals reveals interesting characteristics about them. Effective principals had clear goals, both long- and short-term, and their priorities dealt with the happiness and achievement of students. Effective principals tried to achieve a balance between task and interpersonal relationships, but their first priority was to have a good school and this task orientation took precedence over human relations if need be. These principals applied the task ethic to themselves, and they viewed themselves as instructional leaders who were responsible for the quality of their schools. High teacher expectations were communicated by such principals and were coupled with the assumption that programs would always be changing to better serve learners. Furthermore, effective principals seemed to attend to all aspects of the educational endeavor. They set specific goals and held teachers to them. They also had knowledge of the instructional practices of their teachers, and, in direct and indirect ways, they saw to it that the teachers had the knowledge and skills necessary for program improvement. Effective principals also took actions to secure the necessary support from the community and higher administration for the school improvement efforts they endorsed. According to Leithwood and Montgomery, "rather than being pro-active as the effective principal appeared to be, the typical principal tended to be primarily responsive—responsive to district demands and the demands from the many other sources of problems encountered everyday" (1982: 27).

Hall, Hord, and Griffin (1980) found that in schools where the principal was concerned about the teachers' use of a specific innovation, the manner in which the teachers were using the innovation was more consistent. Stallings and Mohlman (1981), who studied the implementation of a specific program (Effective Use of Time Program), found that in schools with more supportive principals more teachers implemented the training program. In this study, principals were rated as supportive when they were observed to (1) go out of their way to help teachers; (2) be constructive in their criticism and to explain reasons for suggesting change in behavior; (3) share new ideas; (4) set good examples by being on time and staying late; (5) be well prepared; and (6) care for the personal welfare of the teachers.

Little (1981) suggests that to operate as effective facilitators, principals need a certain amount of what might be called organizational potency. She describes a number of ways principals can facilitate the instructional success of teachers. Principals can support certain norms by *announcing* that they hold particular expectations for teachers, for example, at faculty meetings. Moreover, those expectations can be expressed as practices teachers can follow, for instance, by participating in weekly in-service meetings. Principals can also act in such a way that their own behavior provides a *model* for the norms they support. Principals fortify or weaken norms by the way they *sanction* teachers. They can increase or decrease activity through mechanisms such as deciding who can use internal resources (for example, schedules or materials budgets), granting access to outside resources, deciding on special provisions or release time, and informally recognizing a job well done. Finally, principals *protect* teachers who are accomplishing what they want them to be doing. One way they do this job is by acting as an effective "buffer" between the district's needs and the needs of the teachers.

Clearly, the studies of principals, whether in the leadership studies, the studies of effective principals, or the studies of principals as change facilitators, show that the principal is considered to be a prime factor in the process of change and school improvement. Many factors can be reiterated regarding the dimensions of the principal's role that appear to make a difference. What seems useful here is to provide a brief reflection on the three bodies of literature.

The Message from the Literature

Three bodies of literature have been sampled—those regarding leadership, change, and the role of principals. Clearly, management and guidance of any system, educational or otherwise, is necessary to maintain and improve its effectiveness and efficiency. The leadership literature has in large measure centered on the analysis of the traits, behaviors, or styles brought to the role of leader and on the extent to which the situation influences leadership potential. The change literature suggests different roles for the change agent/leader, depending on the perspective taken. The principal literature illuminates how the effective principal behaves. The consistent theme across all three bodies of literature is that leaders are the focal point from which action, and its subsequent effects, emanates. Clearly, the principal is a key leader as the titular head of the school, holding whatever power and authority accompanies the position. The principal, regardless of traits, style, or familiarity with change models, is thus perceived as the best situated leader in the school for making school improvements.

The critical aspect of this leadership role is in the exercise of day-to-day actions that are required to initiate and sustain the change and improvement process. The principal as change facilitator carries special weight in school change. But principals are not the only change facilitators; many of the same skills described for the principal can be effectively used by others. Descriptions of specific concepts and tools for becoming an effective change facilitator fill the remaining chapters of this book.

Chapter 3

The Teacher's Point of View: Stages of Concern

Teacher 1
   Well, I don't see how this is any different from what I have always done.

Teacher 2
   I would like to try a different way of doing this in the fall. If we changed the materials, I think all of the students would have a better understanding.

Curriculum Consultant
   If we have one more meeting where all we do is talk and nothing gets decided, I'm going to scream!

If we had a nickel for every time we, one of our colleagues, or one of our staff members uttered these kinds of statements, we would be rich, even in these inflationary times. The reason these statements sound so familiar is that they summarize feelings and perceptions that are a part of every change. They are typical "concerns" that all of us feel and express. Actually, hearing these statements can be of tremendous use to the concerns-based change facilitator. Change facilitators can categorize concerns statements and adapt their interventions to be responsive to teachers' concerns.

One of the main premises of this book is that principals and other facilitators can be more effective and change can be more successful if the "concerns" of teachers are considered. This assertion is not offered as a simplistic slogan. It is meant to reflect our belief in the importance of the personal side of change, especially from the perspective of the "front line" user. Innovation characteristics have to be considered, and we have already started building a case for the critical difference change facilitators make. Policymakers, administrators, and others will have points of view that must be considered; but in the end, how teachers feel about and perceive change will in large part determine whether or not change actually occurs in classrooms. The first set of CBAM concepts and recommendations therefore, have to do with understanding the dynamics of teachers' perceptions of change, and with adjusting one's facilitating behaviors so that they address change from the teachers' point of view.

This prescription is really neither new nor unique to educational settings. Entertainers, politicians, parents, advertisers, and others interested in gaining acceptance and support for their plans by a client group adjust the presentation of their messages so that they can be understood by their recipients. They strive to communicate so that their messages resonate with the receivers' interests. What is new in the "concerns" theory is that it provides change facilitators with ways to assess and catalog the different perceptions teachers can have. With this diagnostic information in hand, it is possible to be more effective in adjusting interventions so that they are related to teachers' perceptions. Consequently, the teachers receive timely information and assistance that *they* perceive as being more relevant (i.e., useful), and their use of the innovation advances.

The concerns-based perspective does not deny the change facilitator's own point of view, which is also real; however, one of the critical understandings change facilitators must develop is that the form and function of their interventions must be adjusted so that they are synchronized with the viewpoint of the target group (i.e., teachers, parents, or students). The common practice of managing and facilitating only from the change agent's point of view restricts understanding. Frequently, this one-sided view results in teachers hearing different messages from what the change facilitators intended, and little or no advancement in use of the innovation occurs. We do not mean that the facilitator's longer-term strategic objectives must be altered, but reaching those objectives requires starting where people are and moving incrementally in the desired direction.

The concept and theory of concerns described in this chapter has been demonstrated to be an effective way to determine teachers' perceptions and to chart the movement or nonmovement of teachers toward a longer-term objective. Extensive research on teachers' concerns and teachers' concerns about innovations exists. Different ways to assess concerns are available, and they result in direct implications for change facilitating behaviors. In this chapter, we present the concept of concerns, the research background, and concerns theory. We discuss implications for change facilitators and suggest some applications. In later chapters, links between a concerns diagnosis and the facilitator's interventions will be described in detail. How to describe, assess, and interpret the teacher's point of view is the primary topic of this chapter.

The Origins of Concerns Theory

The concept of concerns and the development of concerns theory emerged in the late 1960s from the pioneering research of Frances Fuller and her colleagues at the Research and Development Center for Teacher Education at The University of Texas at Austin. The label for the "concerns" concept was selected during this period. Interestingly, the term itself has been very useful, since it tends to defy definition and yet is readily interpretable using one's own frame of reference.

Teachers' "Problems" and "Satisfactions"

During the last several decades, research has been directed toward teachers' "problems" and "satisfactions." Studies have been done in both the United States (Cruickshank 1981; Thompson 1963; Travers, Rabinowitz, and Nemovicher 1952) and in England (Gabriel 1957; Phillips 1932). From all these studies, consistent findings have emerged. "To summarize the data as it is reported by these investigators, what we know is that beginning teachers are concerned about class control, about their own content adequacy, about the situations in which they teach and about evaluations by their supervisors, by their pupils, and of their pupils by themselves" (Fuller 1969: 210). The studies also reveal that there are patterns to teachers' problems and satisfactions. In particular, teachers who are more mature in their careers mention different kinds of problems and satisfactions than do teachers who have limited experience.

For example, in the Gabriel study (1957), when experienced teachers' satisfactions and problems were contrasted with the satisfactions and problems reported by beginning teachers, some striking differences were noted as well as similarities. Among the significant differences were that experienced teachers more often reported that the slow progress of pupils was a problem, while inexperienced teachers more often reported that criticism from supervisors and maintaining student discipline were problems. For satisfactions, experienced teachers more frequently brought up the success of former pupils, while inexperienced teachers more frequently reported that holidays and praise from inspectors were sources of satisfaction.

These early studies and data became the first indicators that the differing perceptions and needs of teachers are important considerations when developing and delivering teacher interventions. Rather than offering evaluative judgments about these differences in satisfactions and problems, the teacher educator's emphasis should be upon developing an understanding of the implications these differences have for assisting teachers in professional growth. Fuller (1973) and Fuller and Bown (1975) have proposed that typical preservice teacher education programs be responsive to the problems and satisfactions apparently characteristic of students at that time in their professional training. If beginning teachers have different problems and satisfactions than do experienced teachers, then clearly the teacher education experiences each group receives should be different. Beginning and experienced teachers, in general, are asking different questions and have different perceptions of their roles and needs. To be relevant to what a particular group of teachers perceives as problems and satisfactions, then staff development and related experiences should be designed and delivered with those differences in mind.

Teachers' Concerns about Teaching

Another interesting illustration of the kinds of differences and perceptions experience can make is the report by Fuller (1969). In this study, Fuller surveyed one hundred preservice teachers to get their assessment of an educational psychology course they had taken as part of their professional training. Ninety-seven out of the one hundred students saw the course as being of little value and not relevant. Three students rated the course as being very useful and were enthusiastic about it. Frances Fuller examined more closely the three students who had found the course to be a positive experience. She asked, "What happened that made these students value the course?" In reviewing what was known about these students, she found that they were more mature and had had teaching-related experiences. Their "concerns," then, were different from the typically less mature, more inexperienced preservice teacher.

The studies of teachers' problems and satisfactions, in conjunction with clinical work, led Fuller and her colleagues to propose that there were clusters of concerns that could be associated with teachers and their teaching career, and that these concerns in general changed in a predictable fashion as teachers became increasingly experienced and sophisticated about their job (Fuller, Bown, and Peck 1967). Fuller identified and described four major clusters of concerns (unrelated, self, task, and impact) that have subsequently been verified in research she and others have done (George 1978; Babb 1971; Hardy 1977, 1978). All concerns focused on the job of teaching, but each cluster had a different content and dynamic.

UNRELATED CONCERNS. At the beginning of a preservice teacher education program, the potential teacher's concerns tend not to be tied to teaching at all. The individual's concerns focus on topics and questions such as, "Where do I get tickets to the rock concert this weekend?" or "I am concerned about getting a passing grade in the U.S. history course"; or concerns may be expressed about getting along with a roommate. Preservice teachers' initial concerns are not typically about teaching or their role in teaching.

SELF CONCERNS. Concerns in this category are typically observed in preservice teachers as they approach their first field experiences. Their concerns have an egocentrism to them; however, they do focus on teaching. Concerns at this point have to do with feelings of potential inadequacy, self-doubts about the knowledge required, or uncertainty about the situation they are about to face. Typical statements reflective of these types of concerns are: "I wonder if I know enough to teach them." "Will I be able to control them?"

TASK CONCERNS. As preservice teachers become more involved and more comfortable in the school setting and become engaged in the act of teaching, their concerns become more intensely related to the job of teaching. Concerns focus on logistics, preparation of materials, coordination, and scheduling. Typical expressions of concern at this stage include: "I have to spend several hours each night grading papers!" "I never seem to be able to get all of it into the scheduled time." "Here it is only Wednesday, and I already feel like it should be Friday!"

IMPACT CONCERNS. Ultimately, teachers can become predominantly concerned about how their teaching is affecting students and about how they can improve themselves as teachers. These concerns focus on the effects of their teaching and on ways they can be more effective. Sample comments made by teachers who have intense concerns of this type are: "I wonder if they are learning what they need to know?" "I am thinking of some ways that I can change what I am doing to draw in more closely two of my slow learners." "I have just taken this media course. It has given me some really fantastic ideas about how I can incorporate interest centers into my regular lessons."

Fuller's research and theory development about teacher concerns and the preceding work on teachers' problems and satisfactions represent a thirty- to forty-year documentation of reasonably consistent findings regarding how teachers perceive and experience their induction into the profession. Yet, over the period of time that these research findings have been accumulating, teacher education practices at the preservice and inservice levels have changed little. All too frequently, such courses do not address the concerns experienced by teachers at the times teachers express them.

For example, in many preservice teacher education programs, heavy emphasis at the beginning of the professional sequence is placed upon coursework having to do with theories in educational psychology, with the history and philosophy of education, and with highly detailed skill development for observing classrooms and designing tests. These contents are advocated by teacher educators as being essential for becoming an effective teacher. No one is apt to question this argument; however, the placement of these courses early in the training of a teacher appears to be inconsistent with the developing teacher's identified problems, satisfactions, and concerns. Fuller (1973) proposed that there be a systematic process whereby the content and experiences offered in a preservice teacher education program are presented and paced in conjunction with the assessment, arousal, and resolution of teachers' concerns about teaching. She proposed that teacher education experiences be sequenced to answer questions in the order teachers typically ask them.

Teacher Concerns about Change

This excursion into past literature about the problems, satisfactions, and concerns of teachers has been a preview for the more recent research demonstrating that concerns theory does not just apply to preservice teachers or to beginning teachers. In fact, concerns are a phenomenon that occurs to all of us when faced with new experiences, demands for improvement, and changes. Concerns theory applies to teachers, principals, teacher educators, and others from a multiplicity of tasks and roles.

In recent research, we and our colleagues have further pursued the pioneering work of Fuller and have identified a set of characteristic concerns common to most innovations and to the change process in general. These concerns follow the same general trend Fuller outlined—in unrelated, self, task, and impact. In this more recent research, it has been possible to identify concerns in much greater detail and to develop systematic descriptions of them and their interrelationships.

The first step was to develop a definition of what a concern is. The concept of concerns has been described as follows:

> The composite representaton of the feelings, preoccupation, thought, and consideration given to a particular issue or task is

called *concern.* Depending on our personal make-up, knowledge, and experience, each person perceives and mentally contends with a given issue differently; thus there are different kinds of concerns. The issue may be interpreted as an outside threat to one's well-being, or it may be seen as rewarding. There may be an overwhelming feeling of confusion and lack of information about what "it" is. There may be ruminations about the effects. The demand to consider the issue may be self-imposed in the form of a goal or objective that we wish to reach, or the pressure that results in increased attention to the issue may be external. In response to the demand, our minds explore ways, means, potential barriers, possible actions, risks, and rewards in relation to the demand. All in all, the mental activity composed of questioning, analyzing, and re-analyzing, considering alternative actions and reactions, and anticipating consequences is *concern.* An aroused state of personal feelings and thought about a demand as it is perceived is *concern.*

To be concerned means to be in a mentally aroused state about something. The intensity of the arousal will depend on the person's past experiences and associations with the subject of the arousal, as well as how close to the person and how immediate the issue is perceived as being. Close personal involvement is likely to mean more intense (i.e., more highly aroused) concern which will be reflected in greatly increased mental activity, thought, worry, analysis, and anticipation. Through all of this, it is the person's *perceptions* that stimulate concerns, not necessarily the reality of the situation. (Hall, George, and Rutherford 1979: 5)

Definitional work was also done to refine distinctions between different categories of concerns. Since the theory proposed that concerns change over time, the idea of scales or stages of concern was accepted. We do not mean, however, to imply a lock step, one-way progression. Ideally, there is a quasi-developmental pattern to changes in concerns when the change process unfolds although concerns might not follow the theoretical progression for any number of reasons, including the attempted adoption of an inappropriate innovation. The resultant categories are summarized as the seven Stages of Concern about an innovation and are presented as figure 2.

There is more to understanding the dynamics of concerns than simply memorizing the definitions presented in figure 2. Typically, teachers will not have concerns at only one of these

Figure 2
Stages of Concern about the Innovation

Impact

6 REFOCUSING: The focus is on exploration of more universal benefits from the innovation, including the possibility of major changes or replacement with a more powerful alternative. Individual has definite ideas about alternatives to the proposed or existing form of the innovation.

5 COLLABORATION: The focus is on coordination and cooperation with others regarding use of the innovation.

4 CONSEQUENCE: Attention focuses on impact of the innovation on student in his/her immediate sphere of influence. The focus is on relevance of the innovation for students, evaluation of student outcomes, including performance and competencies, and changes needed to increase student outcomes.

Task

3 MANAGEMENT: Attention is focused on the processes and tasks of using the innovation and the best use of information and resources. Issues related to efficiency, organizing, managing, scheduling, and time demands are utmost.

Self

2 PERSONAL: Individual is uncertain about the demands of the innovation, his/her inadequacy to meet those demands, and his/her role with the innovation. This includes analysis of his/her role in relation to the reward structure of the organization, decision making, and consideration of potential conflicts with existing structures or personal commitment. Financial or status implications of the program for self and colleagues may also be reflected.

1 INFORMATIONAL: A general awareness of the innovation and interest in learning more detail about it is indicated. The person seems to be unworried about himself/herself in relation to the innovation. She/he is interested in substantive aspects of the innovation in a selfless manner such as general characteristics, effects, and requirements for use.

Unrelated

0 AWARENESS: Little concern about or involvement with the innovation is indicated.

stages but a combination of concerns reflected in two or more stages that are relatively more intense than their other concerns. Our theory and research have shown that there is a general pattern to the intensity of the different stages of concern, and that changes in this pattern can be linked to the change process as it unfolds.

One way to illustrate this pattern is to use a graphic representation to chart "profiles" of the relative intensities of the different stages of concern. On such a chart, the intensity of the concern in each stage can be compared. Examples of different concerns profiles are illustrated in figure 3. These profiles are consistent with concerns theory and have been found in research to be characteristic of persons as they move through the change process. At the beginning of a change process, the typical "nonuser" has concerns that are relatively high in Stage 0 Awareness, Stage 1 Informational, and Stage 2 Personal. Nonusers are typically more concerned about gaining information about the innovation (Stage 1) and about how change will affect them personally (Stage 2). As they begin to use the new program or innovation, Stage 3 (Management) concerns become more intense; and, when teachers become experienced and skilled with an innovation, the tendency is for concerns at Stages 0, 1, 2, and 3 to decrease in intensity while those in Stages 4, 5, and 6 become more intense (Hall, George, and Rutherford 1979).

Assessing Stages of Concern

The first step in becoming skilled at diagnosing concerns, of course, is to know and understand the concept of Stages of Concern and be able to describe the seven different stages that have been identified (see figure 2). Understanding the concept of concerns is hardly enough, however; systematic ways to assess and interpret indications of concern are also needed.

Three techniques have been developed to assess the Stages of Concern about an innovation. These three procedures are one-legged conferencing, open-ended concerns statements, and the Stages of Concern Questionnaire. Each of these procedures rates differently in reliability, validity, and ease of use. With each system, it is possible to collect usable and comprehensive data about the concerns of individuals or a total faculty involved in

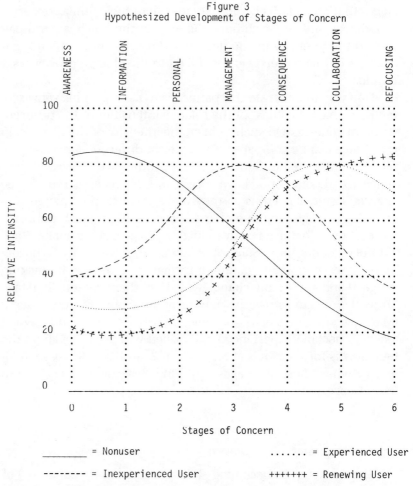

Figure 3
Hypothesized Development of Stages of Concern

_____ = Nonuser   .... = Experienced User

-------- = Inexperienced User   +++++++ = Renewing User

change. Each procedure is applicable to the settings where school-based change facilitators work. The procedures take into account that principals and other school-based change facilitators are constantly on the move, and that teachers are not willing to take extended amounts of time to respond to complicated techniques.

Each procedure has offsetting benefits and disadvantages. For example, the one-legged conferencing can be done informally at any time, but lacks reliability and validity. The Stages of Concern Questionaire is psychometrically rigorous, but requires administration and scoring time and must be interpreted by someone skilled at using it. The open-ended format represents a trade-off between ease of use and psychometrics. It offers a bonus in that concerns are described in the individual's own words. Since there are three approaches, it is possible for change facilitators to have a choice and be able to select the assessment approach most suitable for a given time and need. Each of the procedures is described in more detail in the remainder of this section. Citations are also included so that the reader who wants to know more about the procedures and how to use them will be able to access more technical documents. Training sessions are available from the international cadre of CBAM trainers, listed in Appendix A.

ONE-LEGGED CONFERENCING. The idea of a one-legged conference is borrowed from Sidney Simon (1975), who was interested in value clarification conferences. These informal conferences occur as teachers chat briefly with students in those random, individual contacts that happen in classrooms and around the school. The mechanics for a one-legged concerns interview are similar. The principal or other concerns-based change facilitator takes advantage of any opportunity that presents itself to monitor teacher concerns. The most frequent contact principals have with teachers is in the brief moments of conversation while walking down the hallway, stopping by the teachers' lounge, or chatting briefly before or after a lesson in a classroom. These opportunities provide a very limited amount of time, normally less than two minutes, for assessing concerns and delivering a relevant intervention. To do so requires turning the available time from a purely social encounter to one that is professional in substance. In our research, we have observed that these contacts frequently become lost opportunities. Principals do not take advantage of these one- to two-minute conferences to monitor or facilitate change. All too frequently, they become forgotten moments of informal exchanges of pleasantries.

Interviewing to gain information about concerns requires a specialized set of skills. These include not only being able to ask appropriate questions, but also knowing how to listen and how to follow one question with another. The design is initially to ask an open-ended question. The conference begins with an open question such as, "How's it going with the new reading program?" or "What do you think about the math monitoring system?" Other examples of open-ended questions that can be used to initiate one-legged conferences for concerns are included in figure 4. These questions can be adapted to fit any particular, one-legged conference.

By beginning with an open-ended question, the teacher is given the opportunity to describe his or her concerns, the emphasis of the concerns-based approach. To be effective as a change facilitator, it is important to assess and understand the teacher's concerns so that interventions and other types of support can address them. One way to know what the teachers' concerns are is to have teachers describe them. If the change facilitator begins by asking a more closed question (e.g., Do you like the reading program tests?), all too frequently the conversation moves toward areas of concern to the change facilitator rather than toward concerns of the teacher.

There can be a lot or very little overlap between the concerns the change facilitator has and the concerns the teacher has. Dissimilarity does not mean that the change facilitator's concerns should not be addressed; rather, the change facilitator's concerns should be addressed in terms of the teachers' concerns. Assuming the change facilitator has some appreciation of his or her own concerns, the task in a one-legged conference and in the other concerns-assessing approaches is to determine the teachers' concerns.

After asking the open-ended question, the job of the change facilitator is to *listen* to the teacher's response. The facilitator should analyze the response in terms of the Stages of Concern, looking for indicators and clues that suggest which stage(s) is being expressed. Following this opening discussion, the concerns-based change facilitator should ask probing questions (e.g., Tell me more about what you mean when you say you are interested in useful information). This phase of the interview will help clarify what the teacher's concerns are, and the particular topics that are the most pressing will emerge. Once the Stages of Concern and the focus of the concerns have been diagnosed, it is possible to shift the conference to what needs to happen next. The change facilitator should make recommendations, provide in-

Figure 4
Suggestions for Interviewing for Concerns (SoC)

— To "get at" the client's attitudes, feelings, reactions and
concerns in a one-legged conference —

Use those parts of or whole questions which seem most comfortable to
you. Substitute the name of the innovation at each place "innovation" or
"it" is used in the statement or question.

—Are you aware of the innovation?
—Are you using it?
—I'm interested in anything you'll share with me about the innovation.
—How do you feel about it?
—Any problems or concerns you have about it?
—What do you think of it?
—How does it affect you? Others you're involved with?
—Your reaction to it.
—Your attitude toward it.
—Do you have any reservations about it?
—Would you like any information about it?
—What questions do you have now?

formation, or do something that responds to the identified concerns.

The strategy for the one-legged conference includes the
following: Begin with open-ended question(s), probe to clarify the
Stages of Concern and the particular topics of concern, analyze
teachers' responses in terms of the Stages of Concern definitions,
then intervene to address those concerns. The intervention can
be as simple as offering encouragement, making a commitment to
followup, scheduling a time for further discussion, or suggesting a
concrete activity that can be tried. The key is to address expressed concerns to help resolve them or to introduce new information in order to arouse particular concerns.

The one-legged conference strategy is the most informal and
unobtrusive of the three strategies for assessing concerns. It can
be done whenever one is involved in a face-to-face conversation,
by telephone, in the parking lot, or in the checkout line at the
Safeway grocery. One-legged conferencing takes advantage of
brief moments of contact. In our research, we have found that

change efforts often succeed or fail depending upon how these brief incidents are utilized. If they are overlooked and not utilized as opportunities to facilitate and encourage use of the innovation, then the change effort has less support. If they are utilized to their utmost, many additional points of contact, forms of encouragement, and efforts to resolve concerns do occur. The cumulative effect of these many, little one-legged conferences can strongly impact the ultimate success and effectiveness of a change effort.

OPEN-ENDED STATEMENTS OF CONCERN. There are times when it is useful to have teachers describe in writing their concerns about a particular innovation. Such a procedure has been developed and is called the open-ended statements of concern. A standard format has been established based upon extensive research with this technique, initially developed by Fuller and her colleagues (Fuller and Case 1972). The technique was subsequently used in research on the change process (Newlove and Hall 1976). The design is to give teachers a page with the following statement at the top:

When you think about _____, what are you
concerned about?
(Please be frank and use complete sentences.)

The name of the innovation is written in the space, and the remainder of the page is left blank. This format provides teachers with an opportunity to write a narrative of one or more sentences describing their concerns about the innovation.

The results of the open-ended paragraphs can be content analyzed. The kind of concern reflected in each sentence can be rated, using the Stages of Concern definitions provided in figure 2. The most effective strategy for rating these paragraphs is first to read the entire statement of concern and then to make an overall judgment about whether it represents concerns of the *unrelated, self, task,* or *impact* nature. Following this overall reading, the interpreter does a sentence-by-sentence analysis. Each sentence must be rated in terms of the Stage of Concern it best represents. The set of sentence ratings is then reviewed to see how consistent they are with the initial, overall impression of *self, task,* or *impact* concerns. Examples of ratings for open-ended concerns statements are included as figure 5.

Figure 5
Examples of Open-Ended Concerns Statements

Teacher 1	*SoC Rating*

(I don't have enough time to organize myself each day.)   3

(I'm concerned about not having enough planning and preparation time.) (I'm swamped.)   3, 3

(I find the materials are too fragile for individual use. They are too often broken or end up in somebody's pocket.)   3

Teacher 2

(I'm concerned about learning more about team teaching.)   1

(I find so few articles that give practical ideas about how to begin teaming.)   1

(Now that I've observed teaming in an IGE open classroom, I'm anxious to visit a school where classrooms are separate as in our school, but where teachers team anyway.)   1

Teacher 3

(I am concerned about my particular instructional subject area so that I can change my use of the innovation in such a way that each child will achieve his best through my efforts.)   4

(I am concerned about how I am using the innovation in that I care about how it is affecting students' attitudes toward learning in general and my courses in particular.)   4

(As I use the innovation, I am concerned with the clarity of the objective and the creativity involved in repetition of new ideas so that the student has ample oportunity to *learn* the new concept without becoming bored.)   4

One of the advantages of using the open-ended concerns statement is that one learns a great deal more about *what* the concerns are about. Another way to analyze the statements of concerns, then, is to make a content list of the topics identified in them. For example, in figure 5, the "what" of concerns are as follows:

Teacher 1—The focus of all statements is on issues related to efficiency, organizing, and managing. Time demands of preparation and planning are troublesome. An additional content clue of the concerns regards the less-than-"stout" materials and their lack of durability.

Teacher 2—These statements reflect a healthy, active concern about learning more about team teaching. Apparently, the respondent has done some exploration through articles and observation and is highly interested in learning more about teaming. In the content analysis, the respondent also expresses interest in visiting classrooms.

Teacher 3—Concern about the impact of the innovation on students in his/her immediate sphere of influence is reflected. The focus is on the relevance of the innovation for students, especially on how it impacts student attitudes. Other content of concerns expressed include student learning outcomes and student motivation/boredom.

The open-ended approach to assessing concerns allows teachers to develop a written record describing their concerns at a particular point in time. A disadvantage of this approach is that every teacher's response will not be of the same length and in the same detail. For example, some teachers will only provide single-word answers, making it impossible to identify the Stages of Concern. Some teachers will write a single paragraph, while others will write a detailed page and a half. Thus, the amount of data available for analysis can vary dramatically. One strength of this procedure is that the descriptions are in the respondent's own words and provide the change facilitator with information not only about the intensity of the various Stages of Concern but also about the particular topics of concern. Thus, the concerns-based change facilitator can respond not only to the concerns dynamic but also to the particular focus of those concerns.

THE STAGES OF CONCERN QUESTIONNAIRE (SoCQ). For more systematic study and for research and evaluation efforts where reliability of data is particularly important, the Stages of Concern Questionnaire is the assessment technique to use. This thirty-five-item questionnaire can be used in all educational settings. The questionnaire items should remain unchanged; however, the change facilitator should substitute the innovation name on the cover page and provide a written and perhaps oral rationale for why teachers should respond to the questionnaire. Only ten to fifteen minutes are required for teachers to respond using a seven-point Likert scale for each item. The resultant data can be scored by hand (Parker and Griffin 1979), by mainframe (Hall, George, and Rutherford 1979), or by microcomputer (Brickley 1982). One of the clear strengths of the Stages of Concern Questionnaire is that it has strong psychometric qualities. For example, the test–retest correlation results range from 0.65 to 0.86, and the estimates of internal consistency (alpha coefficients) range from 0.64 to 0.83. Thus, for evaluation efforts or where more systematic and "credible" data are needed, the Stages of Concern Questionnaire becomes useful. The technique allows the collection of data at regular intervals so that a more objective plotting of progress, or lack thereof, can be charted.

Scoring the Stages of Concern Questionnaire data results in profiles (see figure 3). The profiles graphically present the relatively more and relatively less intense Stages of Concern. As a person becomes more skilled at interpreting these concerns profiles, increased information can be gathered about the dynamics of the change process and how it is unfolding. This information, of course, can be used in plans for intervening.

Interpretation of Stages of Concern profiles can be done with varying levels of sophistication. The basic procedure is to identify those Stages of Concern that are relatively more intense by noting the highest "peaks" of the profile, and then to interpret those stages according to the paragraph definitions provided in figure 2. If there is only one peak, the interpretation of the profile is quite simple and straightforward—only one Stage of Concern is intense. If two or three of the stage scores peak, however, the profile interpretation becomes more complex. Interpretation must then take into account that concerns are not singly differentiated but are conglomerated and are represented by the particular stages shown as more intense.

With increasing sophistication, it is also possible to provide clinical interpretation of those Stages of Concern that are of a lower intensity. The lowest scaled scores on the Stages of Concern Questionnaire reveal the stages wherein the respondent indicates little or no concern at the time. In most cases, it would be fruitless to deliver interventions targeted toward those particular Stages of Concern. If concerns are not intense at those stages, respondents are not likely to find interventions targeted there to be particularly relevant or worthwhile. More information on interpreting the Stages of Concern Questionnaire is readily available in Hall, George, and Rutherford's (1979) *Measuring Stages of Concern about the Innovation: A Manual for Use of the SoC Questionnaire.* For those who wish to use the Stages of Concern Questionnaire, it is included as an appendix in that manual, as are the procedures for scoring the SoC Questionnaire.

A Little More about Concerns Theory

In this chapter, we are providing a quick tour of the concept of Stages of Concern. To illustrate some of the subtleties as well as additional power possible through using the Stages of Concern and concerns theory, further discussion and illustrations make up the final parts of this chapter. Additional discussion and illustrations are included in the last two chapters as well.

The concept of Stages of Concern is deceptively simple. It would be quite easy if one could understand concerns simply by superficially assessing the difference between *self*, *task*, and *impact* concerns. Increasing subtlety and complexity in the interpretation of concerns is revealed, however, as one thinks more about the seven different Stages of Concern, their interaction, the possible combinations of less and more intense stages, and the implications that result from considering the dynamics of the arousal and the resolution of concern intensity over time.

Concerns theory and research reveal that concerns change over time in an fairly predictable, developmental manner. If we can predict how concerns will change throughout the phases of the change process, we can design in-service and other intervention activities in advance. These interventions could be designed to address the different concerns as they emerge. For example, it should be possible, at least in general ways, to anticipate the concerns that will be intense at the beginning of a change effort. As the implementation phase arrives, certain other concerns will be likely to appear, and the needed interventions could be anticipated. Assuming the innovation is appropriate, a general picture of how all concerns are likely to evolve can be developed.

Introducing an Innovation

Based on past research and theory, it is possible to predict the most likely concerns profile for a faculty about to embark on a change effort. If no unusual information is known about the innovation or the faculty, then the prospective users of the innovation can be assumed to have the typical "nonusers" concerns profile (see figure 3). That is, their concerns will be more intense on Stage 0 Awareness, Stage 1 Informational, and Stage 2 Personal. Their concerns will be relatively less intense on the impact stages of Stage 4 Consequence, Stage 5 Collaboration, and Stage 6 Refocusing. With this admittedly limited understanding at the time of planning for a change effort, it is possible to make strategic and tactical decisions about how the change process should be launched.

For example, it can be assumed that interventions will need to be designed that address the more intense informational and personal concerns. To address the informational concerns, obviously information should be provided. One of the subtleties of intense informational concerns, however is that they require a particular type and quantity of information. Persons with high informational concerns do not want massive detail and a bombardment of information about the innovation; rather, they need a small amount of information at any one time, but repeated offerings of information. Intervention can be done through a combination of media, ranging from face-to-face conversations, brief reports in staff meetings, the use of newsletters, and press releases. The key is to begin with providing general information using several different media resources, then to gradually increase the amounts.

In addition to informational concerns, nonusers tend to have high Stage 2 Personal concerns. They may be concerned about their capability to function with the innovation or about the ambiguity and uncertainty the introduction of the innovation may cause. They are apt to have concerns about how the principal and other authorities will perceive their use of the innovation, and about the administration's priority for innovation use. These types of personal concerns require specialized interventions. For example, the principal can state in a staff meeting that he or she is very supportive of the innovation. The principal could go further and show excitement about the innovation and its promise. In other contexts, the principal and other change facilitators can anticipate that teachers will feel uncomfortable for a while, and they can express *that it is okay* for teachers to have some feelings of uncertainty at first, that it is a frequent experience in the change process.

When personal concerns are more intense, it is important to have more face-to-face contact and be more encouraging than when other Stages of Concern are intense. For instance, facilitators should visit more often with teachers on a one-to-one basis to offer assistance and encouragement. If the Stage 2 Personal concerns are not resolved but are further heightened, due either to innovation characteristics or uncertainty about the implications of innovation use or the direction of the change process, then the entire evolution of the change process and the potential for the arousal of higher Stages of Concern are endangered. When an individual is primarily concerned about himself or herself, that person does not have much residual energy for concern about the tasks and consequences of innovation use. In general, change facilitators should be supersensitive to the possible arousal of personal concerns and address those concerns to achieve their early resolution. Unless this resolution is accomplished early in a change effort, the implementation phase can become prolonged. The personal concerns of individuals can also "feed" on each other, further heightening them. In the end, many "good" innovations can be lost due to inadequately addressing or assisting teachers in resolving their personal concerns.

The Implementation Phase

During early implementation, as teachers begin to use the innovation, Stage 3 Management concerns typically become more intense. At this point, it is important to provide "how to do it" workshops and in other ways address the constantly changing topics of management concerns. Management concerns change as teachers turn the page in the manual and encounter new tasks and activities to be implemented. They also change based on the trials of daily attempts to use the new method. One implication of our recent research is that Stage 3 Management concerns should not be addressed solely by providing day-long workshops. Rather, various kinds of alternative interventions should be used that allow for quick and idiosyncratic responses to the constantly evolving management concerns. The employment of in-house/resident experts for advice in using the innovation can be helpful. Having a hot line that teachers can call or holding "comfort and caring" sessions in the schools where an expert answers "how to do it questions" will help. Providing newsletters and teachers' manuals that easily and correctly address "how to do it" questions can also be useful.

Due to the diversity of the specific task questions teachers ask, offering an all-day workshop that all teachers must attend becomes problematic. Any one management concern question will be relevant only to a subset of the total group in attendance at the workshop. For example, one subset of participants will have already confronted that question and found an answer. They will rate that particular aspect of the workshop as "boring." Another subset of the faculty will not have reached that activity yet and, therefore, do not have task concerns about that specific item. This second subset, too, will rate the workshop as "boring." The third subset will be involved in the activity and be most interested in the response to the question. They, of course, will rate the workshop as being very relevant. However, for the next question asked, the membership of the subsets will shift, once again likely resulting in a majority not finding the particular question of immediate relevance to them. Thus, the use of alternative mechanisms to all-day "how to do it" workshops needs to be considered for addressing most Stage 3 Management concerns.

The key to remember is that management concerns are intense during the first use of most innovations. Principals and other change facilitators should not be surprised when teachers express them. In fact, based upon research and theory, facilitators should anticipate these management/task concerns by having mechanisms planned and placed in advance to address the implementation phase.

The Arousal of Impact Concerns

The introduction and implementation of an innovation can be judged successful when concerns at Stages 1, 2, and 3 have been resolved. The arousal of *impact* concerns (Stage 4 Consequence, Stage 5 Collaboration, and Stage 6 Refocusing), however, does not necessarily follow. Some teachers naturally begin to express concerns related to student outcomes, however most teachers will need a new round of experiences to arouse impact concerns. Once aroused, impact concerns require additional forms of support and encouragement from the principal and other change facilitators. A new series of requests for resources, staff development, and alternative arrangements will be forthcoming. In the case of impact concerns, the reasons for these requests and changes have to do with concerns for increasing the effectiveness of the use of the innovation; with the self and task concerns, the primary intent was to make use easier and more comfortable for teachers.

For ultimate success from a concerns-based point of view, the resolution of self and task concerns is only part of the final goal. The arousal of impact concerns is also desirable. After all, ideal teachers as represented in the professional literature and in general discussions are primarily concerned about their students' learning and their collegial relationships with other teachers. Teachers can develop these kinds of impact concerns, but only if change facilitators and the context first help them resolve their self and task concerns and then support their arousal of student-oriented concerns. In the various interventions suggested throughout this book, emphasis is placed upon providing theory, concepts, and suggestions for practices that can lead to the arousal of impact concerns on the part of teachers.

Our research clearly demonstrates that the arousal of impact concerns is directly related to what principals and others do and do not do. It is, of course, possible for teachers to experience Stage 4 Consequence concerns and perhaps intense Stage 6 Refocusing concerns on their own. The arousal of Stage 5 Collaboration concerns, though, generally requires encouragement and support from the principal. If there is not sanctioning and encouragement for teachers to work together, then they will be more apt to work independently.

To broaden this point, the arousal of impact concerns at all three stages in large part rests upon the priorities and actions taken by the principal. If emphasis is not placed on what happens with students and good teaching is not encouraged and supported, it is very difficult for teachers by themselves to develop and maintain impact concerns. In many ways, the presence of such concern becomes a strong indicator of school climate. If teachers tend to have stronger impact concerns, the school as a whole is likely to be seen as more productive and student outcomes will tend to be higher. In our research, the more productive schools with higher student outcomes have clearly achieved this goal through a combination of principal leadership and faculty and staff working together. Such coordination regularly occurs in spite of the characteristics of the local context and student population.

Developing the conditions that stimulate teacher impact concerns takes time. In fact, for most innovations and innovation bundles it takes three to five years! Admittedly, some relatively simple innovations such as changing reading textbooks in an elementary school can be accomplished in a year or two, but most innovations represent bigger changes and are not always supported by ongoing change facilitator involvement. In addition, most schools are not given three or four years to implement a particular innovation. More typically several innovations are introduced each year. Unfortunately for teachers and students, in many cases the various innovations do not complement each other, and in some cases, they place conflicting demands on teachers and students. It is possible to see teachers complete the wave sequence of concerns illustrated in figure 3, but it takes time and skill on the part of teachers and change facilitators.

Discussion and Summary

In summary, we suggest that the concerns concept can be used in developing the overall plan for a change process by anticipating the arousal and resolution of the different Stages of Concern. For example, in planning for a change effort, we know that, typically, informational and personal concerns will at first be intense, so in-service and other activities should be designed to address these concerns. An initial, general overview of the innovation and the planned change process can be helpful. In addition, the initial expectations for individuals should be made clear. How much is expected and a reasonable time line for accomplishing these tasks should be introduced. There should be positive and supportive comments about the innovation and teachers' future use of it. After the innovation is introduced and as individuals begin to implement it, they are apt to have higher management concerns. This possibility can be anticipated, and the necessary planning for addressing many of these concerns can be done in advance. Training sessions, visits to locations where implementation has been successful, coaching, and consultation are all support activities that are appropriate. The long-range plan, then, should anticipate individuals' early concerns at Stages 1 and 2, followed by Stage 3 concerns, and initial thought should be given to what will likely be needed to address the future arousal of impact concerns. Such planning is consistent with our position that change is a process, that there is a personal side to that process, and that the concerns-based change facilitator's responsibility is to anticipate and address concerns.

As the change process unfolds, Stages of Concern can be assessed in several ways so that day-to-day interventions, as well as the larger tactical and strategic interventions, can be adjusted. If the principal and other concerns-based change facilitators are using one-legged conferencing and open-ended statements, they will be closely in touch with how things are going. The Stages of Concern Questionnaire (SoCQ) can be used once or twice a year with a representative sample to collect more objective data about progress. Using these data to chart progress has been very useful to upper-level administrators and policymakers, especially for those that are more event oriented. With the SoCQ profiles, progress in the process can be illustrated and logical explanations can be made for why the change is not complete and what is needed next. With study and, when available, training, it is possible to become sensitive to the dynamic of concerns and to become skilled in the unobtrusive and more direct ways of assessing and interpreting Stages of Concern information. These abilities can be a powerful tool for monitoring and a highly effective diagnostic tool for change facilitation.

Discussion Points

There are many different issues that could be addressed in this brief discussion section, however several are particularly important to emphasize.

IT IS OKAY TO HAVE PERSONAL CONCERNS. Stage 2 Personal concerns are a natural and typical part of the change process.

Research and theory demonstrate the regular occurrence of these concerns. Teachers often express discomfort about having personal concerns and frequently change facilitators ignore, downplay, or even become impatient with persons who experience them. Change facilitators and teachers need to recognize that having high personal concerns is justifiable at some points in the change process. It is *not* okay for change facilitators to put down, ignore, or inappropriately address intense personal concerns. In fact, doing so is an almost sure way to endanger the entire change process, and at a minimum, it creates a number of side issues and resistance to change that will then have to be addressed.

Marsh and Jordan-Marsh (1985) have proposed that there are three clusters of concerns within personal concerns: (1) organizational/political/professional. (2) decision-making commitment, and (3) self-task. These clusters can be a way to analyze personal concerns in more depth. Interventions can be planned using the characteristics of each cluster and the relative emphasis a client places on the three clusters in combination. Marsh and Jordan-Marsh turned to the psychological literature on decision making and efficacy (particularly Janis and Mann 1976; and Bandura 1981) for structures and suggestions to use in developing interventions customized to a particular clustering of personal concerns. Probably, similar multidisciplinary analyses can be applied to the dynamics of other Stages of Concern as well.

CHANGE FACILITATORS HAVE CONCERNS, TOO. The concerns theory does not apply only to teachers; it applies to principals and other change facilitators as well (Rutherford, Hall, and George 1982). We all have a strong likelihood of going through similar progressions in our concerns about a change. The difference is in the topic of the concerns rather than in the dynamic of the Stages of Concern themselves. Principals have concerns about their roles as instructional leader and change facilitator. District office persons have concerns, so do parents, company employees, and presidents. Relative to their various roles, individuals can experience self, task, and impact concerns at different times.

Again, it is okay to have concerns at any of these different stages. What is required of principals and other change facilitators is that they recognize their own concerns and that they adjust interventions according to the concerns of their clients. They need to do this adjustment in spite of their own concerns. Accomplishing this task is asking a lot, especially if the facilitator has high personal or management concerns. To put aside the expression of their own personal or management concerns in order to be responsive to and supportive of teachers is a difficult and, in some cases, nearly impossible request. For the success of the change process, however, it is important that leaders not become preoccupied with their own personal and task concerns. If they do, these concerns are likely to be reflected by their staffs.

Ideally, supervisors and consultants who work with principals and other change facilitators will address and resolve the facilitator's concerns. In this way, the concerns-based approach applies regardless of who the change facilitators and clients are. We all have concerns, and we will be most effective and demonstrate the most growth when our concerns are appropriately addressed.

THE ETHICS OF CONCERNS-BASED INTERVENING. A word change facilitators usually try to avoid when thinking about their work is manipulation. Whether we like it or not, the role and responsibility of a change facilitator entails encouraging individuals to change, and some would characterize this task as manipulating what others do. In the concerns-based approach, we advocate that it is inappropriate not to address the concerns teachers and others have in the process of changing. The most human and user-oriented way to work is to understand individuals' needs and to provide facilitation in ways that are in alignment with this diagnosis.

A very poor practice of change facilitators is failing to listen or understand the concerns of the individuals with whom they are working. Disregarding concerns typically results in the facilitator decreeing change. This approach has historically been typical of policymakers, legislators, and others who are organizationally removed from life in the classroom. They seem to have little understanding of the change process as it is experienced by front-line users. From a concerns-based point of view, the ethical approach to change facilitation is to base interventions on the needs of teachers, students, or other clients, not simply to use formal authority to force a change.

Effective change facilitators frequently ask themselves whether what they are doing is "right." There is no simple or concrete answer. However, we have observed that good facilitators do think about the question from time to time and that this questioning in itself seems to clarify what is appropriate. Effective facilitators also have a vision of where the school should be going, defined in large part by what is important for students. Their interventions are designed to facilitate movement toward the vision, which may be the best definition of right we can have.

Most of this discussion has implicitly assumed that the innovation is appropriate. Inappropriate innovations will be expressed in teacher's concerns. The effective change facilitator will hear intense Stage 2 Personal, Stage 3 Management, and "tail up" Stage 6 Refocusing concerns that seriously and sometimes adamantly, question (for right or wrong reasons) whether or not the innovation is appropriate. The effective change facilitator will heed these clues and make adjustments. In some cases, the innovation may be wrong or poorly matched to the local setting. In other instances, special steps need to be taken to address the highly aroused Stage 2 Personal, Stage 3 Management, and Stage 6 Refocusing concerns. For these situations, the reader needs to know more about concerns theory than is presented in this chapter. The various resources cited in this chapter and the rest of the book should be referred to.

Chapter 4

Is It Being Used?
Levels Of Use
Of An Innovation

Teacher A

She handles the home economics program in a well-orchestrated way. She has organized the Textile lab into kits and each year she puts her students through some training sessions on how to work in committees, how to obtain clothing samples and use laboratory equipment, and how to return them for use by others. At the outset it took her some time to get all the wrinkles ironed out, but last year and this year all her systems have operated like clockwork.

Teacher B

He wrote to the sales representative to find out what the physics curriculum looked like. As a result, he went to an inservice opportunity offered by the representative, and now he's visiting a high school using the program. He has talked with his colleagues about whether they think it would work in their department.

Teacher C

Can you believe it? During the Work Day last month she made a bright colored folder for each first grader and pulled the kids math books apart. Instead of giving the whole class the same instruction and assignment as she had been doing, she pulled out the part of the math book each individual pupil was ready for and put it in their folder. Then she grouped the folders according to the objective of the lessons and taught each objective to the pupils who were ready for it. She made instruction and the pupils' practice individualized for them. She is always coming up with new ideas.

These descriptions of teachers are different from those in chapter 3 in a very important way. Did you notice the difference? If you did not, it will become obvious as soon as it is pointed out: These statements are descriptions of behaviors. Affect, perceptions, and feelings are left out; the emphasis is on describing what teachers are *doing* relative to a particular innovation. This behavioral orientation becomes a second important way of understanding and facilitating change.

In our early field work and experience, we observed that teachers and college professors employed a variety of behaviors as the change process unfolded and that there was a pattern to their evolution. Analyzing whether an innovation was used did not involve a simple, dichotomous yes/no question, as had been suggested through the literature and in announcements by policymakers. Asking whether teachers used or did not use an innovation turned out to be too simplistic. Rather, there are "levels" of use that can be identified and distinguished.

As the second diagnostic dimension of the CBAM, eight different Levels of Use of an innovation (LoU) have been identified and operationally defined. As with Stages of Concern, Levels of Use can serve as a valuable diagnostic tool for planning and facilitating the change process. Unlike the Stages of Concern dimension, Levels of use focuses on the behaviors that are or are not taking place in relation to the innovation. Stages of Concern, described in the preceding chapter, can be useful to the facilitator in tracing the feelings and perceptions of individuals as they experience change; however, what people feel and how they perceive a situation can be quite different from what they actually do. These differences can be distinguished conceptually and operationally when both SoC and LoU are addressed.

In this chapter, we describe the eight Levels of Use of an innovation. Research findings and examples from practice are used throughout the chapter. We conclude with a discussion of implications and applications of the Levels of Use diagnostic dimension for planning, facilitating, and monitoring the change process. In chapters 10 and 11, examples of how the SoC and LoU dimensions can be used in combination are presented.

The Levels of Use Concept

Often when an idea is introduced, it is seen as so obvious and makes so much sense that it is difficult to imagine there was a time when the idea was not a part of common knowledge. The work being done regarding Levels of Use is an interesting illustration of this phenomenon. During the 1960s, heavy emphasis was placed on curriculum development; however, little or no attention was given to what happened or what was needed at the classroom level following the initial teacher training and purchase of the related curriculum materials. Follow-up work for facilitating implementation and for evaluating classroom use of the new programs was regularly omitted. Before the mid-1970s, school leaders assumed, at least implicitly, that the use of a new program or promising practice was taking place if the materials had been delivered to the classroom. This assumption was held not only by administrators within a district but also by the developers of the innovations and, what is even more surprising, by the evaluators of the product. Questions about how the new curriculum was faring in classrooms were asked of the principal or someone from the central office. Mailed surveys were commonly used to find out in how many classrooms and schools particular programs or practices were being used. Rarely did evaluators directly observe in classrooms or directly assess the teachers using the new programs and procedures. Thus, it is not particularly surprising that in many of the evaluation studies done earlier, the major finding was that there was "no significant differences" between the old program and the new. We know now that each "user" must be assessed directly if reliable and valid information is to be gathered about whether or not new practices are in use and in what way they are being used in particular classrooms.

From our field work in schools and colleges in the late 1960s and early 1970s, eight different levels for assessing the use of an innovation were identified, operationally defined, and verified. These levels represent different behavioral approaches to the use of an innovation, approaches that move beyond the simple matter of no use versus full use. The Levels of Use definitions are presented in figure 6 and include three "nonuse" descriptions and five "use" descriptions.

A Brief Description of the Levels of Use

When defining the levels, heavy emphasis was placed on developing definitions of what can be seen and observed; each level represents a different behavioral approach. For example, the person at Level of Use 0, Nonuse, is described by the absence of innovation-related behavior. The person is not looking at, reading about, using, or discussing the innovation. All interviews and observations of the person indicate no steps toward involvement with the innovation. Surprisingly, research and evaluation efforts have indicated that in many so-called treatment or experimental schools where a new program is assumed to be in use, there are apt to be one or more teachers at the 0 Level of Use. As was described above, principals and evaluators frequently assume that all teachers in the "using" schools are users, yet direct assessment of individual teachers' Levels of Use may reveal teachers at the 0 Level of Use state. This finding obviously has implications for staff development and related change facilitating activities.

There is a typical progression in a person's movements through the levels of Use. The progression is not locked in step by step, however, in general, people move in sequence from Level of Use 0, Nonuse, to Level of Use IVA, Routine. This progression assumes, of course, that the innovation is appropriate, the principal and other change facilitators do their job, and time is provided. For example, persons who move out of Level of Use 0 typically move to a Level of Use I, Orientation. At this level, behaviors entail looking for information about the innovation, talking to others, attending an orientation workshop, reading descriptive brochures, and conducting a general exploration of the potential for and possibilities of use of the innovation and alternatives. A person at Level of Use I, however, has not made a commitment to use the innovation.

The decision to use an innovation brings a person to a Level of Use II, Preparation. In addition to having made the decision to begin using the innovation, the person at Level of Use II has shifted his/her behavioral pattern to one of preparing materials and space and planning for the first use of the innovation. In

Figure 6
Levels of Use of the Innovation

VI   RENEWAL: State in which the user reevaluates the quality of use of the innovation, seeks major modifications of or alternatives to present innovation to achieve increased impact on clients, examines new developments in the field, and explores new goals for self and the system.

V   INTEGRATION: State in which the user is combining own efforts to use the innovation with related activities of colleagues to achieve a collective impact on clients within their common sphere of influence.

IVB   REFINEMENT: State in which the user varies the use of the innovation to increase the impact on clients within immediate sphere of influence. Variations are based on knowledge of both short- and long-term consequences for clients.

IVA   ROUTINE: Use of the innovation is stabilized. Few if any changes are being made in ongoing use. Little preparation or thought is being given to improving innovation use or its consequences.

III   MECHANICAL USE: State in which the user focuses most effort on the short-term, day-to-day use of the innovation with little time for reflection. Changes in use are made more to meet user needs than client needs. The user is primarily engaged in a stepwise attempt to master the tasks required to use the innovation, often resulting in disjointed and superficial use.

II   PREPARATION: State in which the user is preparing for first use of the innovation.

I   ORIENTATION: State in which the user has recently acquired or is acquiring information about the innovation and/or has recently explored or is exploring its value orientation and its demands upon user and user system.

0   NONUSE: State in which the user has little or no knowledge of the innovation, no involvement with the innovation, and is doing nothing toward becoming involved.

Excerpted from: The LoU Chart: Operational Definitions of Levels of Use of the Innovation. Austin: Research and Development Center for Teacher Education, The University of Texas, 1975.

many instances, the decision to begin its use may not have been made by the individual. Frequently, school staff, district administrators, state agency personnel (and increasingly legislators), as well as the federal government decide that an innovation will be used. Thus, teachers may move into Preparation Level of Use behavior patterns as a consequence of the decisions of others. Regardless, for persons at LoU II, the time for beginning use is clear and behaviors focus on preparing for that first use. Note that the three levels described so far are different states of being a "nonuser."

The first use of an innovation is typically reflected in Level of Use III, Mechanical, behaviors. At this level, there is a tendency for disjointedness and a lack of smoothness in sequencing, pacing, and distributing materials and activities. Individuals at this level cling to the users guide. Inefficiency in the use of time, materials, and resources, and a short-term focus are common. Often, individuals at LoU III exhibit a day-to-day or even hour-to-hour focus, with less clarity about the long-term picture and how the innovation will be used next week or month. Individuals typically remain at the mechanical level for an extended period of time; a year or two is not uncommon for complex innovations and innovation bundles.

As they become experienced in using the new materials and/or procedures, teachers tend to move into Level of Use IVA, Routine. Persons at this Level of Use have established an equilibrium in what they are doing. They know the routines and the longer-term sequence of the innovation's use. Further, there is stability, and they are unchanging in their pattern of use.

The type of changes or modifications a teacher makes is an important clue to determining Levels of Use. For example, teachers at the Routine Level of Use are not making any modifications. They have systems already worked out, and routines are in place. They know where they are going and have no plans to change. In contrast, a teacher at the Mechanical Level of Use is adapting the innovation or their use of it, in many instances doing so on a moment-to-moment and day-to-day basis. They are making changes in schedules, preparation, logistics, the time spent on particular activities, the assignment of students, and grading and reporting procedures. The primary reason for all of these changes at LoU III is to increase efficiency or reduce the task burden in using the innovation.

The LoU III adaptations or the LoU IVA lack of changes can be contrasted with the changes persons at Level of Use IVB, Refinement; V, Integration; and VI, Renewal, make. At these higher levels, adaptations are intended to improve the effectiveness and positive outcomes from using the innovation. Individuals at a Level of Use IVB, Refinement, for example, are working within their classroom to get greater impact from the use of the innovation. Perhaps the refinement is the addition of specially built materials to involve students who can not read at grade level or the addition of another component to a learning center. The LoU IVB teacher might attend a workshop to enhance teaching skills or to explain some particular element of the innovation. The focus is now on increasing effects with students.

Teachers at Level of Use V make a commitment to use the innovation with other teachers. As at Level of Use IVB, changes are made to improve the effectiveness of innovation use. At LoU V, those changes are made to accommodate the related use of one or more other teachers. This use of the innovation enhances the outcomes that can be obtained through coordinated and integrated working efforts.

Individuals at Level of Use VI, Renewal, make major modifications in the innovation or in their innovation use by adding significant new and different components, or perhaps they are exploring alternatives that could be used to replace it altogether. In either case, the purpose is to improve the effects associated with innovation use through major modification or change. Out of the LoU research, a slightly different kind of Level of Use VI person has been identified, referred to as the LoU VI"G" in recognition of John Gardner and his book *Self Renewal* (1964). The Level of Use VIG person makes many small modifications, has an array of ideas, and displays a great deal of creative energy that is focused on working with the innovation. The result is constant alteration and activity, all related to increasing innovation effectiveness.

A More Detailed Definition of Levels of Use

In the research and training work that has been done with Levels of Use, the emphasis has been on operationally defining the concept. Clear definitions are helpful for facilitators and increases reliability and validity estimates for researchers. A set of Decision Points were developed to clarify the distinctions between each Level of Use. These Decision Points make it possible to use one key behavioral act as a basic discriminator of each Level of Use. As a further step in defining the meaning of each level, nearly a thousand behavioral indicators were generated. These indicators were retrieved from field notes and staff discussions about the meaning of each Level of Use. The end product was the clustering of indicators around a set of dimensions or "categories" that cut across the levels. These behavioral indicators and categories are useful for research purposes, since they further clarify the different Levels of Use by distinguishing subparts in each level. The categories are also helpful to facilitators interested in fine-tuning their diagnostic and monitoring skills. The definitions of Levels of Use, the Decision Points, and the categories are summarized in the LoU chart (Hall, Loucks, Rutherford, and Newlove 1975), included as figure 7.

The categories cut across the Levels of Use and have unique sets of behavioral indicators within each level. Interestingly, this work expanded our understanding of what use means. The categories reflect behavior occurring both inside and outside the classroom. What is typically thought of as direct use of the innovation, that is, what happens in classrooms, is grouped under the *Performing* category. All other categories and behavioral indicators represent innovation-related behavior occurring outside the actual classroom. This significant characteristic of the LoU concept should help facilitators appreciate the significance of the range of activities teachers become involved with when an innovation is introduced. The activity that occurs within the classroom plus the innovation-related behaviors exhibited before and after classroom performance combine to form the totality of innovation use. This perspective broadens the change facilitator's field of vision and range of intervention opportunities. In both innovation nonuse and use categories significant amounts of activity occur before and after classroom time.

As already stated, the categories extend across the Levels of Use. For example, the knowledge a person has about an innovation accumulates and becomes increasingly comprehensive and

Figure 7
Levels of Use of the Innovation

CATEGORIES

Scale point definitions of the levels of use of the innovation	Knowledge	Acquiring Information	Sharing	Assessing	Planning	Status Reporting	Performing
Level 0 NON-USE							
Decision Point A Level I ORIENTATION							
Decision Point B Level II PREPARATION							
Decision Point C Level III MECHANICAL USE							
Decision Point D-1 Level IV A ROUTINE							
Decision Point D-2 Level IV B REFINEMENT							
Decision Point E Level V INTEGRATION							
Decision Point F Level VI RENEWAL							

This figure presents the framework of the Levels of Use chart. The text of the chart is provided by category in the following figures:

7A Knowledge
7B Acquiring Information
7C Sharing
7D Assessing
7E Planning
7F Status Reporting
7G Performing

Hall, G.E., Loucks, S.F., Rutherford, W.L., and Newlove, B.W. Levels of Use of the Innovation: A framework for analyzing innovation adoption. The Journal of Teacher Education, 1975, 26 (1), 52–56.

SCALE POINT DEFINITIONS OF THE LEVELS OF USE OF THE INNOVATION

Levels of Use are distinct states that represent observably different types of behavior and patterns of innovation use as exhibited by individuals and groups. These levels characterize a user's development in acquiring new skills and varying use of the innovation. Each level encompasses a range of behaviors, but is limited by a set of identifiable Decision Points. For descriptive purposes, each level is defined by seven categories.

KNOWLEDGE

That which the user knows about characteristics of the innovation, how to use it, and consequences of its use. This is cognitive knowledge related to using the innovation, not feelings or attitudes.

LEVEL 0
NON-USE: State in which the user has little or no knowledge of the innovation, no involvement with the innovation, and is doing nothing toward becoming involved.

Knows nothing about this or similar innovations or has only very limited general knowledge of efforts to develop innovations in the area.

DECISION POINT A:
Takes action to learn more detailed information about the innovation.

LEVEL I
ORIENTATION: State in which the user has recently acquired or is acquiring information about the innovation and/or has recently explored or is exploring its value orientation and its demands upon user and user system.

Knows general information about the innovation such as origin, characteristics, and implementation requirements.

DECISION POINT B:
Makes a decision to use the innovation by establishing a time to begin.

LEVEL II
PREPARATION: State in which the user is preparing for first use of the innovation.

Knows logistical requirements, necessary resources and timing for initial use of the innovation, and details of initial experiences for clients.

DECISION POINT C:
Changes, if any, and use are dominated by user needs.
LEVEL III
MECHANICAL USE: State in which the user focuses most effort on the short-term, day-to-day use of the innovation with little time for reflection. Changes in use are made more to meet user needs than client needs. The user is primarily engaged in a stepwise attempt to master the tasks required to use the innovation, often resulting in disjointed and superficial use.

Knows on a day-to-day basis the requirements for using the innovation. Is more knowledgeable about short-term activities and effects than long-range activities and effects of use of the innovation.

DECISION POINT D-1:
A routine pattern of use is established.

LEVEL IV A
ROUTINE: Use of the innovation is stabilized. Few if any changes are being made in ongoing use. Little preparation or thought is being given to improving innovation use or its consequences.

Knows both short- and long-term requirements for use and how to use the innovation with minimum effort or stress.

DECISION POINT D-2:
Changes use of the innovation based on formal or informal evaluation in order to increase client outcomes.

LEVEL IV B
REFINEMENT: State in which the user varies the use of the innovation to increase the impact on clients within immediate sphere of influence. Variations are based on knowledge of both short- and long-term consequences for clients.

Knows cognitive and affective effects of the innovation on clients and ways for increasing impact on clients.

DECISION POINT E:
Initiates changes in use of innovation based on input of and in coordination with what colleagues are doing.

LEVEL V
INTEGRATION: State in which the user is combining own efforts to use the innovation with related activities of colleagues to achieve a collective impact on clients within their common sphere of influence.

Knows how to coordinate own use of the innovation with colleagues to provide a collective impact on clients.

DECISION POINT F:
Begins exploring alternatives to or major modifications of the innovation presently in use.
LEVEL VI
RENEWAL: State in which the user reevaluates the quality of use of the innovation, seeks major modifications of or alternatives to present innovation to achieve increased impact on clients, examines new developments in the field, and explores new goals for self and the system.

Knows of alternatives that could be used to change or replace the present innovation that would improve the quality of outcomes of its use.

LoU	ACQUIRING INFORMATION Solicits information about the innovation in a variety of ways, including questioning resource persons, corresponding with resource agencies, reviewing printed materials, and making visits.	SHARING Discusses the innovation with others. Shares plans, ideas, resources, outcomes, and problems related to use of the innovation.	ASSESSING Examines the potential or actual use of the innovation or some aspect of it. This can be a mental assessment or can involve actual collection and analysis of data.
LEVEL 0	Takes little or no action to solicit information beyond reviewing descriptive information about this or similar innovations when it happens to come to personal attention.	Is not communicating with others about the innovation beyond possibly acknowledging that the innovation exists.	Takes no action to analyze the innovation, its characteristics, possible use, or consequences of use.
LEVEL I	Seeks descriptive material about the innovation. Seeks opinions and knowledge of others through discussions, visits, or workshops.	Discusses the innovation in general terms and/or exchanges descriptive information, materials, or ideas about the innovation and possible implications of its use.	Analyzes and compares materials, content, requirements for use, evaluation reports, potential outcomes, strengths and weaknesses for purpose of making a decision about use of the innovation.
LEVEL II	Seeks information and resources specifically related to preparation for use of the innovation in own setting.	Discusses resources needed for initial use of the innovation. Joins others in pre-use training, and in planning for resources, logistics, schedules, etc., in preparation for first use.	Analyzes detailed requirements and available resources for initial use of the innovation.
LEVEL III	Solicits management information about such things as logistics, scheduling techniques, and ideas for reducing amount of time and work required of user.	Discusses management and logistical issues related to use of the innovation. Resources and materials are shared for purposes of reducing management, flow and logistical problems related to use of the innovation.	Examines own use of the innovation with respect to problems of logistics, management, time, schedules, resources, and general reactions of clients.
LEVEL IV A	Makes no special efforts to seek information as a part of ongoing use of the innovation.	Describes current use of the innovation with little or no reference to ways of changing use.	Assesses use of the innovation in global terms without reference to making changes. Specific evaluation activities are limited to those that are administratively required with little attention paid to findings for the purpose of changing use.
LEVEL IV B	Solicits information and materials that focus specifically on changing use of the innovation to affect client outcomes.	Discusses own methods of modifying use of the innovation to change client outcomes.	Assesses use of the innovation for the purpose of changing current practices to improve client outcomes.
LEVEL V	Solicits information and opinions for the purpose of collaborating with others in use of the innovation.	Discusses efforts to increase client impact through collaboration with others on personal use of the innovation.	Appraises collaborative use of the innovation in terms of client outcomes and strengths and weaknesses of the integrated effort.
LEVEL VI	Seeks information and materials about other innovations as alternatives to the present innovation or for making major adaptations in the innovation.	Focuses discussions on identification of major alternatives or replacements for the current innovation.	Analyzes advantages and disadvantages of major modifications or alternatives to the present innovation.

LoU	PLANNING Designs and outlines short- and/or long-range steps to be taken during process of innovation adoption, i.e., aligns resources, schedules activities, meets with others to organize and/or coordinate use of the innovation.	STATUS REPORTING Describes personal stand at the present time in relation to use of the innovation.	PERFORMING Carries out the actions and activities entailed in operationalizing the innovation.
LEVEL 0	Schedules no time and specifies no steps for the study or use of the innovation.	Reports little or no personal involvement with the innovation.	Takes no discernible action toward learning about or using the innovation. The innovation and/or its accouterments are not present or in use.
LEVEL I	Plans to gather necessary information and resources as needed to make a decision for or against use of the innovation.	Reports presently orienting self to what the innovation is and is not.	Explores the innovation and requirements for its use by talking to others about it, reviewing descriptive information and sample materials, attending orientation sessions, and observing others using it.
LEVEL II	Identifies steps and procedures entailed in obtaining resources and organizing activities and events for initial use of the innovation.	Reports preparing self for initial use of the innovation.	Studies reference materials in depth, organizes resources and logistics, schedules and receives skill training in preparation for initial use.
LEVEL III	Plans for organizing and managing resources, activities, and events related primarily to immediate ongoing use of the innovation. Planned-for changes address managerial or logistical issues with a short-term perspective.	Reports that logistics, time, management, resource organization, etc., are the focus of most personal efforts to use the innovation.	Manages innovation with varying degrees of efficiency. Often lacks anticipation of immediate consequences. The flow of actions in the user and clients is often disjointed, uneven and uncertain. When changes are made, they are primarily in response to logistical and organizational problems.
LEVEL IV A	Plans intermediate and long-range actions with little projected variation in how the innovation will be used. Planning focuses on routine use of resources, personnel, etc.	Reports that personal use of the innovation is going along satisfactorily with few if any problems.	Uses the innovation smoothly with minimal management problems; over time, there is little variation in pattern of use.
LEVEL IV B	Develops intermediate and long-range plans that anticipate possible and needed steps, resources, and events designed to enhance client outcomes.	Reports varying use of the innovation in order to change client outcomes.	Explores and experiments with alternative combinations of the innovation with existing practices to maximize client involvement and to optimize client outcomes.
LEVEL V	Plans specific actions to coordinate own use of the innovation with others to achieve increased impact on clients.	Reports spending time and energy collaborating with others about integrating own use of the innovation.	Collaborates with others in use of the innovation as a means for expanding the innovation's impact on clients. Changes in use are made in coordination with others.
LEVEL VI	Plans activities that involve pursuit of alternatives to enhance or replace the innovation.	Reports considering major modifications of or alternatives to present use of the innovation.	Explores other innovations that could be used in combination with or in place of the present innovation in an attempt to develop more effective means of achieving client outcomes.

sophisticated as the individual moves to higher Levels of Use. A Level of Use 0, Nonuse, person's knowledge is minimal at best and probably includes inaccuracies, while the person at Level of Use IVB, Refinement, has a great deal of knowledge about using the innovation and the effects of its use. In addition, LoU IVB knowledge includes understanding of the ways variations in use can contribute to increasing positive student outcomes.

Another example of the dimensionality of the LoU categories can be illustrated by analyzing the kinds of information that are sought. The *Acquiring Information* category is designed for this purpose. The person at Level of Use II, Preparation, is looking for information to help prepare for first use. The person at Level of Use IVA, Routine, is not looking for any information ("Although I may read something if it comes across my desk," or they might listen in on a conversation). They do not deliberately go out to acquire information about the innovation.

The *Sharing* category has a special emphasis too. This category is not related to the information one acquires during a conversation with another; rather, it has to do with what people tell others about what they are doing with the innovation. For example, a teacher might describe to another teacher while picking up their mail how he/she uses the innovation.

The *Assessing* category is not only for the formal administration of tests and interpretation of those data, but also includes the moment-to-moment reflection and self-examination a person does regarding an innovation and its use. For example, individuals at LoU III, Mechanical, may spend a great deal of time analyzing and assessing the strengths and weaknesses of their approaches and their various inefficiencies. Teachers working as a part of a collaborative team at LoU V, Integration, are apt to be assessing the merits and weaknesses of their and their colleagues' performances and contemplating what can be done to further refine and improve that working relationship for the express purpose of increasing innovation-related, positive outcomes.

Planning is a particularly useful category for change facilitators. Discovering a teacher's plan provides a good indication of the upcoming resource requirements, potential workshop needs, and other kinds of support that teacher will be needing. For example, a teacher at LoU I, Orientation, might be thinking of attending an orientation workshop or might be making a note to seek out some descriptive information about the innovation and its alternatives. This planning is of a very different form than what would be done by a person at Level of Use VI, Renewal. The latter person could be planning to take a special, two-week summer workshop that will demonstrate a significantly different innovation to replace the "old" innovation.

The *Status Reporting* category includes indicators, such as summary statements, that a person gives about their overall Level of Use. Illustrative of this category is the teacher at the Mechanical Level of Use who describes his/her innovation use as disjointed, that he/she is unsure where to go next. Teachers at LoU IVA, Routine, would indicate that everything is going fine, they know where they are going and have no plans for change. In addition to reporting on their status, this type of expression may relate to some of the other categories as well, for instance, planning.

These categories provide a structure for more detailed diagnoses and a way to organize the many indicators collected for determining a teacher's Level of Use. When all the categorical information is added up, it provides the overall definition for each of the eight levels first introduced in figure 6. In real life, the ratings for these categories will not always fall straight across a particular level. Category ratings at more than one level is a regular occurrence; however, for a given teacher, the categories typically line up fairly close to a particular Level of Use. The skilled Levels of Use assessor is able to use the categories to identify more detailed differences within an overall Level of Use and to use these differences to fine-tune the planning of interventions and to interpret evaluation results. This skill, of course, takes study, training, and practice. A brief description of how LoU assessments are made is presented next.

Assessing Levels of Use

Assessing Levels of Use is more complex and in some ways more subtle than assessing Stages of Concern. LoU is a behaviorally defined variable with a large number of indicators and categorical descriptors. The problem is in trying to identify a sufficient amount of data in a cost-effective way to determine the overall Level of Use of a teacher or set of teachers. To have highest reliability, Levels of Use should be assessed using an intensive observational approach. Most of the categorical information, however, deals with behaviors that occur outside of class periods. An observer would thus have to follow a teacher around school all day. Observations would have to be made during planning periods. The assessor would have to listen in on conversations and telephone calls, and would even need to read correspondence to collect information for each of the categories. Even for research purposes this intensive type of field work is not practical, although the approach was used in the study described later to validate the LoU assessment procedure (Hall and Loucks 1977). An affordable and accurate procedure was needed, which would also be appropriate to the concept.

Since LoU is a behavioral concept, paper/pencil questionnaires will not work. In spite of our best efforts to discourage researchers from building paper/pencil LoU questionnaires, however, several abortive attempts have been made. Attempting to assess Levels of Use with such a questionnaire is similar to attempting to read semaphore signals by turning on the radio: The receiver medium does not fit the format of the message. A behavioral variable cannot be assessed with a nonbehavioral measure. When someone attempts to assess Levels of Use with a questionnaire, the result is a partial assessment of concerns about use rather than a direct description of use or a direct assessment of concerns.

The resolution to this methodological problem was to develop a special type of interview procedure called a focused interview (Foster and Nixon 1975). Since Levels of Use were operationally defined, it was possible to build an interview with a series of branches to it, allowing the interviewer to shift to different parts of the interview guide depending upon the interviewee's answers. The interview is called a focused interview because it starts in an open-ended fashion and proceeds through a sequence of questions that close in on a particular subject. Each of the basic branching questions is followed by a series of level- and category-specific probes. In this way, the trained Levels of Use interviewer is able to collect information from interviewees about what they are doing with the innovation. Becoming skilled in conducting Levels of Use interviews requires training (Loucks, Newlove, and Hall 1975). It is possible, through a three-day intensive training workshop (Newlove 1978), for interviewers to become certified as skilled and reliable in assessing Levels of Use.

One problem the CBAM research staff faced was demonstrating that an interview procedure could be accurate. Since there was no prior assessment procedure to determine the validity of the LoU interview, a validity study was specially designed. For this study, reliable data about Levels of Use were collected using a format different from the LoU interview procedure. The Levels of Use interview procedure was, therefore, compared to LoU ratings field workers obtained by using ethnographic procedures to collect descriptive data. The ethnographic procedures involved day-long observations and interviewing selected teachers. In the validity study, forty-five teachers were interviewed using the standard twenty- to thirty-minute Levels of Use focused interview, and their LoU was assessed by the interviewer. A subset of seventeen teachers was then identified, which included one or more teachers at each LoU. Independently, LoU-trained field workers then observed the selected teachers from the time they arrived at school until they left at the end of the day. The field workers developed comprehensive, narrative descriptions of the teacher behaviors and discussions that indicated Levels of Use. The field researchers then rated the Levels of Use of the teachers they had observed. The correlation between the field worker's rating and the interviewer's rating of Levels of Use was .98. At this point, we felt confident that a trained interviewer using the Levels of Use focused interview procedure could do the job accurately.

For the practitioner, it is not necessary to incorporate all of the rigor of the "formal" Levels of Use interview; however, it certainly can help fine-tune one's diagnostic skill. For change facilitators, the one-legged conference format suggested for the Stages of Concern can be modified and used quite effectively to assess LoU. The suggested sequence of questions to use in a one-legged conference are presented in figure 8. The overall design is the same as that used in the more rigorous research interview. The format begins with a very open question, "Are you using it?"

By starting from this open stance, the interviewees are allowed to present the case for their use or nonuse of the innovation. Each of the open questions is then followed by a series of probes. The design, then, starts with broad questions and gradually focuses to category-specific probes. Each of these probes requires the teacher to describe behavioral actions they have taken or will be taking in the near future. Throughout, the interviewer must keep in mind that, in assessing Levels of Use, the emphasis is on what teachers are doing or not doing with the innovation, not on how they feel about it. For the reader who wishes to know more about assessing Levels of Use, a training manual (Loucks, Newlove, and Hall 1975) is available, and a training workshop is also available through the CBAM cadre listed in Appendix A.

Findings from Research

Numerous research studies have been done using Levels of Use. Some of the key findings and outcomes of this work, those that have implications for school principals and others involved with facilitating change, are briefly highlighted here. References to technical reports and related documents are also included for those who wish to know more.

Typical LoU Distributions

In two large studies (Hall and Loucks 1977), samples were selected to include persons with widely varying amounts of experience with team teaching and instructional modules—the identified innovations. Some subjects had no experience with the innovation, others had five or six years of experience with it. The studies were of teachers teaming in elementary schools and of instructional modules used in schools, colleges, and departments of education. The samples were designed to include the total range of experience, knowledge, and perceptions likely to be associated with adoption of educational innovations. Levels of Use interviews were conducted with each subject twice each school year for two years. The resulting data made it possible to explore what the typical distribution of Levels of Use was and what percentage of the users of an innovation become LoU VI, Renewal, users.

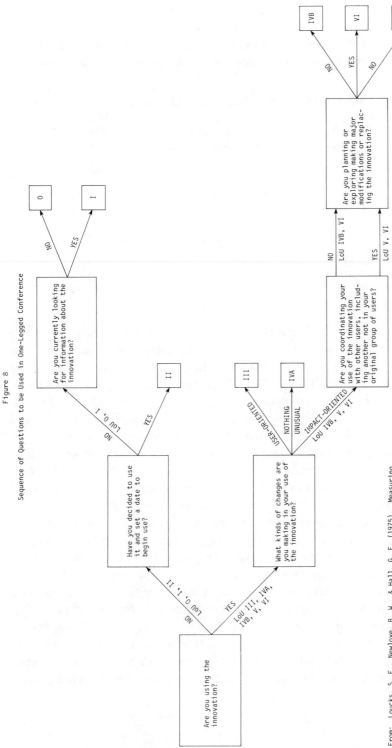

Figure 8

Sequence of Questions to be Used in One-Legged Conference

From: Loucks, S. F., Newlove, B. W., & Hall, G. E. (1975). *Measuring levels of use of the innovation: A manual for trainers, interviewers, and raters* (Report No. 3013). Austin: The University of Texas, Research and Development Center for Teacher Education.

Figure 9
Distribution of Overall Level of Use of Individuals
in Two Cross-Sectional Studies for Two Innovations

Level of Use	Teaming in Elementary Schools	Modules in Teacher Education Institutions
	N = 368	N = 277
0	5%	13%
I	10%	31%
II	2%	9%
III	20%	10%
IVA	55%	18%
IVB	4%	10%
V	4%	6%
VI	1%	2%

The data displayed in figure 9 is a summary of the findings for all the LoU in the two, cross-sectional samplings. It is not surprising that, in the teaming sample, 40 to 50 percent of the users are at the Routine Level of Use. This finding does not mean that the same persons are always at this level. In fact, apparently only about one-third of the LoU IVA, Routine, persons were "career" LoU IVAs. Another third of the routine users were persons "resting" after having arrived at IVA from their earlier, Mechanical Level of Use. The other third of the routine users were those who had previously implemented LoU IVB, V, or VI changes and had once again returned to routine use.

Analyses of the data in these samples also provides information about movement from level to level. Apparently, the normal path for a person is to move in sequence from LoU 0 to LoU IVA; however, once teachers (and professors) reach LoU IVA, a number of different directions become options. Some teachers continue with their present practices and remain at LoU IVA, whereas some move to LoU IVB or V and stay there. Others seem to enter repeated cycles of introducing LoU IVB, V, or VI refinements, which move them temporarily back to LoU III and, in time, to LoU IVA again. These individuals tend to be the professional, energetic, and creative teachers that students, parents, and teacher educators dream of. Unfortunately, these types are fewer in numbers than the dreamers would like. How many teachers and professors regularly move in this cycle is unknown, but clearly their number is tied, in part, to the change facilitating style of the principal and others—the topic of chapter 8.

One question frequently asked is "How desirable is it to have staff move to higher Levels of Use?" If Levels of Use are viewed as a simple line of steps, the logical conclusion would be that all persons should reach Level of Use VI, Renewal. Individuals with a deeper understanding of LoU, though, might consider the consequences of having so many staff members at LoU VI. Level of Use VI, Renewal, faculty are constantly looking for new resources and ideas and are always altering things. They tend to have intense impact-oriented concerns, which results in a great deal of pressure on the facilitators and organization to always do more and constantly rethink things. Teachers at this LoU require a great deal of support, although, in the two cross-sectional studies with large samples, only 2 to 3 percent of the populations were at that level.

First-Time Users and LoU III

Another analysis of the cross-sectional studies indicated that at least 60 to 70 percent of all first-time innovation users were at the Mechanical Level of Use. This finding is a consistent one and has direct implications for planners of change as well as for change facilitators. If nearly all first-time users will be at the Mechanical Level of Use for a period of time, then it is possible to anticipate and plan for the needed staff development and related support Mechanical Level of Use teachers will need. Historically, the need for supporting teachers at the Mechanical Level of Use has not been anticipated, especially when change was assumed to be an event. The "God bless you workshop," provided in late August, leaves teachers on their own to implement the new practice. The how to do it assistance, follow up, and consulting that persons at a Mechanical Level of Use need are not usually provided unless continued use of the innovation is threatened. In many cases, teachers gradually work things out for themselves, but this approach takes time and energy and often leads to inappropriate use. Persons at a Mechanical Level of Use should be provided with the necessary comfort and caring, and what Loucks and Melle (1980) call coaching, so they are able to resolve their mechanical use problems and move on to routine use.

Failing to assist and support innovation users at LoU III is antithetical to the concerns-based perspective. It causes prolonged stress on teachers. Also, because the adaptations made by mechanical use teachers are, by definition, user oriented, the innovation may be changed into less effective configurations, and the continuing inefficiencies in use are likely to lead to less effective outcomes. Prolonged periods of LoU III drain users, leaving less vitality for considering and implementing future changes. That nearly all innovation users experience a period of LoU III behavior at the beginning of implementation is clear. The kinds of support that are effective are also clear. Offering support for this phase needs to become a regular part of change facilitation for all innovation.

When Evaluations Show No Significant Differences

All too frequently, summative evaluation studies have concluded that there were "no significant differences" in student outcomes between the new and old practices. Levels of Use research has provided an interesting insight into why so many of these evaluation studies have come up with such results. For example, Loucks (1975) studied eleven schools that were implementing Individually Guided Education (IGE) and eleven comparison schools not involved with IGE (Watkins and Holley 1975). The schools had been identified by the district as IGE or non-IGE schools three years previously, and special support had been given to the IGE schools. The school district evaluation found no significant differences in student achievement between the two sets of schools. To their credit, the evaluators held off conducting their summative evaluation until the third year of implementation. The implementation of IGE, however, was not documented at the classroom level. With the support of the school district's office of evaluation, Levels of Use data were collected in all IGE and non-IGE schools as part of the Loucks study. Since IGE is an innovation bundle, teachers' Levels of Use were assessed with regard to key innovations within that bundle—individualized instruction in reading and individualized instruction in mathematics. These innovations were selected since it was assumed that their use would be closely associated with the criterion scores on standardized achievement tests.

The general finding from the LoU data was that, in the so-called IGE treatment schools, only 80 percent of the teachers were "users" of individualized instruction in reading and math. In other words, 20 percent of the teachers in the experimental schools were not using individualized instruction. In the comparison schools, 49 percent of the teachers were "users" of individualized instruction. In this case, the treatment and comparison groups were mixed; there was not a pure sample of users in one group and a pure sample of nonusers in the other group. It does not, then, seem surprising that the evaluation results found no significant differences between the two groups. By contrast, when all the LoU-identified users of individualized instruction were compared with the nonusers (LoU 0, I, and II), large, statistically significant differences were identified in favor of individualized instruction.

The point here is not that individualized instruction is better, but that it is critical to document that the treatment group does indeed consist of users and that the comparison group is composed of nonusers. Asking building or district personnel about the use and nonuse of classroom innovations is risky. Direct assessment of the prospective users and nonusers is essential; otherwise, the validity of the findings from summative evaluation studies must be questioned. Importantly, such findings should not be used as a basis for policy decisions. In the IGE example, the district discontinued support for the innovation bundle, when in fact a critical innovation within the bundle was correlated with major, desirable differences in student achievement.

To be most useful, summative evaluations designed to test innovation effectiveness should be done when users in the treatment group are at Level of Use IVA, Routine. These persons have the innovation systems worked out, know where they are going, and use the innovation in a stable pattern. Persons at LoU III,

Mechanical, and LoU IVB, V, and VI are adapting and changing their use of the innovation. The Mechanical Level of Use persons are making changes to they can become more efficient and can "survive" with the innovation, while the Levels of Use IVB, V, and VI persons are making adaptations intended to increase positive outcomes. These adaptations may or may not be consistent with the original developers' vision of the innovation. Additionally, such users may be using the innovation in ways that will mislead a summative evaluation. Using the same rationale, the control group should be composed of persons who are at LoU 0, Nonuse. These persons will not be evidencing any behaviors associated with use of the innovation.

The Relationship of LoU to Student Achievement

Research data is limited on the kinds of outcomes obtained when teachers use an innovation at different Levels of Use. Logic suggests that when teachers reach a Mechanical Level of Use, by definition, they are inefficient users and just becoming familiar with and understanding the innovation materials and processes. At this point, it seems reasonable to predict that student outcomes will be less positive. On the other hand, when persons have reached higher Levels of Use and are making adaptations intended to increase positive outcomes, it seems more appropriate to hypothesize that such outcomes will be more frequent.

The limited amount of research conducted to date on this theory suggests that the real world is more complex. For example, in the Loucks study (1975), when individualized reading was the innovation, a curvelinear relationship was observed, with a general pattern of higher student reading achievement correlated with higher teacher Levels of Use. However, with the same teachers, when individualized instruction in mathematics was the innovation, a different curvelinear relationship was identified that indicated higher achievement at teacher LoU III. This study, however, has limitations and more research needs to be done.

Using Levels of Use

Levels of Use represents the second key diagnostic dimension of the Concerns-Based Adoption Model and provides a useful way to understand and describe implementation at the classroom level. In the final section of this chapter, data are used to illustrate other aspects of Levels of Use and then to indicate implications for staff development, evaluation, planning, and facilitation by principals and other change facilitators. When they understand the concept of Levels of Use, facilitators will be more effective in their role and better able to provide needed assistance to teachers and information for policymakers as the change process unfolds.

Pacing and Phasing the Change Process

Levels of Use data can provide a series of benchmarks that indicate the rate at which change is progressing. Frequently, as already stated, administrators, school board members, and other policymakers unwittingly treat the change process as an event. The decree is made that on September 1st all teachers will use a new program. The expectation is that change is an event, and that delivery of the "box" is equal to ongoing and effective use of the new program. Although this event orientation does not make sense, policymakers have not been given any alternative frameworks that will show whether or not their policies are being implemented. The Levels of Use concept provides this framework for considering and describing the change process in ways that respond to policymakers' needs for accountability. Levels of Use data can be used as mileposts to chart the rate of progress of a particular change and to ascertain when the process has been totally accomplished, or not accomplished.

The implementation of the Revised Science Curriculum (Pratt, Winters, and George 1980) for grades three through six in the Jefferson County, Colorado, Public Schools illustrates this point. In this effort, teachers in grades three to six in eighty elementary schools implemented an activity-oriented science curriculum. The curriculum materials had been developed using the district's comprehensive curriculum development policies and process. The innovation's development involved teacher input, field testing of units, and pilot testing within a few schools. When it was time for the districtwide implementation, the school district committed resources to support the change process, including three, full-day, teacher in-service workshops.

Since the developers of the curriculum were aware of the CBAM model, especially the Stages of Concern and Levels of Use, they recognized it would not be possible to provide the needed support and follow up to teachers in all eighty elementary schools at the same time. The developers further recognized that the best way to deliver the in-service workshops would be to space them over an eighteen-month period and to adjust them to teachers' concerns as they were aroused, rather than attempting to answer questions at times when teachers were not asking them. It was decided to divide the district into thirds, with each third moving into implementation at six-month intervals. This phasing allowed staff developers and curriculum specialists to concentrate their initial implementation efforts on only a third of the district at a time.

As part of this effort, the CBAM staff at the Research and Development Center for Teacher Education monitored the change process in a sample of twenty study schools. Stages of Concern and Levels of Use assessments were completed twice a year. A summary of the LoU data is presented in figure 10. It illustrates the phasing that occurred in implementation and also demonstrates the gradual movement of teachers from nonuse to use. Note the gradual movement from Level of Use 0, Nonuse, toward mechanical use, routine use, and refinement use, as time passes. The movement is reflected in the continual decrease in the proportion of teachers at level of Use 0 and the increase in the number of teachers at mechanical use, routine use, and refinement use levels. These data support the view that change is a process. The data can be used to pace implementation support. They can also be used to report to upper-level decision makers that progress is being made, but that "institutionalization" has not yet been reached.

The Change Process Takes Time and Timing

The JeffCo Science Program is a relatively simple curriculum change and took place within a district highly regarded for its curriculum development and implementation procedures. The curriculum materials received the National Science Teachers Association Search for Excellence in Science Education award (SESE) (Hrebar and Pratt 1983). The research conducted on the im-

Figure 10
Levels of Use Distribution

	0	I	II	III	IVA	IVB	V	VI	
				Phase 1					
FALL 76	5	9	83	1	1	0	0	0	N = 75
SPRING 77	0	4	9	53	24	7	1	1	N = 74
FALL 77	3	3	5	38	35	0	13	3	N = 63
SPRING 78	2	3	2	42	34	13	3	2	N = 62
SPRING 79	6	0	2	23	52	13	0	4	N = 52
				Percent at each LoU					
				Phase 2					
FALL 76	53	3	17	5	17	5	0	0	N = 60
SPRING 77	7	5	43	19	21	3	0	2	N = 58
FALL 77	4	11	11	40	23	6	4	2	N = 53
SPRING 78	9	2	2	44	24	16	0	2	N = 45
SPRING 78	5	0	2	40	40	12	0	2	N = 43
				Percent at each LoU					
				Phase 3					
FALL 76	80	14	1	3	0	0	0	1	N = 69
SPRING 77	66	3	24	6	0	0	0	1	N = 70
FALL 77	12	16	63	4	6	0	0	0	N = 51
SPRING 78	8	14	6	42	22	4	2	2	N = 50
SPRING 79	16	2	0	25	41	12	2	2	N = 51
				Percent at each LoU					

plementation process received the 1984 Professional Service Award of the American Educational Research Association (Hall and Pratt 1984). Even so, a period of three to four years was still necessary for the majority of teachers to move from nonuse to routine use of the innovation. At the end of that time period, there were still a significant number of teachers at a Mechanical Level of Use and a less than hoped for number of teachers at the higher Levels of Use.

The implication for change facilitators is that assisting teachers in the move from nonuse to use requires a comprehensive set of interventions. Assisting moves to ever higher Levels of Use requires an entirely new set of interventions and an additional period of time. Thus, LoU research implies that implementation to the point of institutionalization (most if not all teachers at LoU IVA or higher) will require three to five years.

That it takes three to five years to implement new programs is not a surprise to practitioners, although it is a disappointment to policymakers who usually want to do things more quickly. The reality of the change process is, however, that it does take time; therefore, if worthwhile innovations are to be introduced, implementing one every three to four years would certainly be an improvement over the present practice of attempting five to twenty innovations every eighteen months.

Levels of Use of the innovation is one basis for providing interventions, and the day-to-day interventions facilitators provide and the manner in which support teachers should vary depending on their teachers' Levels of Use. The teachers at a Mechanical Level of Use need timely, specific suggestions to help them become more efficient. Teachers at a Level of Use I, Orientation, are looking for descriptive information, while a teacher at Level of Use IVA needs no particular support unless there is interest in arousing the teacher towards higher Levels of Use. In this case, inservice sessions, consultations, and other kinds of interventions could be designed that might lead to interest in refined innovation approaches. For the LoU IVA teacher, we suggest assessing the concerns of the teacher. Understanding teachers' concerns in conjunction with knowledge of their Levels of Use provides a richer picture and diagnostic basis for designing and facilitating interventions. Some further examples of the use of LoU as a diagnostic tool for interventions can be found in chapter 10. In the next chapter, the third diagnostic dimension of the CBAM model is introduced.

Chapter 5

What Is It? Innovation Configurations

School district A has determined a need for teaching career education and has identified a program designed for its particular student population. How should the different parts of the new program be implemented?

Curriculum staff in school district B have realized that one result of encouraging individual building-level autonomy in curriculum decision-making is that the reading program lacks continuity between grade levels, uniformity within single grades and articulation between schools. How should curriculum articulation be accomplished?

All eighth grade science teachers in junior high school C use a single science program, but over the years each has developed his or her own style of use. Some teachers appear to be achieving better results with students than others. How can they determine what is actually making the difference? And what do they do once they find out? (Hall and Loucks 1981: 46).

These descriptions illustrate some of the underlying issues that emerge when characteristics of an innovation become the focus. What are the key features of an innovation? How can the actual practices in different classrooms be compared? Finally, which way of using a particular innovation component is best? These issues are addressed within the Concerns-Based Adoption

Model by the concept of Innovation Configurations (IC), the third diagnostic dimension of the model. The IC dimension deals direct-ly with characteristics of the innovation and what use means when the innovation is the frame of reference.

The IC dimension was not a part of the original framework of the Concens-Based Adoption Model. It emerged out of the early studies designed to develop reliable and valid procedures for assessing Levels of Use and to test for the existence of each level in real life. The two initial studies involved over four hundred teachers and the innovation of teaming and approximately 350 college faculty involved with the innovation of instructional modules (Hall and Loucks 1977). In both studies, the Levels of Use interview procedure was used twice a year for two years.

In the teaming study, researchers from the Research and Development Center for Teacher Education interviewed teachers in Texas, Nebraska, and Massachusetts to determine their Levels of Use of team teaching. Many teachers were quick to say, "Yes, I am team teaching"; however, when we asked them to describe how they were teaming, the answers varied. For example:

—Teachers in one school described their team as consisting of three teachers and two parent aides, 150 students, an open classroom with a great deal of open space, and constant reorganization of students for instruction in reading, mathematics, and language arts.

—Teaming in a second school consisted of two teachers in the same grade level, both of whom had self-contained classrooms, who met once a month to exchange lesson plans. They kept their students in the same groups and exchanged few teaching respon-sibilities.

—Of course, the infamous "turn teaching," where teachers took turns teaching the whole group, was found too.

This variety of descriptions of teaming led to the basic ques-tion: "What is teaming?" Although the four hundred teachers claimed to be using the innovation, what some teams did was significantly different from what other teams did. The name of the innovation may have been the same, but the operational forms had different components and variations.

The same type of phenomenon was observed with university faculty and their use of instructional modules. For example:

—One college faculty described the instructional modules as a series of self-contained packages that normally took the students about one week to complete. Each "module" consisted of an introductory description of objectives and rationale, a pretest, a posttest, and a set of alternative enabling activities.

—On another campus, college faculty modules consisted of a course syllabus, a large array of instructional objectives, and a list of resources the students could obtain outside class.

These faculties said they were using instructional modules; however, the operational form of these modules varied from faculty member to faculty member and from campus to campus. Again, the question arose, "What is this innovation?"

The differences in how innovations are used led us to propose the concept of Innovation Configurations (Hall and Loucks 1978). We were struck by what the idea of configurations of innovations would mean. For example, staff development would need to be designed differently if it were to address the actual, innovation-related practices of teachers. Second, it seemed quite logical to expect that student outcomes would be different depending on which forms of teaming, instructional modules, or other innovations were actually employed.

This new insight led to an examination of the existing literature and to our subsequent research to develop clearer ways of talking about and defining an innovation or innovative program. We developed procedures to assess the implementation of different configurations of an innovation. The results of this research about Innovation Configurations and its implications for facilitating change are the subject of this chapter. The concept of Innovation Configurations is developed, Innovation Component Checklists are described, and illustrations of methods to assess Innovation Configurations using sample research findings are included. We also discuss implications for change facilitation, for the design of staff development, and for strategic planning. The chapter begins with a brief summary of how others have described innovations.

What the Innovation Literature Says

Innovation definition has been a subject of study for quite

some time. Over time, the conceptual perspectives used to examine the innovation and attributes of innovations have undergone some interesting changes. The aspects of the innovation being examined have shifted, and the point of view for describing an innovation have varied. At least five different orientations have been used to examine and define innovations. These orientations involve examination of the philosophy, goals and outcomes, implementation requirements, or behavioral functions of a given innovation. A brief tour of each of these perspectives for defining innovations can be instructive.

The Perceived Attributes of an Innovation

A very important summary and analysis of the literature was done by Rogers and Shoemaker in their book *Communication of Innovations* (1971). Based upon their comprehensive analysis of the hundreds of studies done of farmers adopting hybrid corn seed, the adoption of penicillin and other miracle drugs by doctors, and technology innovations in Third World countries, Rogers and Shoemaker synthesized a set of "perceived attributes" of innovations. From a perceived attributes perspective, the innovation is defined from the potential adopters' point of view. Rogers and Shoemaker proposed that adopters' perceptions of the innovation can be organized around five attributes:

—Relative Advantage. If an innovation is perceived by potential adopters as having a relative advantage over their present practice, they are more apt to adopt it. In terms of sociology studies, for example, if hybrid corn seed were perceived to have an economic advantage over present practice, it would be more likely to be adopted.

—Compatibility. Innovations that were seen by potential adopters as being compatible with other current practices would have a higher tendency of being adopted. If the innovation were seen as being less compatible, requiring a larger amount of change in practice, and less complementary with other aspects of the present work, it would be less likely to be adopted.

—Complexity. More complex innovations, those that were perceived to be more difficult to adopt because of a large number of components or more technical aspects of their use in terms of the perceptions of potential adopters, would be adopted at a slower rate. If an innovation was seen as relatively simple in terms of its pieces or the processes of its use, it would be adopted more readily.

—Trialability. If a component of an innovation could be tried out, it would be less risky. For example, with hybrid corn seed, it is possible to plant a part of a field with the hybrid corn seed to compare the results with present practice. With ease of trialability, adoption rates would be higher.

—Observability. When the features and benefits of innovations are readily observed, they are more apt to be adopted. Innovations that are subtler in terms of their results or advantages would be adopted at a slower rate.

To extrapolate this idea from rural sociology to education, innovations perceived as having an advantage over present practice (e.g., demonstrate increased scores on standardized achievement tests), being compatible with present practice (e.g., do not require the purchase of additional equipment or materials), being simple to use (e.g, no difficult, complex, or new kinds of procedures or gadgets where training is required to use them), being amenable to trial on an experimental basis (e.g., a volunteer teacher at any school could try a part of the innovation for a six-week period), and having results that are readily observable (e.g., students and teachers are extremely pleased with how it is going), will have higher adoption rates. On the other hand, if the innovation or change in practice falls short in one or more of these areas, it seems reasonable to project that the adoption decision and implementation will be slower.

The perceived attributes perspective of Rogers and Shoemaker has some advantages. It provides a very useful set of categories that change facilitators can use as they plan a change process and that can provide clues about some issues that might be raised in relation to a teacher's perceptions of an innovation. A potential danger is that the definition of the innovation is in terms of perceptions rather than in terms of what the innovation *really* is. The next orientation provides a different way of defining an innovation and represents a different definition of reality.

The Philosophy of an Innovation

Education innovations can also be defined from the point of view of the innovation developer and the philosophical orientaton the developer portrays. This orientation was particularly predominant in the 1960s and early 1970s when a great deal of emphasis was placed on developing the philosophical basis and underlying assumptions of an innovation. For example, in science, mathematics, and social science curricula, resident educational psychologists, learning theorists, and philosophers were enlisted to articulate the philosophical orientation for a curriculum. The Science A Process Approach program (SAPA) used the concept of learning hierarchies developed by Robert Gagne, while the Science Curriculum Improvement Study curriculum (SCIS) employed the psychology of Jean Piaget, and the Elementary Science Study units (ESS) relied upon Jerome Brunner. Not only were the resulting curriculum materials and expected teaching practices designed and sequenced based upon the premises of these different philosophical orientations, but the ultimate approaches to change, staff development, and implementation support for teachers were designed accordingly.

This approach meant, for example, that teachers involved in adopting *Science A Process Approach* learned about behavioral objectives, learning hierarchies, and the importance of the pretest and posttest linked to the instructional activities. The *Elementary Science Study* teachers in their workshops had time for "messing about." In "messing about," there was minimal emphasis on explicitly following the teachers guide and heavy emphasis upon students and teachers freely exploring and examining the materials and processes being introduced. One outcome of these different philosophical orientations was an increased emphasis on and debate regarding the relative importance of content versus process (Parker and Rubin 1966).

From a change process point of view, the philosophical orientation for defining an innovation has important implications for teachers in classrooms who are expected to implement the approach. Frequently, when a philosophical orientation is the basis for defining an innovation, it is difficult to make real and concrete descriptions of practice. What teachers are to do is based on their having internalized the philosophy and theory of the innovation developers. When one is at a Mechanical Level of Use with intense personal and management concerns, it is extremely difficult to think reflectively about an innovation's philosophy. The consequence frequently is increased ambiguity and feelings of uncertainty about what should be happening in the classroom.

Moreover, in terms of concerns theory, this time is when teachers need concrete and specific suggestions, advice, and prescriptive coaching. Innovations defined from a philosophical orientation, however, do not typically provide that detail for early implementors. This incongruence might be one reason why there has been so little real implementation and continuation of many of the curricula developed in the 1960s. If concerns theory is correct, those programs would probably have had higher success rates if the change facilitators had thought more about the needs of teachers at the time of implementation and had taken time to assist teachers in developing confidence and competence in behaving in the manner being advocated by the philosophical orientation.

The Goals and Outcomes of an Innovation

Another orientation for defining an innovation is in terms of its goals and outcomes. This orientation received increased emphasis in the 1970s and 1980s. With the current emphasis on testing, it is likely that goals and outcomes will be emphasized more in the 1990s.

In this orientation, developers and innovation facilitators describe the innovation in terms of what it will accomplish, such as increased standardized achievement test scores or a decrease in vandalism or absenteeism.

A potential disadvantage of a goals and outcomes orientation is that the details of practice are left undefined. Administrators, teachers, and others may not have sufficient understanding to know exactly what they need to do to achieve the outcomes the original developer obtained. It is important to know the goals and outcomes expected from an innovation, but potential users also need to know what to do to achieve those outcomes.

The Implementation Requirements of an Innovation

Defining an innovation in terms of implementation requirements is frequently done as well. When an innovation is defined by its implementation requirements, the emphasis is on specifying what must be present: time requirements, logistics, training that teachers need, grouping of students, personnel requirements, and scheduling and organizational structures associated with the innovation's use. The problem with this orientation is that actual practice in the classroom and what teachers *do* with the textbook and with the twenty-five minutes of scheduled time are not described. Teachers tend to be left on their own in using the prescribed text and related materials. When an innovation is defined by what must be in place, decision makers will have good information about the initial purchase costs but little information about how the materials and resources will be used. Knowing implementation requirements is important, but information about how the innovation works is also important.

A quick examination of early issues of *Educational Programs That Work*, published for the National Diffusion Network, provides excellent illustrations of programs that were defined by their implementation requirements. Interestingly, later issues of this publication reflect how the leadership and participants in the National Diffusion Network learned from their experiences and expanded their definitions of innovations to include not only implementation requirements but also goals and outcomes and what we call Innovation Configuration Components (National Diffusion Network 1980).

The Behaviors/Functions of the Innovation

In the 1970s, Innovation Configuration concept development and work by Treadway (1980) gave thought to defining an innovation in terms of its operational form. When an innovation is defined in this way, the emphasis is on describing what teachers and students *do* on a day-to-day basis with the materials, philosophies, processes, and goals and outcomes that have been presented to them in the name of the innovation. With this perspective, the emphasis is on developing behavioral descriptions and identifying alternative ways the innovation might be made operational in classrooms.

This perspective provides a description of the developer's orientation and what he/she sees occurring in classrooms when the innovation is in use. The developer is asked to describe what is observed in a classroom where the innovation is in use versus what is not observed in a classroom where the innovation is not in use. Procedures are developed to collect data and to document how teachers and classrooms are operating in ways more or less consistent with the developers' model.

The difference between the Innovation Configuration approach in the Concerns-Based Adoption Model and the "functional" approach of Treadway and Horst is that the latter suggest an innovation can be defined by its "functional" components and that any (two or more different) operational patterns that achieve the same function will in theory represent the innovation. From a theoretical point of view, this orientation makes a great deal of sense; however, it runs the risk of limited practicality since very different configurations, requiring widely different support and resources, can emerge to serve the same function. The Innovation Configuration approach also emphasizes functional alternatives but does so with the developer's "archtype" always in mind. Thus, alternative ways an innovation can be implemented and made operational are continually related to the developer's implementation requirements, philosophy, and model.

The Concept of Innovation Configurations and the IC Component Checklist

The emergence of the need for a concept like Innovation Configurations can be traced to national policy and curriculum development decisions of the last several decades. Prior to the launching of Sputnik in 1957, decisions about teaching and curriculum were in the hands of teachers at the local level, and curriculum materials were synonymous with textbooks. After Sputnik, the design and development of curriculum were placed in the hands of national curriculum development groups. Interestingly, one of the espoused objectives of the curriculum development groups of the 1960s was to create curriculum innovations that would be "teacher proof" in implementation in classrooms. The first in what was to become a series of classic studies of classroom implementation (Gallagher 1967) hinted at the fallacy of the teacher proof curriculum assertion. In his study of four high school teachers implementing the same BSCS curriculum, Gallagher systematically documented that each teacher had strikingly different patterns of practice in their classrooms, although they were all teaching with the same BSCS curriculum materials.

The idea that teachers' classroom practices can be quite different from developers' dreams gradually gained attention in the 1970s. The concept of "mutual adaptation" from the Rand Change Agent Study (Rand Study 1975c) recognized the possible differences between developer expectations and local school implementation. The Rand study further concluded that successful implementation required mutual adaptation—that change succeeds when there is some adaptation of the innovation at the particular school site and some adaptation of the local school's practices as the innovation is implemented. Mutual adaptation was the buzzword of the 1970s; however, it began to be abandoned in the 1980s as each local school began creating its own, home-grown programs supported by school district policymakers and those curriculum developers that treated curriculum development as a local cottage industry. In addition, critics of the Rand Change Agent Study pointed out that the innovations studied in that project mandated the process that had become known as mutual adaptation (Datta 1980).

Our early studies of Stages of Concern, Levels of Use, and Innovation Configurations were being done during the heyday of the mutual adaptation concept. We decided not to focus on where the innovation was developed. Instead, we described what teachers and students did with the innovation-related materials and processes daily, rather than narrowly addressing the innovation as described by the developer or district decision makers.

How to collect data about these operational differences and how to summarize these data in ways that could be used by change facilitators, staff developers, evaluators, curriculum developers, and others became a research and development agenda. The strategy that was finally developed to collect and summarize these data entails identifying the basic *components* of an innovation and, within each component, identifying the *variations* that describe how individual teachers might use the components in their classrooms. Perhaps descriptions of three teachers' use of an individualized mathematics curriculum will help illustrate the strategy.

> Mr. R. teaches the objectives in sequence to the whole class at once and uses the work sheets only. He tests the class when they are finished with the worksheets, records the grades, and goes on to the next objective.

> Ms. S. individualizes, assigning students to worksheets and additional materials when needed to achieve an objective. She tests each student as he or she completes the material, recycling when necessary. She records when each objective is achieved on individual record cards.

> Mrs. Z has three math groups, each working on teacher-made materials keyed to different objectives. When each group completes the materials, tests are given to that group. If a student does not pass the tests he or she is moved to a group working on the objective he or she needs to achieve.

> All three teachers may be said to "use" the math program, but they use different *operational forms* of the program. They vary in their use of program components. In other words, they each use a different configuration. (Hall and Loucks 1981: 48)

To analyze the three different configurations described, the *components* or building blocks of the innovation must be identified. In the math program illustrated above, the components are (1) materials used, (2) grouping procedures, (3) kinds of tests used, and (4) uses of test data. For a more process-oriented innovation such as team teaching, examples of components could be (1) the roles of team members, (2) the sharing of responsibilities, and (3) the grouping of students.

Within each component, there will be *variations*. In each classroom or for each team, how teachers actually use the components will vary. For example, in the component "materials" in the math program, variations could be (1) textbook only, (2) teacher-made materials, (3) games, or (4) some combination of these. With the innovation of teaming, the component "grouping students," the variations could be (1) one group of all students, (2) students assigned to achievement groups, or (3) students assigned to individual teachers.

When analysis of an innovation is made in terms of its operational components and the different variations of these components, an Innovation Configuration Component Checklist can be used to summarize the array of possibilities. Two sample configuration checklists are included as figures 11 and 12. When an Innovation Configuration Component Checklist is available for an innovation, it is possible for teachers as well as change facilitators to articulate a clearer understanding of the ways the innovation can be made operational. It is surprising how frequently teachers really want to implement programs in the ways developers espouse but are not clear on how to do it. By presenting teachers with an IC Component Checklist, many, for the first time, become aware of how to make their practice more congruent with the most promising pattern. Other teachers can be reinforced for variations they are already using.

An observer, or teachers themselves, can use an IC Component Checklist to analyze innovation use in the classroom. By circling the variation of each component used, they can make a record of the way it is being used. The resulting, unique combination of circles will represent the pattern or configuration. A combination of circled variations such as Ib, IIa, IIIb . . . on figure 11 would represent one configuration.

Which Configurations Are Better?

Frequently, program developers or policymakers determine that certain configurations are more effective than others. This determination might be based on field testing and evaluation of the innovation, or more likely, it might reflect philosophical or legal positions. In any case, when certain components and variations have value over others, it is possible to reflect a preference within the IC Component Checklist. One way is to scale the variations within a component from "ideal" to "acceptable" to "unacceptable." In figure 11, the components are listed in this way, with the variations toward the left of each component being determined as the more ideal variation.

The process for determining the ideal variation is not reflected in the component checklist; however, it is strongly recommended that policymakers, administrators, change facilitators, evaluators, and teachers, *prior* to implementing an in-

Figure 11
Innovation Configuration Components and Variations of a
Continuous-Progress Mathematics Curriculum

Teacher _____ Observer _____

I.   Instructional Materials

a.	b.	c.	d.
program materials only	program materials plus	text only	teacher made materials only

II. Grouping

a.	b.	c.	d.
completely individualized	small groups	large homogeneous group	large heterogeneous group

III. Testing Component

a.	b.	c.	d.
each student tests themselves as they complete each objective	testing done weekly with test results fed back to students	testing done once every six weeks with nothing done with test results	no regular testing except standardized achievement tests required by district

novation, come to a consensus on what represents appropriate classroom practice. Frequently, this decision is not made and is left to chance, with teachers discovering for themselves what use of the innovation means. Often the definition of what represents appropriate practice evolves; in other cases, clarification of expectations is not made until problems arise after implementation begins. Delaying the determination of appropriate practices results in teachers implementing configurations that at some later time are judged to be less than ideal. Another problem occurs when policymakers change their acceptable use configuration definitions after experience has been gained and then inform early adopters that they are "out of compliance" with the new innovation use definitions. It is more appropriate and supportive of teacher morale to provide guidelines on appropriate configurations before implementation begins.

This discussion does not mean there always have to be more and less acceptable configurations. Quite conceivably in some change efforts, any configuration of an innovation will be acceptable. If so, this decision should be made public prior to implementation.

Another approach is to phase in the components of an innovation by encouraging the user to start with less rigorous variations of components. In later stages of the change process, increased emphasis can be placed on implementing more ideal variations of certain components or full configurations. The main point again is that, at the beginning of an implementation effort, key decision makers, evaluators, and facilitators should agree about what implementation is all about, and this information should be readily available to all prospective users. In addition, evaluators should not be making summative evaluation decisions until after teachers have implemented acceptable innovation configurations.

There are two other techniques that can help guide evaluators, policymakers, facilitators, and teachers in defining acceptable and ideal practices. The first is to identify "critical" components of an innovation and to distinguish these from the "related" components. If the decision-making group decides that certain components are essential to use the innovation, these components can be marked with an asterisk and placed at the beginning of the IC Component Checklist. The "nice-to-have," related

Figure 12
Learning with Art Configuration Checklist

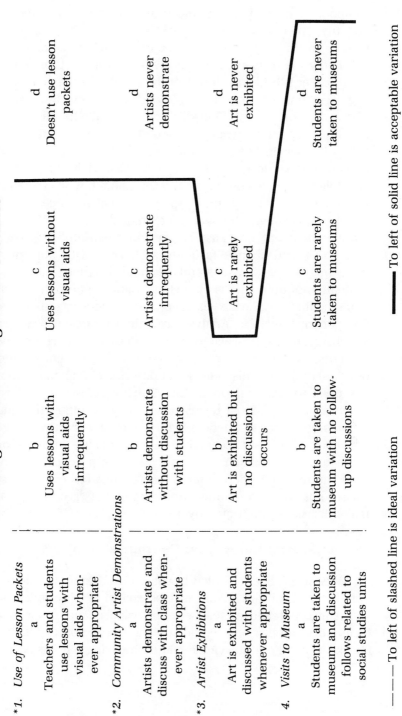

1. Use of Lesson Packets

a
Teachers and students use lessons with visual aids whenever appropriate

b
Uses lessons with visual aids infrequently

c
Uses lessons without visual aids

d
Doesn't use lesson packets

2. Community Artist Demonstrations

a
Artists demonstrate and discuss with class whenever appropriate

b
Artists demonstrate without discussion with students

c
Artists demonstrate infrequently

d
Artists never demonstrate

3. Artist Exhibitions

a
Art is exhibited and discussed with students whenever appropriate

b
Art is exhibited but no discussion occurs

c
Art is rarely exhibited

d
Art is never exhibited

4. *Visits to Museum*

a
Students are taken to museum and discussion follows related to social studies units

b
Students are taken to museum with no follow-up discussions

c
Students are rarely taken to museums

d
Students are never taken to museums

———— To left of solid line is acceptable variation

------ To left of slashed line is ideal variation

* Critical Components

components of the innovation can be listed after the critical components. The IC Component Checklist in figure 12 exemplifies this format. In this way, change facilitators, teachers, and evaluators will know the priority areas and where to spend their time.

Another useful way to reflect the value of certain components and variations is to draw vertical, solid, and dashed lines, also part of the IC Component Checklist in figure 12. In this case, the developer or other group decided that those variations to the right of the solid line are "unacceptable." The component variations falling between the solid and the dashed lines represent acceptable variations of use for each component, while variations to the left of the dashed lines represent ideal practices and most closely approximate the developer's model.

A component checklist is particularly useful for teachers, evaluators, and change facilitators charged with implementing programs to particular standards and in those cases where evaluation of outcomes is important. Data can be collected about implementation in each classroom and summarized on the IC Component Checklist. Analyses can then be made to determine which variations are related to outcomes, and, therefore, which components/variations are more essential to implement. Ideally, developers will do this determination prior to implementation. In any case, the IC Component Checklist provides a useful way to describe in operational terms what using an innovation means, provides guidance to teachers in implementing practices judged to be more and less acceptable, and provides information to evaluators about which forms of classroom practice meet or exceed the minimum definition of use. Evaluators can then select classrooms where key innovation components are being used to make decisions about effectiveness.

Measuring Innovation Configurations

Once it has been decided to use an Innovation Configuration Component Checklist, data must be collected to complete it. As was suggested above, teachers, principals, and other change facilitators can circle variations on the Innovation Configuration checklist based on interviewing and observing what is occurring in classrooms. How reliable and valid these ratings will be depends in part on the data collection procedure used (e.g., interview versus classroom observation) and in part on the type of component being assessed. For example, teachers could be asked through an interview procedure to describe the variation of a grouping component they were using, and there could be reasonable confidence that the report was valid. Data about a component dealing with teaching behavior, however, should probably be collected through direct classroom observation. Asking teachers to estimate the ratio of open to closed questions they use in instruction is not a very accurate procedure. Direct classroom observation is also needed to rate an IC checklist component dealing with teacher/student interaction. These and a number of other measurement problems have been considered in the research conducted on the IC checklist.

A manual describing in detail the procedures for developing an Innovation Component Checklist and addressing some of the more technical research issues has been developed (Heck, Steigelbauer, Hall, and Loucks 1981). The checklist development procedure requires a special orientation and entails more than developers sitting down by themselves to sketch out components and component variations. It requires a systematic analysis of the innovation, and an interactive process works best. When developers attempt the task by themselves, they have a tendency to describe philosophical orientation, goals, outcomes, and implementation requirements rather than operational forms. Developers find the interactive process of describing and clarifying IC components and component variations to be instructive and useful.

An outline of the recommended procedure for developing an IC Component Checklist is presented in figure 13. The task does not threaten teachers, developers, evaluators, or change facilitators. The process begins with reviewing any documents and materials that describe the innovation and its components. The innovation developers and any related facilitators and trainers are then interviewed about the innovation *in terms of classroom practice*. Following this procedure the first draft of IC components and variations can be made.

Figure 13
A Procedure for Identifying Innovation Configurations

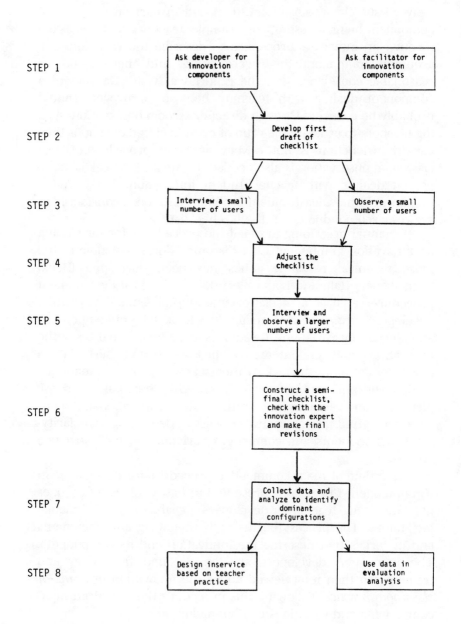

The second step entails observing and interviewing a small number of users with a wide range of experience, skill, and appropriateness of use of the innovation. The product from this step is an adjusted component checklist that includes descriptions of components and variations from teachers. If possible, this is a good time to check back with the developer if he or she is not directly involved in the ongoing checklist building process. It is important to have the developer's model in mind, including their vision and dream of ideal use, as the components and variations are being identified. The IC checklist should also include variations the developer has not envisioned.

The subsequent steps in IC Component Checklist development entail refining the checklist by collecting data from a larger sample of users. Once there is agreement about the number, sequence of components, and component variations, the checklist can be made available for use in staff development and evaluation applicatons. The key in developing the checklist is to keep in mind three questions: (1) What are the key components? (2) What will teachers and students be doing when the innovation is in use? (3) What will be observed in the classroom? These development steps are only highlighted in this chapter since the technical manual is readily available through the Research and Development Center for Teacher Education (Heck, Stiegelbauer, Hall, and Loucks 1981) or through ERIC (ERIC ED 204 147).

The important process to remember is where decision makers, change facilitators, evaluators, and, hopefully, teachers, come together to ask the basic question: What does use of this innovation mean in the classroom? When this process is carried out and a consensus is reached, a major step toward making a successful change has been taken. When all the key actors share the same image(s) of how the innovation is to be operationalized and of what its essential components, its ideal and unacceptable variations are, the possibilities for successful classroom implementation and subsequent expected effects are greatly enhanced. All too frequently, change processes are carried out with no clear and concrete description of what the innovation is. This lack of specificity increases teacher frustration and informational and personal concerns. It almost certainly insures that, when the summative evaluation is done, the evaluator will once again report "no significant difference" between the new program and the old way. This implication and others of Innovation Configurations are explored further in the final section of this chapter. Before that, some of the research applications of IC are summarized.

Findings from Research with Innovation Configurations

Some research findings are described here that illustrate the utility and the heuristic potential of the concept of Innovation Configurations. The findings selected for description reveal implications for planning and designing future change processes.

Configurations of Team Teaching

As was described earlier, one of the original studies of the concept of Innovation Configurations investigated more than four hundred elementary school teachers involved in team teaching in schools in Texas, Nebraska, and Massachusetts. A surprising array of patterns of team teaching was found as the data were collected. An analysis of the different patterns of teaming was done by Rutherford (1981). He identified eight configurations of teams, summarized in figure 14. Although the eight configurations do not represent all possible combinations of components and variations, they do summarize those most frequently observed. Several of the configurations were similar across most variations, but the differences were significant in the operation of the teams and have direct implications for instruction and staff development.

Fidelity Orientation

One of the ongoing debates in education is the degree of fidelity, or adherence to the developer's model, that can be expected from schools and individual teachers. This ideological debate is one of those for which there is no absolute answer but about which everyone has an opinion. Whatever the answer, it certainly depends on the characteristics of the innovation, the users, the clients, and the context.

The 1970s and 1980s have been a time of distaste for "high" fidelity orientations, where teachers are expected to adhere close-

Figure 14
Patterns of Teaming

Type 1: A team (or unit) of three to five teachers share a common group of students and most, if not all, students have some contact with each teacher during the course of the day. Each teacher teaches all subjects, but to different groups of children. Much of the instructional planning in the team is done cooperatively, although each teacher maintains his or her own particular teaching style and is ultimately responsible for the content of the subjects he or she teaches. Children are easily and commonly shifted from one group to another as their needs require.

Type 2: Teams are much the same as Type 1, except that certain instructional activities are planned for the entire team by one person. For example, one teacher might plan a two-week unit on science that is taught by all teachers. All teachers have responsibility for planning such a unit in some subject areas.

Type 3: Teams have much the same organizational pattern and regular interaction as Types 1 and 2, but teaching assignments are based more on skills than on subject areas. All teachers may be teaching math, but instead of teaching all skills to their group, they may teach only certain math skills, i.e., division or subtraction. In this pattern, students move from level to level as their skill needs change, and the skills a teacher teaches change as pupil needs require.

Type 4: Teams are organizationally the same as Type 1-3. In this pattern, however, cooperative planning does not necessarily encompass all the teaching activities of the team. Instead, there is one common endeavor, such as an enrichment center or learning center, that accommodates all children in the unit and is planned cooperatively. Teachers decide on the materials and tasks to be included in the center, or the rules for its operation, and on the responsibilities of each teacher relative to the center. Planning for instruction in the various subjects is not usually shared except for the general exchange of ideas.

Type 5: Teams meet together regularly and share a common group of children, but they do little cooperative planning beyond sharing general ideas or providing support for each other.

Figure 14 (Cont'd)
Patterns of Teaming

Sometimes these teams establish some team standards, such as how to discipline children, that they plan cooperatively.

Type 6:   Teams vary from those above in that they do not share a common group of students. Early in the year, children are assigned out to various teachers, usually on the basis of achievement level, and they usually remain in that group for the remainder of the year. It is possible for a child to be moved from one teacher to another, but few are shifted. In this pattern, a child is usually taught by at least two teachers in the team, but never goes to all team members. When these teams meet, their discussions usually center around matters such as scheduling, administrative details or resources that concern the entire team.

Type 7:   This is a less frequently noted teaming pattern. These teams get together principally for the identifying and sharing of ideas and resources. They share no children, and team members generally function independently of each other, except for the sharing of resources. Occasionally, they will shift an individual child from one teacher to another.

Type 8:   In this pattern, two (or more) teachers teach one group of children at the same time. Interestingly, many teachers seemed to feel that this type of teaching is the true model of teaming, but we found very few who did this.

Type 9:   This is an organizational pattern that was found to some degree in all of the above patterns. When teams are large in number—usually six or more—there is a tendency to form two or three sub-teams. When this is done, the sub-teams become virtually independent of each other except for meeting together for administrative purposes.

Rutherford, W. L. (1981). *Team teaching: How do teachers use it?* Austin: The University of Texas at Austin, Research and Development Center for Teacher Education.

ly to a developer's model. In extremely "high" fidelity examples, only one configuration of the innovation is seen as acceptable. The general argument against this perspective is that teachers will not accept a high fidelity implementation, making it impossible to "impose" the innovation on them. From a concerns-based perspective, a fidelity approach is possible, and, as with any other strategy, there are inherent weaknesses and advantages that can be anticipated. The key is to compensate for the weaknesses and to take advantage of the strengths. For example, a fidelity approach runs the risk of teachers having higher Stage 2 Personal concerns, so extra interventions will be needed that anticipate the arousal of these concerns.

One example that demonstrates that a high fidelity approach can succeed comes from the work of Reid and her associates with the *Exemplary Center for Reading Instruction (ECRI)*. As part of a national study of the implementation of National Diffusion Network programs, data were collected on the implementation of ECRI (Reid 1980). The developers of ECRI maintained there was only one acceptable configuration of this program. Their staff development program and all the materials supported and directed teachers in exactly how to conduct the ECRI program. In the study, an Innovation Configuration Component Checklist was developed for ECRI, and IC data were collected in the sample sites. The data consistently showed that teachers were, in fact, using the first variation of each component on the ECRI component checklist. Because the developers were clear and worked over time to support teachers in their movement toward the one acceptable configuration, and because the use of ECRI made noticeable differences with students, a fidelity implementation was achieved.

Very few developers are as highly prescriptive as those of ECRI. It is extremely rare to see an IC Component Checklist where only the first variation of each component is both acceptable and ideal. More frequently, some variation is tolerated for critical components, and increased amounts of variation are accepted with regard to related components. ECRI does illustrate, however, that under certain conditions a high fidelity orientation can result in successful implementation in many classrooms. Such implementation success requires that change facilitators and teachers share a common image of innovation use and that ongoing support and coaching interventions for teachers are provided. In addition, positive student effects obviously encourage teachers to achieve high fidelity use. The successful implementation of most high fidelity innovations requires skilled change facilitators.

A Variation on the Standard IC Component Checklist

A slightly different variation of the Innovation Configuration checklist was used in the science department of Jefferson County, Colorado (Melle and Pratt 1981). In the implementation of a revised science curriculum for grades three through six, a JeffCo science implementation checklist was developed. The checklist included "variations," which are highlighted in figure 15. One difference between this and the standard IC Component Checklist is that the labels for the ideal and unacceptable variations are "Best Practices Working," "Getting a Good Start," and "Outside Intended Program."

Also, components on this checklist combine implementation requirements, such as the amount of prescribed teaching time, with standard behavioral components. In our Innovation Configurations work, we develop a separate list of implementation requirements. In the JeffCo Science checklist, school board policy established some of the implementation requirement components. The checklist translated board policy into information and provided the kinds of detail that enabled teachers and change facilitators to move in the desired directions. The Jeffco science checklist was also used to study the relationship of implementation to learning outcomes (Pratt, Winters, and George 1980). The findings showed that student outcomes in science achievement were consistent with their teachers' implementations of more or less ideal configurations of the program.

No Fidelity Is Okay Too!

There are a number of times and many reasons for not indicating ideal and unacceptable variations, or critical and related components. Some innovations do not have a fidelity orientation. The developer(s) declines to nominate practices that are more or less desirable, and anything is acceptable. In other cases, there may be external reasons for not advocating certain components and variations. In these cases, the IC Component Checklist is useful in that it leaves the interpretation of use to the users. The

Figure 15
Example of a Component Described

Is Science Taught According to R-1 Guide?

Outside Intended Program	Getting a Good Start	Best Practices Working
A. During the school year the teaching covers less than 85% of the objectives and activities. The teacher may or may not cover units in the guide. If units are taught, more activities are omitted than included.	A. During the school year 85% of the objectives and 85% of the activities are taught. The teacher covers the units as written and spends the allotted time (see #1). Some units may be abbreviated because an extra amount of time was spent on another unit.	A. During the school year the teacher teaches all units, all objectives of each unit and 90% of the activities. At the end of some objectives teacher uses Optional Activities to extend the unit with small groups of students.
B. Objectives or activities are not sequenced. Objectives may be used but teacher-made activities are used to accomplish the objectives.	B. The teacher can: —Point in the guide to the objective that is currently being taught. —Describe what objectives and activities went before and what objectives will come after current activities.	B. The teacher can relate what objective is being studied and how the activity pertains to accomplishing the objective. He/she can relate what objectives preceded and will succeed the objective being taught.
C. Supplementary media is frequently used in addition to or to the exclusion of hands-on activities.	C. Teacher uses supplementary media sparingly.	C. Teacher uses supplementary media sparingly and can demonstrate how supplements which are used support the objectives being taught.

implementation checklist for the Ginn and Company Reading Program (GRP) (1984) is a good example of this situation. The GRP implementation checklist does not identify critical and related components or ideal and unacceptable variations. Based on their knowledge of reading, instructional design, and research on teaching, the publishers did have opinions about what would be more and less appropriate in classroom practice, yet they did not think it was appropriate or possible to prescribe to all schools how the reading program should be used. By preserving a left to right sequencing, they were able to reflect their position about variations for each component. This checklist, a part of which is presented in figure 16, illustrates, for a nonfidelity orientation, the usefulness of the checklist tool for facilitating implementation and clarifying directions for teachers, principals, and others. The checklist is presented by the publisher to principals, teachers, and reading consultants so that all can think more clearly about the different ways the Ginn Reading Program can be used.

Implications and Issues of Innovation Configurations

Many of the implications and issues related to the concept of Innovation Configurations have already been introduced. Some of these are worth highlighting here, and a few others that are important to consider are included as well.

I. THE CONCEPT OF INNOVATION CONFIGURATIONS WORKS WITH ALL SIZES AND TYPES OF PROGRAMS AND PROCESSES. The concept of Innovation Configurations can be applied to old or new programs. The concept can be applied to regular practices in the teaching of a particular subject matter, to the organizational arrangements between teachers, and to use of a process such as Reality Therapy (Glasser 1969). It is not restricted to major changes. In all cases, if there is some conception of use, it is possible to identify components and component variations. The components and variations will describe the different ways the program or process can be made operational.

Collecting data to complete the checklist for some programs and processes may be problematic. For example, when implementing Reality Therapy, separate component checklists

Figure 16
The Ginn Reading Program Components

For each component, circle the item that best describes how that component is used. Use the Notes and Observations section to record additional teaching strategies.

Components					Notes & Observations
1. Student placement—What materials do you use to place students that are new to the program?					
(a)	(b)	(c)	(d)	(e)	
GRP Placement Test and other available information	Transition charts and information available from student files	GRP Placement Test only	Transition Chart only	Teacher judgement only	
2. Use of the Teacher's Edition—How closely do you follow the Teacher's Edition?					
(a)	(b)	(c)	(d)		
Follow the T.E. in general, but make adaptatons based upon pupil needs	Follow the T.E. closely	Follow the T.E. in general, but make adaptation and additions based upon teacher needs	Do not follow the T.E.		

Figure 16 (Cont'd)
The Ginn Reading Program Components

3. Sections of the Lesson Plan—Which section(s) within each part of the lesson plan do you use?

Part 1	Part 2	Part 3	Part 4
1. Introducing vocabulary	1. Guiding reading	1. Decoding	1. Language
2. Preparing for Compre-hension	2. Discussing the selection	2. Vocabulary	2. Literature
	3. Focus questions	3. Comprehension	3. Creativity
		4. Life-Study Skills	4. Arts and Careers

should be developed for each of the user groups. There could be one IC Component Checklist for teachers, another for the principal, and another for counselors. The different "units of adoption" would need their own IC Component Checklists.

II. WHEN DOES A VARIATION BECOME A COMPONENT, WHEN DOES A COMPONENT BECOME AN INNOVATION, AND WHEN DOES AN INNOVATION BECOME AN INNOVATION BUNDLE? This issue is another way of asking, What is an innovation? Clearly, all innovations are not the same size and there is not a clear demarcation between a variation and a component of an innovation. This decision, in many ways, is a judgment call based on how the IC Component Checklist will be used and the level of detail needed. An innovation could be summarized with from four to six components on one IC checklist, or there could be fifteen to twenty different components, depending upon the scope and complexity of the innovation and the detail of information desired.

An interesting conceptual issue and, at the same time, a very practical problem has to do with the number of innovations that exist within a particular change process. Too often there is not an innovation but an *innovation bundle*, a set of two or more interrelated innovations that are being implemented at the same time. Some examples of innovation bundles that have received widespread use are Individually Guided Education (IGE), Competency-Based Teacher Education (CBTE), mainstreaming, and bilingual education. These cases are not single innovations but, rather, large, complex, and multifaceted innovation bundles. Frequently, change facilitators are confused about the existence of more then one innovation in a bundle and attempt implementing them all with the same set of staff development procedures and other facilitation activities. This mistake tends to cause teacher confusion, and in some cases interference can occur between the different innovations in the bundle.

A more effective change process can occur and be evaluated if the innovations within the bundle are distinguished and separate IC Component Checklists developed for each one. A strategic plan that phases in the different innovations within the bundle can then be developed, and staff development and other facilitative supports can be designed in consistent ways. Subsequent summative evaluations will then be done with these distinctions in mind.

III. With IC Component Data, Staff Development Can be More Closely Designed and Targeted. Staff developers are continually challenged with designing workshops to support change. In many instances, they attempt to move beyond the "good time" workshops typically offered at the beginning of the school year. Increasing emphasis is therefore placed on phased and content-specific workshops to support the change process as it is occurring, for it is difficult to predetermine the workshop contents that will be needed.

With Innovation Configurations data in summary form, as is illustrated in figure 17, it is possible to identify the innovation variations and components that are being implemented effectively and to identify the one or two components that are not being utilized as well. Those components that call for more staff development will be the ones, as is reflected in figure 17, where the majority of the teachers are using variations that tend towards the "right" side of the component checklist.

In the figure 17 example, staff development workshops should be designed to help teachers learn to use program-required objectives to drive their classroom instruction, rather than being guided by the textbook sequence of objectives. It is also clear that the text is not being enhanced by the use of the activity kits as instructional resources. With this analysis, staff developers now know that they should address the kits and their use in the program in the next workshop.

Another example of using IC data for staff development is being tried in the Lincoln Public Schools (Nebraska). IC checklists were developed for key curriculum areas by teams of principals, teachers, and curriculum specialists. These checklists were then used by principals to monitor classroom practice. They summarized their findings across classrooms and used the diagnostic data as the basis for developing their staff development and school improvement plans.

Using IC data for planning can result in more relevant staff development for teachers and, ultimately, more successful implementation of the innovation. By analyzing the Innovation Configurations being used by teachers, problem areas quickly

Figure 17
Summary of Data for Teachers in School
MATH CHECKLIST

Component 1: *Objectives/Planning*

  30% Teaches program objectives in sequence*
  65% Teaches text objectives sequence
  5% Teaches other objectives

Component 2: *Instructional Resources*

  10% Uses text and Activity Kits*
  85% Uses text only
  5% Uses Activity Kits only

Component 3: *Testing*

  100% Uses Mastery Test at recommended time*

Component 4: *Use of Test Results*

  5% Each student's instruction is *individualized* on basis of test
    results
  25% Group(s) change; students are reassigned frequently
  65% Group(s) remain intact; students receive extra help as needed
  5% Group(s) remain intact; any review is done by group

Component 5: *Record Keeping*

  100% Current information recorded*

*essential (required by district)

emerge. Because the emphasis is placed on the innovation rather than on teachers, suggestions for changing practices are more easily accepted. Of course, when this information is combined with information about Stages of Concern and Levels of Use, an even more effective training experience can be designed.

IV. WHAT DO YOU DO ABOUT HIGH AND LOW FIDELITY? Some change and adaptation in innovation use is normally accepted or tolerated. But some of these configurations are too far removed to belong to *the* innovation. Reaching agreement on what represents such a "drastic mutation" of an innovation is often difficult without formal discussions. Without discussion, there often is an area or array of drastic mutations. As illustrated in figure 18, the configurations of use within that area can be acceptable to some, but unacceptable to others.

Figure 18
Configuration Continuum

Using "Car" as the Innovation

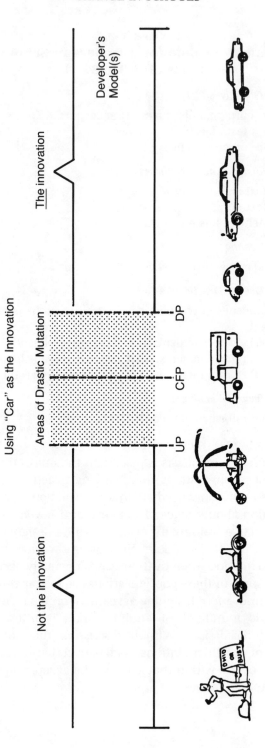

Points of Drastic Mutation
UP — User's Point
CFP — Change Facilitator's Point
DP — Developer's Point

At the beginning of the change process, it is important for someone to make decisions regarding how much teacher variation and of what nature to encourage, or about how much restriction should be placed on teacher creativity and classroom adaptation of a program or process. When there is consensus, and all parties understand the objectives and goals of implementation at the school and classroom level, the change process can proceed more effectively and drastic mutation can be kept to a minimum. The decision-making process should include all the key actors and take long-term goals and objectives into account, as well as initial implementation needs.

An effect observed in several studies, to be addressed more directly in subsequent chapters, regards the role of the principal in determining fidelity. In our studies, there have been intriguing school-by-school differences in Innovation Configurations data. In one large-scale study of a mathematics curriculum implementation, some schools were observed to have relatively consistent configuration patterns among all teachers in the school. In other schools in the same district with access to the same resources and staff development opportunities, configurations varied greatly among teachers. One conclusion was that the principals and other school-based change facilitators made a difference in the amount of configuration variation within a particular school. It is quite conceivable that principals and teachers in some schools came to an agreement on using a particular configuration or a limited set of configurations. The corollary seems to be that, in other schools, each teacher was left to do whatever they wished, resulting in different configurations of the same innovation.

Related to the preceding discussion of fidelity, it is quite conceivable that even within the limits set by the district, individual schools still have room for variation. How much variation will each school want, and how will decisions about consistency or lack of consistency be made within each school? Use of the IC Component Checklist can support school-level discussions about the variations possible in each component and what is desirable for each component. In the discussions, the IC checklist could be useful not only for developing staff agreements, but for setting priorities for resources and for supporting the change process.

V. How Can All of the Information About An Innovation Be Summarized in One Place? A concise way for outlining innovation information is to use the idea of Key Elements. Key elements consists of three lists: (1) implementation requirements, (2) IC Component Checklist, and (3) goals and outcomes. A portfolio that includes these three lists provides a brief yet thorough description of an innovation. With this information, decision makers, evaluators, teachers, principals, and others can learn a great deal about the characteristics and expectations of an innovation. With the Key Elements, decisions can be made about adopting the innovation, monitoring implementation, refining practices, and evaluating effects. Developed from a wide array of experiences, model building, and research, Key Elements represent the frameworks for answering what appears to be a very simple question: What is an innovation?

Summary

In this chapter, the third diagnostic dimension of the Concerns-Based Adoption Model, Innovation Configurations, was examined. The concept of Innovation Configurations, the IC Component Checklist, and ways to use the checklist were introduced. The discussion included some of the implications of viewing the innovation from its use at the classroom level. Now that the three diagnostic dimensions have been described, it is time to shift the discussion to an analysis of interventions—the actions of change facilitators. These actions are explored in the next two chapters.

Chapter 6

Little Things
Mean A Lot:
Incident Interventions

As the curriculum consultant and teacher walk down the hallway to lunch, the consultant asks, "How is it going with the life science program since I sent the five microscopes over?" The teacher responds enthusiastically but a bit sheepishly, "It was really a boost to the motivation of the seventh graders. But could you stop by after class today and show me how to make those new type slides?"

In the weekly staff meeting the assistant principal provided an information handout and a brief lecture, and then directed teachers to solve two problems in the metric math curricula. Teachers who asked "good" questions about the problem activities were rewarded with a set of posters illustrating metric measures.

The Director of Instruction mailed to all teachers and administrators the first biweekly newsletter, containing a column highlighting exemplary teacher practices with the expository writing program.

A tired-looking teacher standing in the school office at his mailbox read a "Happy Gram" from the principal complimenting him on his successful field trip earlier in the day with the new environmental ed unit. The weary teacher smiled broadly, "I sure needed that!" Three days later when the teacher profusely thanked her, the principal puzzled, "Did I really do something that great?"

The three diagnostic dimensions of the Concerns-Based Adoption Model were described in the three previous chapters; now we move to the concept of interventions. From a concerns-based point of view, it is insufficient simply to assess teachers' and other clients' concerns and use of a particular program or process; it is the reponsibility of the concerns-based change facilitator to "do something" on the basis of the assessment—to intervene.

Interestingly, practitioners and the literature rarely address directly what to do. There has been an implicit expectation that change facilitators, including principals, assistant principals, curriculum consultants, and others, will take various actions to make change occur. Detailed analyses of what these different actions are, or should be, have not, however, been systematically described. The concept of intervening only recently has been defined in any systematic way, although there has been an extensive array of case studies analyzing change outcomes. In general, these recent studies focus on the more global structure of interventions and the overall "game plan" that unfolds during the course of a change process. Typically, what is not described are the day-to-day behaviors of principals, staff developers, teachers, and others involved in facilitating and, in some cases, inhibiting the change process. Based on research with CBAM concepts, it is clear that these day-to-day actions, or interventions, are keys to the success or failure of change attempts. Indeed, these interventions are the keys to understanding the dynamics of facilitating change.

The name *incident* intervention has been assigned to these small moment-to-moment and day-to-day actions. The change process can be analyzed using the incident interventions that occur daily, and it is clear that these incidents make a significant difference in the outcome of the change process. Further, there are patterns and trends in the ways these individual incidents are connected and sequenced throughout the school year and during the change process.

Frequently, policymakers, administrators, staff developers, evaluators, and researchers think of interventions as consisting only of workshops. In fact, interventions come in many other shapes and sizes. As the examples at the beginning of this chapter illustrate, incident interventions can be face-to-face, but they can also occur through other media such as in print and by telephone. Incident interventions can involve a few or many people. They can take thirty seconds or three hours. Finally, there are many of them.

When we and our colleagues began defining interventions and developing procedures to classify them, there were serious and intense debates. After extensive analysis of the literature and two years of collecting ethnographic data on interventions in several schools and school districts, the CBAM research staff finally agreed upon a definition: An intervention is an action or event or a set of actions or events that influences use of the innovation.

The thrust of this chapter is to describe ways to analyze the smallest of interventions—incidents—and to draw implications for practice. A classification system for identifying kinds of incident interventions and a system for dissecting these interventions into their subdimensions are also described. The chapter includes a summary of intervention findings from the study of elementary school principals as they facilitated implementation of new curriculum programs. It concludes with some implications and recommendations for change facilitator practice. In chapter 7, another part of the intervention analytical framework is introduced. This idea can be used to analyze the accumulation of incidents and examine the interrelationships of interventions as they occur throughout an entire change process.

The Many Shapes of Incident Interventions

Each incident intervention by itself typically has little effect on the overall change process. Most of them are not consciously noticed either by the recipient or the change facilitator who delivers them. A few "critical" incidents are remembered by everyone, but the more numerous, everyday incidents are quickly forgotten by most people. Yet, a surprising number of these incident interventions occur during the implementation of even relatively simple curriculum innovations. In the Principal Teacher Interaction Study (Hord, Huling, and Stiegelbauer 1983), nearly two thousand incidents were identified that occurred during the implementation of relatively simple curriculum innovations in nine elementary schools during one school year. While collecting the data, it was observed that principals and other change facilitators had quickly lost track of the incidents they had made. When reminded of particular incidents, they did not always remember them or did not think of them as having been particularly significant. Frequently, principals were apologetic for having spent time doing some of those "little" things; teachers in the study did not always remember interventions either. Yet, the incidents did occur, and their effects accumulated. A structure was needed to classify and sort the incidents that were identified.

Incident interventions can be categorized in a number of ways. The definitions developed for the different types or "sublevels" of incident interventions are presented in figure 19. An example of an incident intervention for each sublevel, drawn from the studies of principals, follows.

ISOLATED INCIDENT. The dean chatted with the biology teacher and recommended that he wear his jacket during school duty hours. This suggestion is an isolated action, with no link to the particular biology program being implemented in this teacher's classroom. The casual suggestion remained separated from other biology program-related actions.

SIMPLE INCIDENT. The math coordinator telephoned and told the assistant principal that the teachers were not using the new math materials. The coordinator is intervening with the assistant principal via the telephone with a straightforward message that potentially could be quite powerful, depending on how the assistant principal perceives the intervention and what follow-up actions are taken with the teachers.

CHAIN INCIDENT. The social studies resource teacher contacted each teacher to request a student project for the social studies fair. As a result of the resource teacher's identical action with each teacher, the teachers had a short-term, concrete program goal to work toward. The project was not only concrete for the teachers but highly visible to students and parents. It resulted in encouragement of program use by teachers, increased student motivation and productivity, and parent approval.

REPEATED INCIDENT. Three times last week the associate superintendent for instruction asked the principal if he had picked up the reading teachers' guides from the warehouse. A pa-

Figure 19
Definitions of Incident Interventions

	Definition	Indicators	Example
INCIDENT	An incident is the singular occurrence of an action or event. They may be one of a kind happenings or they may aggregate into tactics and strategies.	Is the smallest sized intervention. Can be targeted at one or more individuals. Covers a small amount of time. Is a single action or event.	
Sublevels			
Isolated	Is a single action separated in space, time or purpose from other actions.	Has no identifiable link to other interventions. Takes little time or space.	A casual suggestion. A visit by an Australian educator for a few hours.
Simple	Is a single action or interaction that is functionally related to other interventions.	Can be linked to other incident interventions. Is the smallest intervention.	A facilitator telling another to visit a particular school to provide assistance. A facilitator asking a teacher how use of the innovation is going.
Chain	Is a series of the same simple incident delivered to different targets.	Is the same basic action repeated with different targets. Contains the same source and function.	The facilitator visiting each primary teacher to collect samples of pupils' work related to the innovation.

Figure 19 (Cont'd)

	Definition	Indicators	Example
Repeated	Is a series of the same simple incident delivered to the same target more than once.	Contains the same source, target and function. Done two or more times to the same target.	The facilitator visiting the kindergarten teacher three times to ask for pupils' work related to the innovation.
Complex	Is a set of related simple actions within a short time frame.	Consists of two or more simple incidents that are different in some ways. Takes little time, typically 5 minutes to one hour.	A brief staff meeting during which several decisions are made. A conference in which the facilitator may provide feedback to the user and a plan developed for improving use.

tient superintendent continued to target the same intervention at the same individual. Did the "reluctant" principal then act? Yes, this time persistence paid off!

COMPLEX INCIDENT. The principal conducted an hour-long, in-service workshop with teachers. This complex incident consisted of a series of simple, innovation-related incidents organized around the content and activities of a workshop. The interactions of the principal and faculty through these simple incidents combined to make a complex incident that provided clarification of program goals and objectives for the teachers.

Charting the Flow of Incident Interventions

It is rare for more than a few incident interventions to occur in isolation from each other. There is usually interconnectedness and sequencing to incident interventions; one incident triggers another, it causes another, and so forth. Over the course of a school year, most incidents become connected to each other. To help illustrate this interconnectedness of incident interventions, a mapping procedure has been developed (Zigarmi and Goldstein 1979). The procedure requires identifying each intervention, describing it, and plotting it on a time line to chart its connections to other incident interventions that came before and after.

One of the requirements for charting is a one- or two-sentence description of each intervention. The information to be included in the description answers the questions, Who did what, to whom, for what reason, where, and how? Zigarmi and Goldstein (1979:7) found that it was useful when writing the sentences to "use adverbial phrases to show whether the action occurred once or was repeated" and to indicate how much time (i.e., duration) the intervention required. They also found that writing descriptions in the present tense aided understanding. Having the intervention descriptions typed on individual slips of paper or cards made it possible to move them around. Another productive way to chart interventions is to use long sheets of computer paper with each page representing a week or a month and the whole length of computer paper representing the entire period of study.

Drawing from the work by Zigarmi and Goldstein, a sample analysis of a "map" is presented in figure 20. Note that in this map the perspective of the change facilitator is kept constant when describing what the principal and the resource teacher are doing. Maintaining the facilitator perspective keeps the overall picture of interventions and their interconnectedness organized around one point of view. In this brief map (figure 20), the incidents are placed vertically along a time line by months. The interventions that occur within the month are arranged horizontally. The map reveals the way in which the principal and resource teacher planned and intervened. The map also provides insights about how the resource teacher gave the principal feedback about the progress of the change process. In this account, it is clear that the principal and resource teacher worked as a team in facilitating program implementation. They not only met together to make plans, but frequently met together with teachers to implement their plans. In addition, each facilitator met individually with teachers.

The Anatomy of an Intervention

Another way to understand interventions is to explore the internal parts of each intervention. Questions like the following can then be examined: Who initiates the most interventions? Where are the different locations for interventions? How frequently are interventions aimed at individual teachers, groups of teachers, or the faculty as a whole? What is the purpose of each intervention? What proportion of the interventions are face-to-face versus some other medium? How long does the average intervention take?

These and other questions can be closely examined by using a detailed coding structure—the Anatomy of Interventions—that breaks each intervention into its subparts (see figure 21) (Hord, Hall, and Zigarmi, 1980). The subparts that can be coded are source, target, function, medium, flow, and location. With this coding system, change facilitators can think more critically about each intervention they deliver. Information about a series of incident interventions allows one to look at the various patterns of where, how, when, and for what purpose interventions are typically being made.

Figure 20
Hawthorn School Critical Incident Chart and Time Line

Legend: [ ] = critical incidents

Aug. 1980	CBAM workshop for principals.		District workshop for resource teachers regarding composition.
Sept. 1980	*9/4; 9/24-29* Principal meets with each teacher about their goals for the year.	*9/9; 9/16* Principal meets with resource teacher to plan for the year.	*9/3* District workshop for teachers on composition/ Sourcebook.
Oct. 1980	*10/14* Principal has staff meeting regarding composition.	*10/23* Principal meets with resource teacher regarding composition.	*10/22* Resource teacher meets with each teacher about their concerns
	Teachers state confusion about program's review committee plan.		
Nov. 1980	*11/10* Principal & resource teacher meet to plan composition of committee.	*11/10* Principal & resource teacher meet with each committee member.	Principal meets with individual teachers to encourage work on composition-related activities.
	Resource teacher tells principal of district ideas to clarify innovation.	*11/25* Resource teacher meets with committee in 2 sections—upper and lower grades.	*11/25* Committee teachers meet with others at grade level.
Dec. 1980	*12/1; 12/15* Principal & resource teacher meet to plan composition committee.	*12/10* Resource teacher meets with committee sections to review scope & sequence.	*12/16* Resource teacher discusses scope & sequence with each teacher.

Figure 20 (Cont'd)

12/1 Composition discussed at staff meeting.	*12/18* Resource teacher meets with committee sections to plan.

To illustrate the coding system, an example of a chain incident intervention and its codings can be explained.

CHAIN INCIDENT INTERVENTION. *The principal telephones the chairman of the Principal's Committee, the area math coordinator, and the assistant superintendent to check out the rumor about a further delay in delivery of the promised math materials.* Each action was targeted at individuals and consumed only a few minutes of time, therefore each is an incident. Because the same action was directed at three different targets, the intervention sublevel is "chain" (coded 4). The source of the incident is the principal (coded 6A), while the various targets were the Principals' Committee chairperson (8C), the area math coordinator (8B), and the assistant superintendent (8A). The function of this chain incident was to gain information about materials; thus, it falls under the 1000 function—Developing Supportive Organizational Arrangements— and is an "E" (seeking or providing materials, information, space, other resources). The function code is then 1E. The medium was by telephone and would be coded 4. Flow was one-way (1). The location subsumed the school and was within the immediate user system (the district) and would therefore be coded 2. The composite code for this chain intervention would be:

4	6A	8C, 8B, 8A	1E	4	1	2
sublevel	source	target	function	medium	flow	location

Most of the coding decisions are straightforward, though a few may seem a little peculiar (e.g., the flow code). To maintain consistency, a set of coding rules has been developed. For example, the rules regarding the definition of "flow" state that, to be two-way, there must be initiation by both parties. In this case, the principal did all the initiating, thus the one-way coding.

By using the Anatomy of an Intervention framework, change facilitators can examine their interventions by systematically coding their activities or simply by reflecting on their interventions with the scheme in mind. The coded data can reveal gaps in

Figure 21: Subparts of Incident Interventions

SUBLEVELS OF INCIDENTS
1. Isolated
2. Simple
3. Complex
4. Chain
5. Repeated
6. Blank (specify)

SUBLEVELS OF TACTICS
11. Single Complex
12. Chain
13. Blank (specify)

SOURCE
1. Clients
2. An individual user
3. Subset(s) of primary or potential users
   A. as individuals
   B. as groups
   C. as a whole group
4. All primary/potential users
   A. as individuals
   B. as groups
   C. as a whole
5. Implementation site resource people
6. Implementation site decision makers
   A. principal
   B. asst. principal
   C. other (specify)
7. Innovation facilitators
8. Immediate user system
   A. decision makers
   B. resource people
   C. other (specify)
9. Extended user system member(s) (specify)
10. Events
11. Blank (specify)
    A. CBAM

TARGET
1. Clients
2. An individual user
3. Subset(s) of primary or potential users
   A. as individuals
   B. as groups
   C. as a whole subset
4. All primary/potential users
   A. as individuals
   B. as groups
   C. as a whole
5. Implementation site resource people
6. Implementation site decision makers
   A. principal
   B. asst. principal
   C. other (specify)
7. Innovation facilitators
8. Immediate user system
   A. decision makers
   B. resource people
   C. other (specify)
9. Extended user system member(s) (specify)
10. The change effort/process
11. Blank (specify)
    A. CBAM

FUNCTION
1000. Developing Supportive or Organizational Arrangements and Resources
   A. policy/global rule/major decision making
   B. planning
   C. managing (e.g., scheduling)
   D. staffing or restructuring roles
   E. seeking or providing materials, information, space, other resources
   F. other (specify)
2000. Training
   A. teaching new knowledge, skills
   B. reviewing
   C. clarifying
   D. other (specify)
3000. Consulting and Reinforcing
   A. promoting and encouraging change in innovation use
   B. reinforcing/supporting present innovation use
   C. consulting—problem solving
   D. information sharing (internal communication, e.g., newsletters)
   E. other (specify)
4000. Monitoring and Evaluating
   A. information gathering (data collecting, pulsing, probing)
   B. data analysis processing
   C. reporting
   D. transferring data
   E. other (specify)
5000. Communicating Externally
   A. informing outsiders
   B. other (specify)
6000. Dissemination
   A. gaining support of outsiders
   B. encouraging/promoting use of innovation by outsiders
   C. other (specify)
7000. Impeding Use
   A. discouraging use
   B. interrupting use
   C. other (specify)
8000. Expressing and Responding to Concerns
   A. complimenting, praising
   B. joking, fooling around
   C. apologizing
   D. peacemaking, reconciling, reassuring, down playing
   E. acknowledging
   F. complaining, criticizing
   G. reprimanding
   H. belittling, sarcasm
   I. blank (specify)

MEDIUM
1. Face to face
2. Written
3. Audio-visual
4. Telephone
5. Public media
6. None
7. Blank (specify)

FLOW
1. One way
2. Interactive
3. None
4. Blank (specify)

LOCATION
1. Implementation site
   A. office
   B. classrooms
   C. other (specify)
2. Immediate user system
   A. central office
   B. training site
   C. other (specify)
3. Extended user system
4. Blank (specify)

Expanded from Hord, S. M., Hall, G. E., and Zigarmi, P. Anatomy of incident and tactic interventions: Dimension, design. Austin: Research and Development Center for Teacher Education, The University of Texas, 1980.

the facilitator's attention to "targets," "functions," or other "sources" who could provide interventions effectively. Ruminations might lead facilitators to think about intervening with particular targets or about using particular functions. All in all, the Intervention Anatomy provides a structure that has proven useful for analyzing the individual interventions a change facilitator makes. It can be used to compare and contrast or summarize the interventions made by a number of facilitators. An overview of some research findings using this framework is presented in the next section.

Findings from the Analysis of Incident Interventions

The Principal-Teacher Interaction Study (PTI) was designed specifically to look at the incident intervention behaviors of principals. In this study, the interventions made by principals and others while they were facilitating teachers' use of new curriculum programs were systematically documented. Nine elementary school principals and their faculties were studied for one year. The schools came from three widely separated geographical areas (Florida, Colorado, and California) and represented three different years of experience in implementing three different curriculum innovations. The innovations were all districtwide initiatives: one in writing composition, one in objective-based mathematics, and one a student-oriented science program. Based on the field work, it seems reasonable to suggest that each of the innovations was similar in size and in its ease of being implemented and that the district characteristics were similar.

All innovation-related incident interventions made at the district level, as well as by school-based administrators and teachers, were included in the study. The documentation procedure was based on logs maintained by the principals and assistant principals, on research staff observations of selected interventions, on face-to-face interviews, and on weekly debriefing telephone interviews conducted by the research staff (Goldstein and Rutherford 1982). In the telephone and face-to-face interviews, the principal and other change facilitators were asked to identify interventions they had made, to describe interventions others had made, and to provide detailed information about each intervention that could be used to code its various subparts.

The Anatomy of Interventions scheme was used to codify all identified interventions (Hord and Hall, 1982). The data were coded specifically to identify and describe the who, what, where, when, how, and why of the interventions these individuals made, as illustrated previously. It was then possible to compare and contrast the activities of the different change facilitators in each of the nine study schools. The tables presented in this chapter are summaries of these analyses. The findings illustrate how the incident intervention coding system can be used to develop specific information about intervention activity. The findings provide new insights about the roles of elementary school principals and others as change facilitators.

Summary of Findings

The abundant data from the PTI study schools were sifted and sorted, analyzed and interpreted (Hord, Huling, and Stiegelbauer, 1983). To summarize what was learned about the intervention behaviors of principals and others in these school improvement efforts, a series of tables are presented. We have included a brief description of each table and descriptions of our impressions and hypotheses. Many of the apparent patterns and trends in the data do not make clear sense (or are misleading) without other information about the site context, the actors, and institutional history. We will be reasonably brief in presenting background information, however, since the main purpose here is to illustrate the kinds of analyses and findings that can be generated from systematically collected, incident intervention data (Hord and Huling-Austin 1986).

Table 1: Number of Incidents for Each School

The total number of interventions (N = 1855) in all schools (see table 1) in the PTI study indicated that a great deal of activity occurred around implementing the different curriculum innovations. Yet each of the innovations studied accounted for only a small portion of the school's total instructional program and the daily activity of the various facilitators. The large number of in-

terventions related to relatively typical changes is a clear indicator of how complex the change process is.

Surprisingly, the PTI data did not reveal any overall relationship between the total number of incident interventions for each
set of schools and the year of implementation (California, implementation year one = 517, Florida, year two = 684, Colorado,
year three = 654). The data indicate that there were high rates of
intervention activity in the schools even during the second and
third year of innovation implementation. We viewed the innovations as being similar in size and the sample schools and districts
as similar, therefore leading us to conclude that the change process is not complete after the first year of innovation use. Principals and other change facilitators continued to make innovation-
related interventions to support innovation use for a number of
years. The significance of the first CBAM assumption (change is a
process, not an event) is thusly underscored.

There are other patterns in these data that will be explained
in the discussions of the remaining tables, but one pattern should
be addressed here. There was wide variation in the number of incident interventions within the California schools, which were in
their first year of implementing a writing composition curriculum
(schools 24, 25, and 26). One explanation could be that the
number of incident interventions at school 26 was under-
represented. The data collector felt she was not able to get much
incident information from the school informants. The principal at
this school tended to gloss over reports of incidents in favor of
reporting on more global events. District administrators' opinions
and our analysis of principal facilitator style (see chapter 8) tended to confirm, however, that there was relatively less innovation-
related activity in this school.

Regardless of the depth of data sampled in school 26, there
were a large number of incident interventions identified at each
school site. The average number per school was more than two
hundred. Many little things were apparently being done in each
school to facilitate implementation of the innovations.

Table 2: All Incidents by Sublevel

Incident sublevels include *isolated*, a single action separated in
space, time, and place from other actions (as in a short visit to the

school by another educator); *simple*, a single action functionally related to other interventions; *chain*, a series of the same simple incident delivered to different targets; *repeated*, a series of the same simple incident delivered to the same target more than once (as in a series of observations of the same teacher); and *complex*, a set of related, simple actions within a short time frame (such as a brief staff meeting in which several decisons are made).

In every school, the most frequent incidents were by far simple—approximately 70 per cent. A statistical test that identified expected differences (Brown 1974, 1979) in these types of data revealed that the Colorado schools had significantly fewer simple incidents than would be expected, significantly more isolated incidents than expected, and significantly more repeated incidents than expected. The Florida schools were identified as having more complex incidents than the other two groups of schools. This difference is probably explained by the occurrence of training sessions for large groups of teachers, coded as complex incident interventions. School 39 had more isolated incidents, which supported the research staff's impression that interventions did not "hang together" in any systematic way in that school. There appeared to be a lack of consistent vision for where the school was going and little structured thinking about implementation.

Interpretation of the findings suggests that the facilitation of any new program requires a variety of incident subtypes. Possibly the relative proportion of particular incident sublevels is dependent upon the characteristics of the innovation. For example, innovations that require an extraordinary amount of training would have higher proportions of complex incidents. This subject could be the object of future research. For now, all we can say is that each type was used and that simple incidents were the most frequent.

INTERVENTIONS OVER TIME. These observations on the number and kinds of incident interventions required during the three different years of the three different change efforts support the assertion that change is a process not an event. Successful change requires more than one year, and the second and third years appear to need as much facilitating time and energy as year one. If this pattern is true, there are direct implications for the widely

Table 1: Overall Distributions of Incidents in the Nine Schools (in raw counts)
(Schools Grouped by District)

	California Year 1			Florida Year 2			Colorado Year 3			
	24	25	26	11	12	13	37	38	39	
INTERVENTIONS										
Incidents	109	334	74	239	191	254	172	236	246	1855

Table 2: All Incidents by Sublevels (in percentages)
(Schools Grouped by District)

	California Year 1			Florida Year 2			Colorado Year 3			Average	Frequency
	24	25	26	11	12	13	37	38	39		
Sublevels											
1. Isolated	4	1	4	1		2		1	8	2	40
2. Simple	72	56	78	63	56	72	66	85	83	69	1285
3. Complex	15	17	16	20	21	10	12	6	5	13	247
4. Chain	8	23	1	7	23	12	12	3	3	12	213
5. Repeated	2	2		9		4	10	5	1	4	69
6. Blank (Specify)						1					1
Total Number	109	334	74	239	191	254	172	236	246		1855

used practice of adding new innovations to a school after only one year of experience with a current innovation. The Stages of Concern, Levels of Use, and Innovation Configurations data described in the preceding chapters documents that changes in teacher practice are not likely to happen instantaneously. Nor is institutionalization of new ideas into classroom practices accomplished in one year. The introduction of an additional new program while teachers are involved in the second year of implementing program number one is likely to be a self-defeating strategy in terms of teacher development. Change facilitators will not have the time to provide all the needed interventions when multiple adoption design (i.e., m.a.d. strategy) is used. Intervening takes time. The number of incident interventions observed in the PTI study shows that facilitating teachers' change of classroom practice is a multiyear task for principals and others.

Table 3: All Incidents by Source

Table 3 is a summary of the intervention frequencies of the different role groups (i.e., sources). The data clearly indicate that principals found time to make many interventions. They averaged 31 per cent of the total number of interventions made, varying from a low of 17 per cent to a high of 52 per cent. Another immediate impression from table 3 is that there are a number of different people initiating interventions. For example, in schools 13 and 39, the assistant principals were particularly active. These same two schools, unlike the other schools, did not have as many interventions coming from sources outside the school, such as from district-level resource people. The statistical "cell search" procedure (Brown 1974, 1979) identified the Florida schools as having significantly more 8B resource people, such as district-level curriculum consultants, and 8A decision makers (for example, the director of curriculum) acting as sources than would be expected. This result can probably be attributed to schools 11 and 12. Administrators at school 11 had a well-developed working relationship with the district math curriculum coordinator (8B). This coordinator served as a staff development resource person to the school. He worked closely with the school in supplying training and consultation with teachers. The principal was interactive with a number of district decision makers, and these persons also provided interventions (i.e., supplying information and visiting the school to see how it was going). School 12 was a Title 1 school and had an array of federally funded programs supporting additional personnel in the school. In addition, a district-level facilitator was especially active in this school, where the principal was less active.

Individual teachers were also sources of interventions, as shown by codes 2, 3A, and 4A, the California schools having significantly more individual teachers as sources. Teachers modeled for and consulted with each other and exchanged ideas with the principal and resource teachers. They may not have been official facilitators but they were making interventions as individuals and as groups to develop and maintain the use of the innovation.

Interestingly, the total number of interventions (shown at the bottom of table 3) did not vary greatly with the presence or absence of an assistant principal. For example, the school with the least number of interventions had an assistant principal, while the school with the most interventions did not. Apparently, when an assistant principal was present, the job of facilitating the implementation was divided between the principal and the assistant principal.

The data in table 3 indicate that principals (coded 6A, with 31 per cent of the interventions), innovation facilitators at either the district or school sites (coded 7, 15 per cent), site resource personnel (coded 5, 13 per cent), individual teachers (coded 2, 3A, 4A, 12.5 per cent), assistant principals (6B, 10 per cent), as well as district decision makers and district resource people (coded 8A and 8B, 4 percent and 8 per cent) were active in facilitating the implementation of the innovations. The relative importance of their roles varied from school to school, district to district, and innovation to innovation, as well as with the change facilitating style of the principal (more on this point in chapter 8). In schools where there was an on-site resource person (coded 5), usually there was not a strong district resource person (coded 7 or 8B), and vice versa (for more on this point see chapter 9). In schools where the assistant principal served as an important change facilitator, other resource personnel, if present in the school, did not have as strong an effect on facilitation. In other schools, however, the principal and other personnel exhibited more evenly distributed interventions.

Table 3: All Incidents by Source (in percentages) (Schools Grouped by District)

Sources	California Year 1			Florida Year 2			Colorado Year 3			Average	Frequency
	24	25	26	11	12	13	37	38	39		
1. Students		1						1		1	3
2. An Individual Teacher	10	12	3	5	9	16	9	13	6	10	186
3A. Subset-as Individuals	4	3		4	1	1	4	1	1	2	38
3B. Subset as Groups		1		1					1	1	5
3C. Subset-as Whole Subset	1	1	1	3	1	1	2	1		1	18
4. All Teachers		1		1						1	2
4A. All Teachers-as Individuals		1		1	1					1	8
4B. All Teachers-as Groups				1						1	2
4C. All Teachers-as a Whole		1								1	2
5. Imple. Site Resource People		43		2	2	33		1	1	13	238

Table 3 (Cont'd)

	California Year 1			Florida Year 2			Colorado Year 3			
6A. Principal	50	26	34	27	17	20	36	52	31	583
6B. Assistant Principal			5	13	9	19	35	35	10	187
7. Innovation Facilitators	20	2	45	9			46	28	15	278
8A. I.U.S.-Decision Makers	8	4	10	10	8	3	1	1	4	83
8B. I.U.S.-Resource People	2	1		11	49	5	1	1	8	141
8C. I.U.S.-Other (Specify)		1		1			1	1		5
9. Extended User System	3	2		4			1	1	1	25
10. Change Effort	1	1		1			1	1	1	6
11. Blank	1		1	1	2				1	7
11A. Blank-CBAM	1		1	7	1	2		1	1	26
11B. Blank-(specify)		3				1			1	12
Total Number	109	334	74	239	191	254	172	236	246	1855

NOT A SINGLE-PERSON JOB. Despite the enormous importance of the principal's role in change, the data indicate that the principals did not do all the intervening. Some principals in the PTI study looked to their own staff and developed additional resources to support teachers. These principals creatively structured existing, in-school resources and made specific staff reassignments so that others could help facilitate. For example, one principal reassigned a classroom teacher to a new role as innovation facilitator. District-level and other outside personnel were also carefully orchestrated in some schools. Where principals had other concerns and did not facilitate, outside facilitators took the initiative. In one such case (e.g., school 12), a district consultant provided a large number of interventions to assist teachers. Apparently, then, leadership in school improvement is shared, involving persons with a variety of roles and functions (Hord, Stiegelbauer, and Hall 1984). The principal does not perform this function alone (subject to be discussed in chapter 9).

These patterns suggest to us that some of the activities related to facilitation can be assumed by, carried by, or divided among personnel other than the principal, though the principal still remains the leading force. By using district administrators and decision makers, as well as individual teachers, as sources, change process facilitation involves the whole academic community, not just the school administration and resource people. What these various sources did varied by district, innovation, and the interventions of others. They all were active however, a significant point for planning and evaluating future change efforts.

Table 4: All Incidents by Target

Targets refer to those individuals or groups at whom interventions are directed. In the PTI study, there was a greater variety of targets (see table 4) than sources. Teachers, either as individuals or as a group (coded 2–4C), were the targets of approximately 60 per cent of the incidents, except in school 11. The frequency of individual teachers as targets seems to be related to the year of implementation or to the districts: the third-year implementation district, Colorado, had the most teachers individually targeted; the second-year implementation district, Florida, the second most; and the first year, California, the least. The Colorado district, in particular, targeted individual teachers more often in all three schools (37, 38, 39). The frequencies in Colorado can be attributed to the individualized focus of the innovation for that year, which included an individual improvement plan for each teacher, and to the increasing need for individualized teacher attention as implementation process progressed.

The pattern of placing increased emphasis on individual teachers as the change process unfolds makes sense in terms of SoC, LoU, and IC. At the beginning of implementation, most teachers have higher self and task concerns; as a group, then, they have very similar concerns. At this time, they are at a mechanical use level. As the change process continues, teachers' use of the innovation and their concerns will be more varied, necessitating more individualized intervention.

The second most frequent target listed in table 4 is the principal. The Colorado school principals were targeted significantly more than expected. Other data indicate that the sources targeting the principal included district personnel, in-house assisting facilitators, and teachers. In school 39 of the Colorado group, the principal (6A) and assistant principal (6B) each accounted for 35 per cent of the interventions (table 3), but in the same school, the principal is a target three times as often as the assistant principal (table 4). One interpretation of this result is that, although both the principal and the assistant principal contribute to the facilitation process, the process is still directed by the principal, and any feedback about results comes to him or her.

Other targets include on-site resource personnel (5 per cent) and innovation facilitators (6 per cent). District-level decision makers (2 per cent), students (clients, 2 per cent) and people in the extended user system, such as parents (2 per cent), were also targeted although to lesser degrees.

MANY PERSONS RECEIVE INTERVENTIONS. In any change process, because of the variety of activities involved (workshops, phone calls to parents, hallway discussions with teachers), there is likely to be a broad diversity of targets. What is especially important to observe, however, is the exchange between the two most frequent targets—the users of the innovation (the teachers) and the principals as change facilitators. A surprising finding in the

Table 4: All Incidents by Target (in percentages) (Schools Grouped by District)

Targets	California Year 1			Florida Year 2			Colorado Year 3			Average	Frequency
	24	25	26	11	12	13	37	38	39		
1. Students	12	5		1	1		1	4		2	31
2. An Individual Teacher	7	15	8	10	13	13	33	44	43	22	415
3A. Subset-as Individuals	8	6	1	5	23	30	12	2	3	10	194
3B. Subset as Groups		1	1	1	1	2		1	1	1	26
3C. Subset-as Whole Subset	13	1		8	16		13	7	9	9	171
4. All Teachers										1	3
4A. All Teachers-as Individuals	5	12	5	4	4	9	2	3	2	6	106
4B. All Teachers-as Groups	2	1	1	1					1	1	10
4C. All Teachers-as a Whole	31	8	19	10	13	7	2	3	3	9	162
5. Imple. Site Resource People		20		2	2	4	3	2	4	6	100

Table 4 (Cont'd)

	California Year 1		Florida Year 2			Colorado Year 3				
	14	20	17	12	4	24	17	13	14	
6A. Principal	8		16	5	12					256
6B. Assistant Principal								4	5	87
6C. Imple. Site Dec. Maker-Other					1			1	2	
7. Innovation Facilitators	4	2	8		4	9	13	11	6	112
8A. I.U.S.-Decision Makers		2	3	2	3		2	1	2	31
8B. I.U.S.-Resource People	3	1	7	5	4		1	1	2	44
8C. I.U.S.-Other (Specify)	3	1	3			2	1	1	1	15
9. Extended User System	2		3	2				1	2	28
10. Change Effort	3	1	1	2	2		2	2	2	36
11. Blank	1									7
11A. Blank-CBAM	2	1	1	1			1		1	9
11B. Blank-(specify)	2	2			1				1	9
Total Number	109	334	74	239	191	254	172	236	246	1855

source data was the frequency with which principals, assistant principals, resource teachers, and other facilitators were targets of interventions. Obviously, there was a high degree of interaction among the various change facilitators and between teachers and facilitators about the implementation process. Both these relationships would certainly be desirable and necessary for effective implementation. The exact nature of the exchanges between facilitators (e.g., the principal, the assistant principal, and resource teachers) at any given school varied given the exact roles of the persons involved. At least in these study schools, however, interventions flowed both ways. Consideration of facilitators as frequent intervention targets and study of the content of such interventions are areas for investigation. A closer examination of the specific nature of these interactions, in terms of sources and functions, might tell us a lot about the dynamics of leadership and the content of training for change facilitators.

ANOTHER FINDING HAS PLANNING IMPLICATIONS. The PTI study used a cross-sectional design. The schools were in different years of implementation, therefore interpretations of changes across years is risky, especially if there were systematic differences across districts. Earlier in this chapter, we observed that the characteristics of the districts were similar. No obvious, major differences in policies, products, personnel, types of buildings and teacher experience, or kinds of students were noted. The districts were different in terms of the year of implementation (first, second, and third), and the innovations were different in content (writing composition, mathematics, and science), although similar in design and emphasis. The research staff concluded that some of the district differences in the change process experience were due to the difference in the year of implementation of the innovation. As long as our assumptions about similarity hold, the data show that, as the change process progressed, teachers were more frequently targeted as individuals. As we pointed out, this pattern certainly makes sense in terms of concerns theory. During the first year of a change, most teachers start at the same point, and interventions can therefore be focused toward groups of teachers. During the ensuing years, teacher growth and skill in the use of the innovation develop at varying rates and in varying ways. Teachers then require more individualized interventions.

Planning for change could anticipate this pattern, and staff development and other interventions could be adjusted accordingly. Early in the change process, the same interventions can be done for everyone. As the change process "matures," more school-specific and subgroup-customized interventions will be needed. Again, having a multi-year perspective is the key to planning and facilitating change.

Table 5: All Incidents by Function

Function coding represents the intent or purpose of each intervention. Eight function classifications were used to analyze the PTI data:

> 1000) Developing supportive organizational arrangements includes planning, managing, and providing materials, resources, space 2000) Training means teaching new knowledge and skills, reviewing, and clarifying 3000) Providing consultation and reinforcement includes promoting innovation use, problem solving 4000) Monitoring and evaluating represents data collecting, analyzing, reporting, and transferring data 5000) External communication refers to informing outsiders 6000) Dissemination is gaining support of outsiders and promoting the use of the innovation by outsiders 7000) Impeding includes discouraging or interrupting use 8000) Expressing and responding to concerns includes complimenting, praising, acknowledging, complaining, and reprimanding.

Interventions for at least five of the eight functions were documented in each study school; one school had interventions representing all eight functions. This finding suggests that there is a wide range of purposes to the interventions that are a part of the change process. A summary of the function coding is presented in table 5.

The 1000 functions—supporting arrangements—were the most frequent interventions in seven of the nine schools. Formal training—the 2000 functions—occurred in all the schools but were less frequent than 3000—consultation and reinforcement—and 4000—monitoring and evaluation—functions. Although the number of formal training interventions was lower, it is likely that the total time and number of people affected by

Table 5: All Incidents by Function (in percentages) (Schools Grouped by District)

Functions	California Year 1			Florida Year 2			Colorado Year 3			Avg.	Freq.
	24	25	26	11	12	13	37	38	39		
1000. Developing Supp./Org. Argmnts.	38	33	45	54	33	24	43	28	34	36	660
2000. Training	8	4	14	12	16	3	6	2	4	7	128
3000. Consulting & Reinforcing	30	26	24	17	27	54	12	10	16	24	448
4000. Monitoring	19	20	10	12	21	16	33	37	27	22	416
5000. Communicating Externally	2	3	1	1	1	1		4	1	2	29
6000. Disseminating			1	1						1	2
7000. Impeding Use	1		1							1	2
8000. Expressing/Resp. to Concerns	2	12	3	4	2	2	5	19	18	9	159
9000. Blank (Specify)		2	1	1			1	1	1	1	11
Total Number	109	334	74	239	191	254	172	236	246		1855

such training sessions increases the significance of these interventions. Within districts, there was a wide variation in the frequency of the formal training function. Colorado schools as a group had significantly fewer training and consultation/reinforcement interventions and significantly higher percentages of monitoring/evaluation interventions. The first result is likely due to less training needed in the third year of an implementation program, while the latter result is probably due to a monitoring component that was integrated into the innovation during the third year.

ALL BASES HAVE TO BE COVERED. The most frequently observed functions were 1000, developing supportive organization arrangements, 3000, consulting and reinforcing, and 4000, monitoring. The provision of resources and arrangements was important for each year of the three change efforts. Ordering books and materials, arranging for equipment, and organizing schedules, for instance, were part of the facilitators' roles in each district's implementation. Managing the logistics and supplying the resources needed for innovations can reduce user frustration and contribute to more efficient implementation. These details must be done, and they apparently continue during the first three years of an implementation. Facilitators who feel they are always attending to the nitty gritty are apparently doing just that.

The low incidence of formal training interventions in the data, especially in the first year, was surprising, though all schools provided training to varying degrees. It was expected that more formal training would be conducted in the first-year schools, since teachers were becoming acquainted with a new program. The training incidents, though few in number, may have been of such duration and complexity that there were proportionately higher effects.

A frequently observed intervention addressed problem solving, a subpart of 3000, consultation and reinforcement. This subfunction concerns the one-to-one interactions with teachers about their innovation-related problems and concerns. Such interventions respond to teachers' needs for information, encouragement, and personalized assistance. We would expect such interventions to occur, and they were provided by several sources in each site, including the principals.

Collecting information about individual teachers as they worked to implement a change was a frequently observed subfunction of the monitoring category. Information about teacher practices made it possible to select or design more appropriate interventions to help teachers improve their practice. Ideally, this function serves as a prior step to consultation interventions and seemed to be used for this purpose in the study schools. These interventions were conducted by a variety of sources besides the principal.

Table 6: All Incidents by Medium/Flow/Location

The "medium" of an intervention is the mode or form of the action. The medium could be face-to-face or in a written or audiovisual format—communication by telephone or through public media channels such as newspaper, radio, television or journals. "Flow" refers to the direction of the action. It can be one way or directed to one or more persons; or the flow could be interactive, an exchange of actions between the intervenor (or source) and the individual(s) being targeted. "Location" is where the intervention takes place, such as in classrooms or an office in the central administration building. The frequency distributions for the flow, medium, and location of the incident interventions observed in the PTI study are summarized in table 6.

Face-to-face was clearly the dominant medium for intervening. Written formats accounted for a small 12 percent of the interventions. Interactive flow was the most frequent occurrence, however, there was a 26 percent average number of one-way interventions. The statistical analysis indicated that in the California schools there was significantly more one-way flow. This difference was due to one very active and directive principal.

The majority of interventions occurred at the school/implementation site (coded $1 + 1A + 1B + 1C = 82$ percent), which seems reasonable. Interventions in school 12 occurred mainly in the Media Center, an excellent, new, centrally located facility where many workshops were scheduled. Fifty-three percent of the interventions in school 13 occurred in teachers' classrooms; while, at the other extreme, no classroom interventions were reported in school 26.

THE MEDIUM IS THE MESSAGE. In the nine elementary schools studied, face-to-face interaction was by far the most frequent mode of intervention. Written communication was next, and telephone communication, third. The dominance of face-to-face

Table 6: All Incidents by Medium/Flow/Location (in percentages)
(Schools Grouped by District)

	California Year 1			Florida Year 2			Colorado Year 3				Freq.
	24	25	26	11	12	13	37	38	39	Avg.	
Medium											
1. Face-to-Face	77	82	74	65	87	91	74	84	83	81	1498
2. Written	16	14	15	20	10	5	12	8	9	12	219
3. Audio Visual	1	1	1			1		1	1	1	6
4. Telephone	4	2	8	12	2	3	13	5	6	6	105
5. None/Other	2	1	1	4		1	1	2	2	2	27
Flow											
1. One-Way	30	34	38	43	16	5	31	22	25	26	488
2. Interactive	69	65	61	54	84	92	68	76	73	72	1339
3. None/Other	1	1	1	3		3	1	2	1	2	28
Location											
1. Implementation Site	55	26	72	18	2	10	36	10	21	22	408
1A. Imple. Site-Office	20	7	4	18	26	28	2	38	36	21	394
1B. Imple. Site-Classroom	9	23		16	18	53	22	22	27	24	451
1C. Imple. Site-Other	6	33	7	10	34	8	6	16	2	15	282
2. Immediate User System	6	8	16	26	19	1	32	13	11	14	258
3. Extended User System	3	3	1	12	2	1	2	2	1	3	55
4. Blank (Specify)	1	1		1		1			1	1	7
Total Number	109	334	74	239	191	254	172	236	246		1855

interaction is perhaps a reflection of the principals' preference for less structured methods of communication, but more likely it is a result of the "immediacy" of the change process. There is not usually time to write text. Most intervention activity is in response to immediate inquiries and needs that do not allow the delay required for the production of written interventions. This reality probably explains why the face-to-face medium is so frequent, which leads us to another question: Is all the time spent in face-to-face intervening the most appropriate and most effective means of facilitating? Is it possible that an increased use of other media could get some of the facilitating job done more effectively? If so, understanding when and how to use other formats could release time and energy for performing more interventions.

The high frequency of interactive flow in the interventions indicates that the facilitators were not isolated from their constituencies. What is surprising is the relatively high proportion of interventions that were one way. One-way flow is defined as an intervention primarily one way in direction, but the medium can be face-to-face, by telephone, as well as written. In a one-way intervention, the source of the intervention structures the agenda, the target doing little other than receiving the intervention. In some schools, nearly one-third of all interventions were one way. Clearly, these change facilitators were "directive" more of the time. A next subject for research might be to explore the value and significance of having more or less one-way incident interventions. How does the ratio of one-way to two-way interventions relate to the arousal and resolution of concerns?

Also to be expected was that most interventions took place at the school sites. Schools were not, however, isolated from contact with district personnel. Some schools showed a high involvement of persons from outside the school, as well as frequent interventions that occurred off campus. Differences in these patterns were not related to district, year of implementation, or innovation factors. One hypothesis is that the change facilitator style of the principal was related to the degree of outside involvement. The data appeared to be much more consistent when grouped by the facilitating style of the school leader, suggesting that style is a meaningful organizing factor. This point is further discussed in chapter 8.

Discussion and Implications of Incident Interventions for Change Facilitation

For practitioners involved in school improvement, the PTI data provide additional insights into the process and suggest some important considerations. Though much of what has been reported from the PTI study appears to be stating the obvious, it is important to acknowledge what the data reinforce, the idea that change and improvement do not happen overnight or over one year. Furthermore, the day-to-day actions at the incident level are the building blocks; there are many incident interventions, and these accumulate to make change in school a reality. Intervening engages many actors who work with many targets in a variety of ways to make change happen.

Assuming that the findings from the PTI study are reasonable, there are significant implications for change facilitation. First, school principals, other within-school facilitators, and outside agents can use the Intervention Anatomy coding system and the findings from the PTI study to critique their practices in planning and monitoring the change process. Some of the more salient implications of the coding system and the study findings are summarized in the following statements.

1. THE QUANTITY OF DAY-TO-DAY INCIDENT INTERVENTIONS ARE CRITICAL TO OVERALL IMPLEMENTATION SUCCESS. There is no question that the number of incident interventions makes a major difference in implementation success. In a related data analysis (Huling, Hall, Hord, and Rutherford 1983), the number of interventions correlated positively with implementation success, defined by advancements in SoC, LoU, and IC. These findings suggest that facilitators need to be sensitive to the number of incidents that occur during the course of any school year that relate to any particular program or process. Further, the PTI study data show that a number of actors besides the principal regularly make incident interventions. All facilitators should be cognizant of how their interventions interrelate with the interventions of others.

2. CHANGE FACILITATORS NEED TO USE VARIOUS TECHNIQUES AND PROCEDURES TO MONITOR THEIR OWN INTERVENTION BEHAVIOR. The sublevel definitions of incident interventions and the Anatomy of Intervention codes are practical tools change facilitators can use to

monitor their practices. These individuals do not have to become highly reliable and skilled in coding or take significant amounts of time to document their actions, write up descriptions, or computer analyze their interventions; but they can think critically about the interventions they make or plan to make in light of sublevels and target, function, mode, flow, and location categories. By analyzing their interventions, they can become more sensitive to how they spend their time and to what works. They can thus become more skilled in setting priorities about the design and timing of their interventions. A change facilitator can not be everywhere at once, providing all the interventions that would be useful. Carefully considering the various aspects of an intervention can result in improved design and delivery of interventions and more efficient use of facilitator energies.

3. CONSIDERING THE FUNCTIONS OF INTERVENTIONS IS ALSO IMPORTANT. Based on the data collected in the PTI study, it is clear that the complete set of intervention functions must be performed. It is not sufficient to provide only interventions that handle organizational arrangements; coaching and reinforcing are other functions that must be done. Formal training is obviously necessary, and informal monitoring of imlementation must occur regularly. Apparently, the more effective change facilitators distribute their interventions among the various functions and do not overly concentrate on one functional class. Furthermore, there do not appear to be certain intervention functions characteristic solely of the principalship or other positions. Instead, each facilitator intervenes across a variety of functions.

4. VARIOUS TYPES OF INTERVENTIONS ARE NEEDED IF A CHANGE PROCESS IS TO BE SUCCESSFUL, BUT ALL DO NOT NEED TO BE PROVIDED BY THE PRINCIPAL OR ANY OTHER SINGLE CHANGE FACILITATOR. In earlier research, Hall, Rutherford, and Griffin (1982) hypothesized that three different priorities could be assigned to the principal's intervention role. An illustration of this analysis is included as figure 22. It is proposed that there is a certain, minimum set of interventions (Priority I) that principals must provide. The Priority II set are interventions that either principals can do or that can be done by some other change facilitator(s). The Priority III set of interventions are events that are not likely to be the main responsibility of the principal. Principals do not have the time and, in many cases, do not

have the specific technical knowledge for such coaching. In successful change processes, all three priorities of interventions are addressed. Principals, however, should not be expected to perform the interventions in all the three groups. If a principal is not particularly skilled in intervening or is not very knowlegeable about the innovation, the principal will probably confine his/her activity to providing Priority I interventions. Other change facilitators should be identified and sanctioned to provide Priority II and Priority III interventions. In this way, the composite set of interventions can be provided and the onus is not on the principal alone. In the end, however, whatever the principal does not do, others must do; and there is a minimum set the principal must do if the change process is to be successful.

5. THERE NEEDS TO BE AN ASSESSMENT OF TEACHERS AND OTHER TARGETS BEFORE INTERVENTION OCCURS. One of the reasons for delaying the discussion of interventions until this point in the book is our strong belief that a concerns-based diagnosis is essential before designing and delivering interventions. Only with on-going knowledge of teacher's Stages of Concern, Levels of Use, and Innovation Configuration is it possible to design and deliver interventions optimally. Principals and other change facilitators may be very skilled in the actual delivery of interventions, but without diagnostic data, the interventions may serve no more useful purpose than the proverbial cannon loose on the ship deck. Interventions must be logically related to the needs of teachers and the use of the innovation. Extended discussions of the relationship between concerns-based diagnoses and interventions is presented in the last two chapters of this book.

6. ALL INCIDENT INTERVENTIONS ARE NOT PRE-PLANNED. Incident interventions can be sorted into three clusters based on opportunity. One opportunity is when the chance to intervene *comes to* the change facilitator, for example, when teachers walk up to the principal and initiate an innovation-related discussion. Another kind of opportunity is when the change facilitator *takes advantage* of a situation. For example, when a teacher comes into the office to pick up his/her mail, the change facilitator can have a one-legged conference with the teacher regarding some aspect of innovation use. Less effective change facilitators appear to waste these opportunities on social commentary. Another kind of in-

Figure 22
A Possible Framework for Identifying Critical Principal Tasks in Facilitating School Change

Intervention Source	Example Action/Task	Potential Effects
Priority I		
Principal must do	Sanctioning	Permits activity to occur
Priority II		
Principal can or someone else must do	Push	Makes priorities clear
Priority III		
Not the principal's job	Day-to-day innovation specific technical assistance	Resolve specific concerns

tervention opportunity *is created* by the change facilitator. The facilitator consciously plans an incident intervention and goes out of his or her way to deliver it. For example, a principal decides a teacher needs an encouraging word. She goes across the building to pop her head in the classroom during the teacher's break to let him know she is pleased with his progress.

These three kinds of intervention opportunities regularly occur. The more effective change facilitators recognize more of these events as intervention opportunities and do something with them. Less engaged facilitators seem not to realize they can or should be more assertive or creative in finding and using intervention opportunities, or they simply do not know what to do. Reviewing the Intervention Anatomy and the PTI data presented in this chapter should give the latter individuals more ideas.

7. IT IS FUN TO THINK ABOUT EVERYDAY NAMES FOR CERTAIN CLASSES OF INTERVENTIONS. One of the useful and in some ways more entertaining activities is to think up descriptive names for various interventions, for example, Zaps and Zots. The reader is already familiar with incident interventions that take the form of Zaps—those little sharp digs that some seem to use so regularly. In contrast to the Zap is the Zot, a southwestern, native American term for a particularly high quality piece of turquoise. In intervention parlance, then, a Zot is an intervention that brings a shining glow of satisfaction and warmth to the target.

Summary

In this chapter, the concept of incident interventions and a conceptual framework and coding scheme for analyzing them has been described. Incident interventions do not typically occur in isolation from each other; rather, they tend to be sequenced and cluster around common themes and issues. The aggregations of incident interventions represent "levels" of interventions. In the next chapter, these higher levels of interventions and the full Intervention Taxonomy are described.

Chapter *7*

How Do Interventions Fit Into an Overall Plan? The Intervention Taxonomy

A District Intervention Game Plan

Central office science coordinators planned the implementation of an inquiry-type, process-oriented science curriculum in eighty elementary schools. During the first year of implementation, they did the following:

—The schools were divided into three, equal-sized groups and introduced to the program at six-month intervals. This phasing was done in order to provide effective levels of initial implementation support to each school within the limits of available resources and number of central office staff.

—Twenty-three elementary teachers were selected and trained as in-service leaders for the delivery of program-related training to teachers.

—Three months prior to disseminating the materials, principals were given a half-day orientation. This session gave the principals a head start on becoming familiar with the new curriculum and district expectations.

—Teachers in each school received a one-hour, up-beat orientation session about the new program and the time line for its implementation. At this time, teachers were given the teachers' manuals so that, if they wished, they could become familiar with the program several months prior to implementation.

—The coordinators and in-service leaders directed the teachers in three full days of release time in-service. The days were scheduled at three-month intervals so that the session could address concerns about particular units near the time the units were to be taught.

—Between in-service sessions, central office staff and especially knowledgeable resource teachers held "comfort and caring sessions" in each school and met with individual teachers to help them resolve implementation problems.

—Trained staff regularly collected data regarding teachers' Stages of Concern, Levels of Use, and the configurations of the program being used. These data were used by the facilitators in planning the next interventions and in progress reports to district administrators and the school board.

An Elementary School Intervention Game Plan

An administrative team composed of the principal, assistant principal, and primary grade resource teacher planned and guided the implementation of an innovative communication curriculum. The assistant principal served as facilitator for the upper elementary grades, while the resource teacher served the primary teachers.

—District-level facilitators arranged in-service sessions to provide training for the three, school-based change facilitators before training teachers.

—Before the start of the school year, the team provided orientation and training sessions for the teachers.

—Monthly, hour-long faculty meetings were used to support teachers in using the curriculum guides and new materials for the objective-referenced program.

—A survey of teachers was done every six weeks to obtain their feedback about the program, its materials, and resources.

—A monthly news sheet was produced and circulated to teachers to provide helpful hints and answers to the most typical questions.

—On a daily basis, the three facilitators responded to teachers' needs and problems by supplying materials and help in using the program in the classrooms.

A High School Intervention Game Plan

When the total faculty agreed it wanted to incorporate computers as a problem-solving tool in all departments, the principal and a math resource teacher took the lead in facilitating the implementation plan. The plan included procuring and installing the computers, a maintenance plan for the machines, and a security policy.

—The school enlisted a consultant from the state education department for advice in determining equipment needs and designing the building's computer system.

—A professor from a nearby college was employed as consultant to provide support to the two facilitators.

—The consultant trained the principal and math resource teacher and one teacher from each department in microcomputer operations.

—These facilitators then became "turn key" trainers for the other teachers.

—The consultant spent one full day in the building per week the first three months, and a half day for the next three months.

—The turn key trainers met weekly with the consultant to solve problems, share resources, and make plans for how to assist teachers.

—The principal and math resource teacher monitored program implementation across the school, calling on teachers to ascertain how computers were being used in classrooms.

—Progress was reported to parents and the community, who were vitally interested in the program and pressing for information.

Each of these three descriptions summarizes the wide range of actions and events that occur during the first year of an innovation implementation. Similar descriptions could be developed for the second, third, and perhaps additional years. As the change process unfolds, many interventions occur, and these can be clustered and organized into an overall picture or game plan. The key to understanding and analyzing the overall intervention game plan is first to recognize the occurrence and characteristics of incident interventions. For this reason, the concept of incident interventions was introduced first, in chapter 6. Understanding and appreciating the significance of incident interventions is critical to successful change.

With this background, it is a short step to develop the larger framework showing how incidents connect and accumulate as the change process unfolds. Incident interventions are the building blocks in this framework and are used to define these larger interventions. For research purposes, it became important to develop this classification system—the Intervention Taxonomy (Hall and Hord 1984)—as a way to describe, analyze, and organize the large array of interventions being observed. This intervention classification system is useful for change facilitators in designing future interventions and in monitoring their intervention behavior, as well as for evaluating the effects of past actions.

The names of the different levels of interventions were chosen because of their use in everyday conversation and, in some cases, other disciplines. The traditional labels, "strategy" and "tactic," were used for this work since they have had long-standing use in policy development and in the military. In an analogy from the athletic world, the concept of a "game plan" was found to be useful in representing the total scheme of interventions. "Game plan components" then emerged out of data analysis work, during which it made sense to develop functional clusters of strategies.

The other major class of interventions explored in this chapter is called "mushrooms." A mushroom is a different class of intervention that was defined more recently in our research. Mushrooms tend to develop around the edges of a change process, as do biological mushrooms. Typically, they are not detected until they have been growing for some time. Mushrooms can be poisonous or nutritious to a change process and must be carefully monitored. Mushrooms and the other levels of the Intervention Taxonomy are described in detail in the next section.

Detailed Description of Intervention Levels

Definition and description of the different levels of interventions can be approached from several directions. One starting point is at the incident level, building from the small, singular occurrence of incident interventions to the large and broad in scope, policy class of interventions. Since incident interventions were described in the preceding chapter, a better sense of the totality can best be developed by next describing the policy level and gradually work back down to the incident level.

One guiding principle to keep in mind in this presentation is that the definitions of each intervention level are *relative* to each other. Each intervention level is defined in part through comparison with the intervention levels next to it. For most purposes, it is not necessary to have everyone agree on whether or not a particular intervention is a tactic or a strategy; rather, the emphasis is on keeping interventions of relatively similar sizes assigned to the same level. The intervention levels are on a sliding scale that can be expanded or contracted to whatever extent necessary to include all innovation-related interventions in any given change process. Definitions, descriptors, and some examples of the Levels of Interventions are presented in figure 23. In the next several pages, we provide elaborations and more illustrations of each level.

Policy Level Interventions

Policies are a part of all organizations, and many policies are written down and documented in handbooks, manuals, minutes of meetings, and corporate documents. These written records are referred to as *formal* policies. In addition, there are many *informal* policies and norms within any organization. Policies, both formal and informal, set the parameters within which each change process must unfold.

Policies are the broadest and most encompassing interventions, because policy decisions typically affect an entire organization and for an extended time. Many come from external sources such as state and federal governments and can be used to initiate change (e.g., PL 94–142), to disrupt a change already underway (e.g., a board decision to remove financial support), or to advance a change effort (e.g., the promotion of a key innovation advocate).

That policies can affect the change process is obvious, and the potential effects of policies when viewed as interventions are frequently anticipated by those planning change. For example, a school that operates under a district policy allowing in-service for teachers only within the teacher's duty day is constrained by this circumstance when there are needs for faculty development. This policy involves more than the implementation of a particular innovation, yet it affects the implementation plan and therefore meets the basic definition of an intervention introduced in chapter 6.

Formal policy is generally written and can be described by members of the organization. Statements of formal policy are easy to obtain by reviewing official documents. Formal policy is usually determined by persons within positions of authority in the organization. Some examples of formal policy in schools would be:

—all high school teachers will assume weekly duties as hall monitors;

—all students will maintain a grade point average of 2.0 to participate in sports activities.

Informal policy is not usually written down, although it shapes the behavior of members in the organization. Informal policies are often rooted in subgroup norms and may not be recognized or accepted by all members of the organization. The consequence of violating an informal policy is more likely to be peer disapproval than sanctions imposed by the formal organization. Examples of informal policy are:

—don't send many students to the vice principal for disciplinary actions or you will find yourself receiving close supervision;

—smoking is not accepted in the school building although there is a "smoking lounge."

It is important to reemphasize that most policy-level interventions, formal and informal, are not specific to an innovation; rather, they are targeted toward organization-wide, long-term behavior. They can, however, affect and set limits on particular change processes. Policies tend to be in place for an extended

Figure 23

LEVEL	DEFINITION	DESCRIPTORS	EXAMPLES
POLICY	A policy is a rule or guideline that reflects or directs the procedures, decisions and actions of an organization and the individuals within it.	Affects most, if not all individuals. Is in effect for extended periods of time (years). Refers to more than just the innovation being implemented.	
Formal Policy	An official rule, procedure or decision of the organization.	Is an explicit statement. Is published in the records of the organization. Is officially sanctioned by authority. Can be invoked to control behavior. Is put into effect at an identifiable time.	Travel funds are available for project participants. Students are not permitted to smoke in the building. The union contract states that only credentialed teachers will be used as substitutes.

Figure 23 (Cont'd)

LEVEL	DEFINITION	DESCRIPTORS	EXAMPLES
Informal Policy	An unofficial but accepted rule, procedure or guideline.	Is implicit and not written down. May be in contradiction with formal policy. Is not readily identified or communicated. Is derived from group expectations and norms. Can result in group censure for non-compliance.	Teachers and students should be involved in the establishment of school regulations. Parents will be included in some training for innovations being utilized with their children.
GAME PLAN	A game plan is the overall plan and design of the interventions that are made to implement an innovation.	Affects all persons who are directly or indirectly involved. Lasts the full time period of the change process. Encompasses all aspects of the implementation effort. May or may not be explicit.	The new curriculum will be phased in one grade level at a time over seven years beginning with a preschool workshop followed by three inservice sessions across the year. After an initial awareness and information session and delivery of the innovation kit, teachers will independently implement it in their classrooms in ways that best serve their needs.

Figure 23 (Cont'd)

LEVEL	DEFINITION	DESCRIPTORS	EXAMPLES
GAME PLAN COMPONENT	GPC's are the six major functional clusters of innovation-related interventions.	Clusters all interventions into functional groupings. Covers the entire time period of the change process. Includes all actors and events. In combination covers all interventions of the game plan.	
GPC 1: Developing Supportive Organizational Arrangements	Actions taken to develop policies, plan, manage staff, funds, restrucure roles and provide space, materials, and resources to establish and maintainuse of the innovation.	Covers logistical and scheduling activities. Includes planning and decision making about the change process, schedules and people.	Hiring new staff. Seeking/receiving funds. Providing innovation-related equipment.
GPC 2: Training	Actions taken to develop positive attitudes, knowledge and skills in relation to innovation use, through formal,	Covers formal organized training activities. May be provided for users, administrators or others.	Holding workshops/ Modeling/demonstrating use of the innovation. Observing and providing feedback related to a pre-specified task.

Figure 23 (Cont'd)

LEVEL	DEFINITION	DESCRIPTORS	EXAMPLES
	structured and/or planned activities.	Is normally scheduled and announced in advance.	
GPC 3: Providing Consultation and Reinforcement	Actions (often idiosyncratic, problem-specific, targeted at an individual or small group) taken to encourage and to assist individuals in solving problems related to innovation implementation.	Is focused on consulting and coaching users/ nonusers. Is typified by one-on-one problem solving and informal sharing of tips.	Holding brief conversations about how it is going. Facilitating a problem-solving group. Providing "comfort and caring" sessions.
GPC 4: Monitoring and Evaluation	Actions taken to gather, analyze or report data about the implementation and outcomes of a change effort.	Includes formal and informal assessments. Includes assessment, analysis interpretation and feedback.	analyzing pre-post learner assessments. Administering end-of-workshop questionnaire. Conferencing with teachers to suvey how the new program is going.
GPC 5: External Communication	Actions taken to inform and/or gain the support of indi-	Describes what is being done with the innovation.	Reporting to the Board of Education Making presentations at

Figure 23 (Cont'd)

LEVEL	DEFINITION	DESCRIPTORS	EXAMPLES
	viduals or groups external to the users.		conferences. Developing a public relations campaign.
GPC 6: Dissemination	Actions taken to broadcast innovation information and materials to encourage others to adopt the innovation.	Recruits others to also adopt the innovation.	Mailing descriptive brochures to potential adopters. Making charge-free demonstrations kits available. Training and providing regional innovation representatives.
STRATEGY	A strategy is a framework for translating theory and assumptions at the game plan level into concrete action to be taken.	Impacts most, if not all, users. Covers a large portion of the change process time period.	The change facilitator works with each individual user throughout the change effort. Ongoing training sessions are held throughout the course of the implementation effort.
TACTIC	A tactic operationalizes strategies, and is an inter-related set of small actions intention-	Affects many innovation users but not necessarily all of them.	

Figure 23 (Cont'd)

LEVEL	DEFINITION	DESCRIPTORS	EXAMPLES
	ally taken to affect attitudes toward or use of the innovation.	Covers a shorter time period than a strategy.	
Single-Complex	An interrelated set or collection of different incident interventions that occurs once during a relatively short time frame.	Is made up of many incident interventions. Takes from an hour to several days. Contains incident interventions different from one another yet related.	A day-long workshop. A summer college course.
Chain	An ongoing series or repetitions of the same basic incident.	Is repeated with different targets or purposes. There are some common dimensions to each repetition.	A series of short meetings with the same group over a period of time. A series of similar meetings with different groups. A series of radio broadcasts made about the project during one month.

period of time, and thus represent one source of stability for an organization and its members.

Intervention Game Plan

As part of our sports folklore, coaches develop "game plans" for athletic contests. In football, game plans have become remarkably detailed and sophisticated. Computer analyses are made of players' athletic capabilities, statistical analyses are done on the frequency of use of various "plays," and the tendencies of coaches and players to do particular things under certain conditions are catalogued. Using this information, offensive and defensive strategies are developed so that further specialization and detailed planning can occur. All of these bits and pieces, then, are used to develop a plan of plays. Sophistication and skill in developing game plans has been identified as a key factor in the success of many coaches. Game plans can be associated with the loss of a game when unanticipated plays are run by the opposing team or when miscues occur in the execution of plays used by the home team. In those cases, the plan must be adapted or modified in some way to respond to the unfolding pattern of the game. Still, game plans serve as a guide on how to approach the management of play.

The concept of a game plan also applies to the change process and interventions. Change facilitators can systematically develop and implement an intervention game plan. Aspects of an intervention game plan have been incorporated in standard management practices such as strategic planning, management by objectives, development of operational plans, zero based budgeting, and so on. When managers and other change facilitators are clear about the direction in which they are going and the set of interventions they plan to use to move in that direction, their actions will be more efficient. In addition, there will be more continuity in and interrelationships between interventions, and, consequently, the change process will advance in a more focused way. Progress, of course, depends upon whether the intervention game plan and the innovation are appropriate.

We do not mean to imply that the game plan cannot be adjusted or adapted as the change process evolves. As was mentioned above, coaches change their game plans, and change facilitators should too. With a plan in mind at the outset, however, it is much easier to adjust and adapt as the unexpected occurs and still maintain an overall perspective.

Too frequently, change facilitators have been observed who do not have an intervention game plan in mind, even implicitly. Serendipity seems to rule, and as various needs arise and events occur, interventions are made one at a time. A consequence of the serendipity approach is a lack of continuity and an accumulation of effect across interventions. It also results in more isolated and random interventions, and these change facilitators have to spend more time reacting to "brush fires." Having a game plan in mind provides the larger perspective necessary to plan and monitor in ways that insure that day-to-day interventions add up positively.

Brief descriptions of some intervention game plans were presented in the introduction to this chapter. Whether it is specified in advance or described in retrospect, a game plan is a map of all the actions taken to influence adoption, implementation, and use of a particular innovation in a given setting. Ideally, change facilitators and others have this gestalt in mind, and there is an internal consistency and an overall perspective on how the change process is to be facilitated.

Game Plan Components

This level of interventions emerged from our attempts to cluster interventions into meaningful groupings. Through this process, some functional relationships of interventions, in terms of their combined purposes and effects, were discovered. The functional categories that emerged were surprisingly similar to the function codes that had been earlier identified when analyzing the internal parts of incident interventions (see chapter 6). This clustering of interventions into functional groupings led to the definition of six, regularly found game plan components. Each of the game plan components (GPCs) is defined in figure 23.

Although all six GPCs are meaningful and important to consider in intervention planning, there are times when some of the GPCs do not require interventions. For example, in one high school district, there were no GPC5 external communication interventions and no interest in disseminating the newly developed restaurant management program beyond the district. As a consequence, no GPC6 dissemination interventions (see figure 24) occurred. Although the innovation could conceivably have been of regional or national interest, no actions were taken to inform others about the existence of the innovation, and when change facilitators were asked about the omission, they said it was deliberate. Five to six years after successful implementation of the innovation in the district, the change facilitators did become interested in national dissemination of their innovation, and GPC6 dissemination-type strategies, tactics, and incident interventions began to occur.

In addition to their value in planning, game plan components are useful in analyzing how a change process is going. In the Principal Teacher Interaction Study, for example, the researchers expected principals to spend most of their time performing GPC 1, developing arrangements, and GPC4, monitoring, interventions. They were surprised to find that the principals in the study also spent a relatively large proportion of their time in GPC3, consultation and reinforcement, interventions and some effort in GPC2, training. The game plan components thus became an analytical tool to help researchers as well as practitioners see how the principals allocated their intervention activity.

It is clear from this research that interventions in the first four game plan components are essential for a change process to be successful. Through planning and monitoring, it is possible for change facilitators to consider the various game plan components and to make sure these types of interventions are provided. The game plan components cover the entire period of the change process and impact all actors and events. The intervention examples described under the strategy and tactic discussion in the next section were picked to illustrate each game plan component.

Strategy Level Interventions

Strategies translate game plan components into major actions designed to accomplish particular change process objectives. This definition is consistent with the use of the term in other areas such as management by objectives (MBO) and strategic planning.

Strategic interventions have continuity over an extended period of time and are related to a specific topic or innovation task. Also, strategies tend to reflect the philosophy and assumptions of the change facilitators. For example, if the change

Figure 24
Restaurant Case Study
Game Plan Map

GPC 1	GPC 2	GPC 3	GPC 4
Plan and organize ways to improve restaurant appearance and to increase restaurant profit.	Provide service personnel with training to improve service, increase productivity, and increase food sales.	Devise systems to motivate improved performance among service personnel.	Establish systems for monitoring sales and service.
S. Investigate ways of increasing profit-margin on menu items	S. Train service personnel in improved service techniques	S. Implement a system through which service personnel will periodically meet informally with management to share problems and discuss ways of improving service and increasing sales	S. Monitor service employee productivity in terms of dollars sold
S. Improve building exterior and interior to make restaurant more attractive	S. Train service personnel in selling the product	S. Establish a system for rewarding outstanding performance among staff	S. Implement system for customers to do on-going evaluation of the service
S. Improve atmosphere and decor of restaurant			

Figure 24 (Cont'd)

GPC 1	GPC 2	GPC 3	GPC 4
T. Acquire new service goods for restaurant (linens, uniforms, menus, etc.)			
I. Meet with uniform salesman			
I. Ask staff to look at menu samples & choose one			
I. Sign one-year contract with new linen service			
T. Re-decorate interior			
I. Arrange appointment with plant company			
I. Meet with interior decorator			
I. Phone decorator to inform her of choice in wallpaper			

facilitator believes in an individual development model of change, she or he would be apt to phase in innovation components a few at a time, and a training strategy would be offered that took developmental differences into account. The timing of the training would vary, depending on Stages of Concern and Levels of Use. In contrast, the change facilitator working from the assumptions of the organizational development model (Schmuck and Miles 1971) would be more likely to target interventions at groups of users and to include training that emphasized group process skills. In both cases, many actions would be taken over time that, in combination, comprised sets of strategies. Those strategies in part reflect assumptions about change, as well as demonstrate particular objectives of the change process.

The following are some other examples of strategies.

—The assistant principal maintains an up-to-date inventory of stocks and supplies of consumable innovation materials (GPC1).

—The math curriculum coordinator visits the school twice a month to provide new teachers in-service workshops on teaching upcoming lessons (GPC2).

—Science resource teachers tour the school building daily to hold one-on-one coaching sessions with teachers about using the hands-on activities for pupils (GPC3).

—The principal requests each teacher to turn in weekly lesson plans in order to ascertain what is going on with the expository reading program (GPC4).

—The speech teacher manages the school's weekly call-in radio broadcast to respond to parents' questions about affective education (GPC5).

—The PR Cadre makes monthly appearances at parent association meetings to encourage citywide adoption of soccer safety kits (GPC6).

Frequently in planning for change, strategies are the largest level of interventions considered. The fact that strategies can be clustered in various ways to form game plan components and that the entire overview of the plan for facilitating change needs to be conceptualized is frequently overlooked. Another incomplete approach is to consider strategies only in terms of typical job functions, such as training, and administrative tasks, such as materials procurement, rather than in terms of long-range change goals. By linking strategies to change process objectives, it is much easier to see the total game plan and to plan for missing interventions.

Tactic Level Interventions

Tactics are the interventions most change facilitators think of when asked about their facilitation activities. Interventions such as workshops, regularly scheduled meetings, repeated classroom visits, or regularly published newsletters are the kinds of tactics change facilitators identify. Most change facilitators are not aware that these tactic-level interventions can be clustered around common themes to form strategies, and that a particular tactic-level intervention is comprised of many, simple incident interventions. Most change processes include a large number of tactic-level interventions. They represent major operational chunks of the intervention game plan.

A tactic is an interrelated set of small actions intentionally taken to affect attitudes toward or use of an innovation. Tactics can be planned, and their effects can be monitored. By definition, tactics can last from a few hours to several days and are typically targeted toward a group, subgroup, or all the prospective users of an innovation rather than toward a single individual. Some additional examples of tactics follow.

—Parents organized a five-day work session to help teachers prepare needed materials (GPC1).

—The drama department held a day-long workshop in creative dramatics for the middle school teachers (GPC2).

—The business education supervisor used October to make a weekly visit to each department head in the city to respond to each head's concerns about computer-related instruction (GPC3).

—The safety inspector sent a series of three surveys the third week in May to get feedback from different groups of students who ride the bus (GPC4).

Note that each of these tactics is relatively easy to observe, in part because of their relatively short duration, but also because they are behavioral and task specific. These characteristics are probably the reason change facilitators think of tactics first. They are close at hand, yet a larger unit than individual incidents. It is much more difficult to keep in mind interventions that occur throughout an entire school year and to conceptualize their pattern—the purpose of strategies, game plan components, and the intervention game plan.

Mushrooms

One research discovery has been that some interventions have effects that are not planned or intended. These "unsponsored" interventions are not "owned" by a source such as a school principal or a central office curriculum coordinator. Many of them appear to grow in strength and impact with time, especially when they are not noticed by any of the change facilitators. Due to this tendency to emerge gradually and to lack a readily identifiable sponsor, this special class of interventions was named mushrooms. The map of a mushroom is presented in figure 25.

To understand the mushroom, read the map in figure 25 from left to right. The initial actions that spawned the development of the mushroom were a series of incident interventions associated with a particular change facilitator. In the example in figure 25, one planned tactic for the change process was to use regularly scheduled, faculty team meetings for providing teachers with additional coaching and consultation in their use of the innovation.

During the year, the change facilitator missed many of these meetings. These absences are called *thematic actions*. At the first absence an *unplanned effect* of teachers missing out on their training in the program occurred, and the *immediate change facilitator reaction* was to explain to teachers why he had missed the meeting. One such series of action/effect/reaction occurrences would typically not have much effect on a change process. However, as it turned out, this occurrence was not isolated. Over the course of the school year, the thematic action of the change facilitator was repeated, and these actions accumulated into a theme—the weekly team meetings were not being used to support teachers in their use of the program. The *accumulating effect* was that less attention was given to using the innovation.

Figure 25
Intervention Mushroom Map: The Decline of Team Meetings

SPONSORED ACTIONS	THEMATIC ACTIONS	UNPLANNED EFFECTS	IMMEDIATE CHANGE FACILITATOR REACTIONS
Fall 1976 — Team meeting, 10/26/76	Change facilitator (C.F.) misses team meeting because he is working with a student	Teachers miss out on training in Reality Therapy.	Change facilitator comes to end of meeting to explain why he was gone.
Team P meeting, 11/2/76	C.F. misses meeting due to meeting with principal.	Teachers miss out on training in Reality Therapy.	No Response Identified
Spring 1977 — Team meetings, 1/17-25/77	C.F. cancels meetings due to CBAM interviews and his evaluation project.	"	"
Team meetings, 2/21/77	C.F. misses meetings due to doctor's appointment; does not inform teachers in advance.	"	"
Team M meeting, 2/23/77	C.F. cancels team meeting due to the absence of a teacher.	"	"
Team meeting, April 1977	No satellite meetings for three weeks: CBAM interviews, C.F.'s data collection spring break.	"	"
Fall 1977 — Team N satellite meetings, Oct.-Nov., 1977	Teachers schedule parent conferences during meeting time.	"	"
Team meetings, 10/25-27/77	Team meetings cancelled for CBAM interviews	"	"
Team meetings, 11/28/77	C.F. attends workshop instead of team meetings.	"	"

ACCUM. EFFECTS: Less attention to Reality Therapy.

OVERALL ACTION: NONE

THEME:
Weekly team meetings for training in Reality Therapy are often over-ridden by other activities.

Typically, many more change facilitator reactions can be documented than are identified in figure 25. This column is notably blank. The researchers were unable to identify any instances, after the first time, in which the change facilitator responded to missed meetings. What was even more problematic was that the change facilitator made no attempt to attend to the accumulating mushroom. If there had been any immediate change facilitator reactions to the specific thematic actions, these would have been noted. Also, if an attempt had been made by the change facilitator to address the overall accumulating mushroom, this intervention would have been described in the *overall action* circle in figure 25. But no actions were noted in this case, and the mushroom continued to grow.

Mushrooms will develop around most change processes. They cannot be identified in advance, although to some degree they might be anticipated. Change facilitators need to tune their antennae to the possibility of mushrooms and, when they begin to emerge, design and implement immediate reactions targeted at the entire phenomenon. More effective change facilitators are skilled in early detection of mushrooms and in addressing them. Less effective change facilitators often miss the mushroom all together.

Another aspect of mushroom theory is that there can be both positive and negative mushrooms, just as botanical mushrooms can be nutritious or poisonous. Some can greatly enhance a change process, while others may be harmful to it. The mushroom mapped in figure 25 was obviously deleterious. Examples of positive mushrooms might include teachers talking to each other about how excited they are about an innovation, parents becoming increasingly involved in a school that had not planned for their involvement, or teachers providing ongoing, positive support to change facilitators for the work they are doing.

Another example we found of a positive mushroom involved an elementary school principal. The school clerk who typically distributed incoming new math materials was on extended sick leave. So that teachers would continue to receive the materials quickly, the principal delivered them weekly to each teacher's classroom. After several weekly math deliveries, the principal noticed that teachers were telling him about their math program experiences during the visits. They were also stopping by his office to share "good things" about math, more so than about other subjects. Through the "grapevine," he heard that teachers' perceptions were that math had become a priority. At this point, the school clerk returned to duty, but the principal decided to continue the deliveries. He made opportunities to go to classrooms to take math materials, to tell teachers individually about math in-service meetings, and to visit about math. As a result of these "casual" interventions, teacher energy and enthusiasm grew.

The sponsored actions—the delivery of math materials to each room—accumulated into unplanned effects and a mushroom intervention. Teachers began to describe to the principal what was going on in math, thus, more attention and priority was given to teaching mathematics and to supporting teachers in that subject. In a map of this mushroom intervention, the overall action circle would surround a description of the principal's decision to maintain his weekly contact with teachers.

An array of mushrooms can be identified and mapped. The challenge is for change facilitators to be aware of the mushroom phenomenon and to be more sensitive to their emergence. Some mushrooms can be killed with one swift blow; however, some mushroom interventions can only be cut back and will gradually grow again. We have had some experience with these "evergreen" mushrooms in our research office. At one time or another, there have been instances when two staff members pair off against a third and carry on an increasing flurry of unnecessary and, in some cases, unkind comments about the other(s). In these cases, the chief administrator would implement various incident interventions to quell the mushroom. These incident interventions varied from individual conversations to sitting down with all three and asking them to work it out. Each time, the mushroom-related activities would subside for a period of time, only to build again. Until a major change in personnel assignments is made, a mushroom of this type appears to be unconquerable.

The responsibility of the change facilitator is to be sensitive to mushrooms and to their potential to affect the change process positively or negatively. Since mushrooms tend to grow around the edges and emerge gradually, the sooner they can be recognized, the more successful will be interventions designed to enhance or destroy them.

The term "mushroom" is an appropriate metaphor for this class of interventions. Mushrooms usually grow in obscure locations; they are found in the shade and off the beaten path. They emerge gradually or, all of a sudden, pop up. Sometimes mushrooms stand alone; other times, there are an assortment of contrasting shapes and colors. The same descriptions apply to intervention mushrooms. Intervention mushrooms usually develop gradually; they are easily missed and difficult to identify. If left unattended, they develop momentum and accumulate effects that can exert a new and sometimes profound influence on a change process. This accumulating set of effects becomes a new intervention.

Research on the Levels of Interventions

As in the preceding chapters, findings from research studies are used in this chapter to illustrate interventions and their dynamics. For those studies, procedures and techniques were developed for collecting information about interventions and for charting their flow. The mapping technique introduced briefly in chapter 6 has been particularly helpful in understanding the dynamics of the intervention process. In this section, some additional maps/catalogs are introduced that illustrate how the different levels of interventions interrelate. For those involved in managing change processes, mapping/cataloging interventions can help in planning as well as in monitoring progress. Two variations of the mapping/cataloging procedure are illustrated in this section. The first maps levels of interventions across time; the second catalogs interventions by game plan components.

Charting Interventions Across Time

The most useful and instructive tool for analyzing the total game plan of interventions is to plot interventions along a time line. Figure 26 is an excerpt from a three-year map of interventions for one particular intervention game plan. This plan was for implementing a districtwide elementary math program in forty schools. The three-year plan included a pilot of the program during the first year. Modifications were made in the program during the second year as a result of that pilot, and preparations were made to begin implementation with all teachers in the third year. Interventions were planned in all GPCs except dissemination (GPC6). Strategies were developed within each GPC, and tactics operationalized the strategies. This map provided overall direction and guidance for implementing the program in the schools. Incident-level interventions were designed within the larger levels to address and respond to short-term needs.

Cataloging Interventions by Game Plan Components

About four years into the research on interventions, game plan components as a level began to emerge. In the first studies that used game plan components, strategies were clustered in similar ways. Much to our surprise, the major functions in each of the game plan components remained relatively consistent across different change efforts. This consistency led to the establishment of the six GPCs described earlier. These GPC labels can be used to cluster different strategies, tactics, and incident interventions. With this approach, it is possible to identify quickly those GPCs where interventions are lacking and those GPCs where a number of interventions have been made. It is interesting to note that the GPC cataloging of interventions for the high school restaurant management course in figure 27 reveals that GPCs 3, 4, and 6 had no strategy or tactic interventions to operationalize them. The change facilitators in charge of this effort had unconsciously ignored activity in those areas, and the GPC cataloging reflected this omission.

Weaving It all Together

In this chapter, the different levels of interventions have been described and illustrated. In addition, some mapping and cataloging procedures were used to analyze interventions. One long-range goal of our research is to develop an entire series of frameworks that can be used as diagnostic and prescriptive models for a concerns-based approach to facilitating change. One of these conceptual frameworks has been developed to explain interrelationships between the different levels of interventions (presented in figure 28).

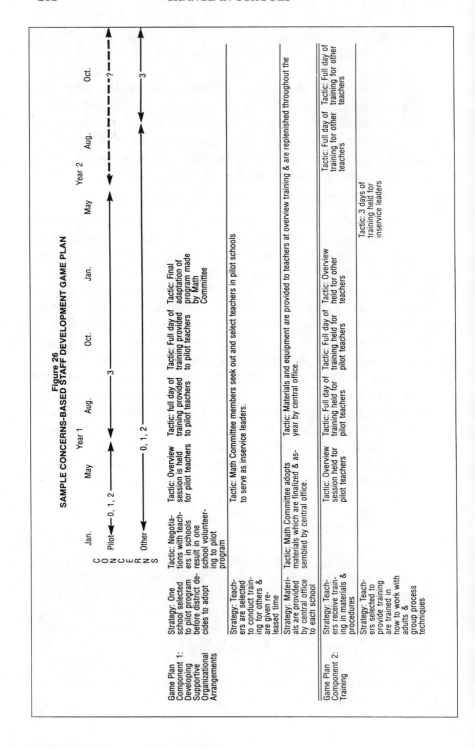

Figure 26
SAMPLE CONCERNS-BASED STAFF DEVELOPMENT GAME PLAN

Game Plan Component	Strategy	Tactic
Game Plan Component 3: Providing Consultation & Reinforcement	Strategy: Math coordinator is on call for school visits & consultation	Tactic: Math coordinator takes call & responds to problems in schools over the phone.
		Tactic: Math coordinator visits schools when asked to provide assistance, consultation, problem solving.
	Strategy: Math coordinator makes scheduled "comfort & caring" visits frequently to every school	Tactic: Twice a month, Math coordinator makes scheduled afternoon visit to each school to assist individual teachers and principal.
Game Plan Component 4: Monitoring & Evaluation	Strategy: Periodically concerns of teachers are assessed and discussed by Math Committee	Tactic: SoCQ is given to teachers in all schools in April and September (Year 2), in May and September (Year 3), and in February and May (Year 4).
		Tactic: Math Committee meets each time SoCQ data are available to adjust plans.
	Strategy: Math Committee visits pilot school during pilot & continues to meet to share data & impressions	Tactic: Each member of the Math Committee pays at least 2 visits to the pilot school between September and April.
		Tactic: During Math Committee meetings, data are shared about these visits.
	Strategy: No summative data are collected until year 4	
Game Plan Component 5: External Communication	Strategy: Bi-monthly reports are made to the state certification board about implementation progress	Tactic: A full day review of teacher feedback of materials, teachers progress in the program and student's accomplishments is held on alternate months
	Strategy: On the first Tuesday of every month a radio broadcast to the community highlights the program	

Figure 27
Case Study of Restaurant Management Course
Fiscal Year Game Plan: Mushrooms/Wine/Buffalo Wings

GPC 1:	GPC 2:	GPC 3:	GPC 4:	GPC 5:	GPC 6:
All facilities and amenities will be overhauled for efficiency and effectiveness	Training in selling the Three High profit Items will be provided to wait service teams and entire staff	Teams will work together to provide positive feedback and productive critiquing of each individual's progress toward profit goals	Teams will monitor each other's work in order to to provide feedback to each other	Monthly, the low performing team will personally visit the restaurant's home office to report to The Cartel of Investors	Monthly, the high performing team will personally visit the publication office of of Gourmet Restaurants International in Gstaad Switzerland to demonstrate their techniques to promote utilization by others
S: The inventory of stock and storage records will be changed over to computerized formats	S: The teams will be trained in collaborative/cooperative skills that focus of productivity			S: Teams will develop skills of presenting clear, concise and precise monthly audits	
S: New sources and possibilities for rapid foodstuffs suppliers will be identified and fiscally sound long term relationships developed	S: The teams will be trained in wine promotion				
S: Kitchen facilities will undergo redesign and reorganization for streamlining and efficiency	During the summer a series of lectures will be provided by a wine consultant				
	T: During the fall winetast-labs will occur				
	Incid: Visit to a wine steward				
	T: In the spring a weekly series of wine news bulletins will be disseminated				

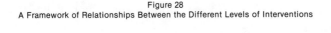

Figure 28
A Framework of Relationships Between the Different Levels of Interventions

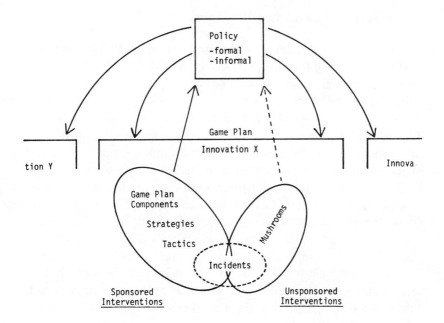

In the framework presented in figure 28 the levels of unsponsored and sponsored interventions are shown as different "wings" of the framework. Policy interventions serve as an umbrella over all other levels of interventions and cover multiple, innovation-specific, intervention game plans.

Out of this "butterfly" diagram, it is possible to develop further questions and hypotheses about the relationships between interventions and about the dynamics of interventions. For example, what are some possible mushroom equivalents to the "levels" that have been defined on the sponsored side? Are there optimal ratios of strategies to tactics or of strategies to incidents, or do these ratios vary by GPC? The heuristic potential of the framework means that it can serve to frame additional research, as well as to guide facilitator practice. There is an important need to broaden the amount of research and increase the depth of understanding about interventions and their roles in change facilitation.

Discussion and Implications

A wide array of implications and recommendations can be drawn from the intervention research and theory that have been described in this and the preceding chapters. A few of these points are highlighted here.

1. IDENTIFYING, ANALYZING, AND CLASSIFYING INTERVENTIONS ACCORDING TO LEVELS IS RELATIVE, NOT ABSOLUTE. Examples of interventions at different levels were provided in these chapters; however, some of the examples could have been classified at a higher or lower level. Classifying a particular intervention as an incident, tactic, or strategy is done in terms of the total array of identified interventions. The idea is not to become overly preoccupied with whether a particular intervention is an incident or a tactic, but rather to place all interventions of roughly the same size at the same level, then to place relatively larger interventions at the next higher level and relatively smaller interventions at the next lower level. The levels of interventions are a relative scale rather than an absolute set of categories.

In a research study, it is possible for a trained research team to reliably assign relative levels to a particular set of intervention data. Unless a person is involved in a research study, however, it is more important to be aware of the relative size and scope than it is to have absolute agreement on the placement of particular interventions.

2. A CHANGE PROCESS SUCCEEDS OR FAILS AT THE INCIDENT LEVEL. Incidents are the basic building blocks for higher level, sponsored interventions, as well as the primary source of mushrooms. There appears to be too little appreciation on the part of policymakers, researchers, and many practitioners for just how much action and initiative is required to accomplish successful implementation. The incident interventions employed for any change process quickly accumulate, and apparently they are the key to the suc-

cess or failure of a change process. For example, in the Principal Teacher Interaction Study, a statistically significant correlation of .61 was found between the number of incident interventions and the principal change facilitator style (Hall, Rutherford, Hord, and Huling-Austin 1984). Further, principal style correlated .74 with implementation success (Huling, Hall, Hord, and Rutherford 1983). Of course, quality of incident interventions must be considered, but the total count appears to be a strong predictor.

Many persons who are in change facilitator roles tend to remove themselves from the nitty-gritty incident level and day-to-day work with individuals and small groups. Facilitators who do not consider the incident level of the change process to be important or leave it to others or to chance are left with an increased likelihood of a poor quality implementation or outright failure. The incident level is where the individual user's concens and problems are or are not resolved. Interventions at that level, therefore, result in subtle behavior changes that can make the differences that culminate in a successful change process.

3. HOW LONG A MUSHROOM BUILDS IS RELATED TO THE CLINICAL SKILL OF THE CHANGE FACILITATOR. The lives of mushrooms in change processes are surprisingly varied. We noted above that the ability to detect mushrooms seems to differ considerably among change facilitators. In several field sites, facilitators were quick to recognize the potential of an emerging mushroom and would do something about them at an early stage. If a mushroom was counterproductive to the change process, counteractions were immediately initiated. If the mushroom was positive in nature, it was capitalized. In other field sites, as illustrated in figure 25, mushrooms grew to highly negative proportions but were never recognized and directly attended to by the change facilitators.

A critical ability of effective change facilitators is to identify and manage mushrooms. Initial data in support of this hypothesis was found in the Principal Teacher Interaction Study, where in the more successful implementing schools, few, if any, mushrooms were identified. In the less successful schools, mushrooms were more readily found. It is questionable whether all change facilitators can be trained in early detection of mushrooms. As will be described in the next chapter, research on change facilitator styles suggests that some facilitators exhibit a natural sensitivity to this type of phenomena, while others seem to be less predisposed or able to anticipate and identify emerging mushrooms.

4. DEVELOPING STEREOTYPIC NAMES FOR INTERVENTIONS MAY BE USEFUL. As was mentioned at the end of the preceding chapter, giving particular interventions common names can be helpful. Since no intervention is all good or all bad but contains a combination of potential strengths and inherent weaknesses, part of the naming game includes identifying the potentials of identified interventions. Brief summaries of some stereotypic tactics/strategies are presented in figure 29. We strive for a stereotypic name that suggests some of the advantages and disadvantages that are a part of the intervention. The names also make the concepts easier for change facilitators and researchers to keep in mind.

The change facilitator must consider the inherent advantages and disadvantages in interventions. Once a particular strategy or tactic is selected, the skilled facilitator will launch a set of related incidents and tactics to compensate for the disadvantages and to maximize the advantages. For example, there has been a great deal of discussion and debate regarding the use of mandates and decrees. There seems to be a preoccupation with what are seen as the weaknesses of this strategy (e.g., lack of ownership), without recognizing that mandates and decrees also have strengths (e.g., clear indication of priority). No intervention is all positive or all negative in its benefits and its costs. The analytical change facilitator keeps in mind the advantages and disadvantages of particular interventions and proceeds accordingly. The use of stereotypic names can remind change facilitators of the interventions' strengths and weaknesses and of the need to accommodate these factors in their change process planning.

In Summary

An initial intervention game plan with many strategies and tactics can be planned in advance. It is possible and helpful to identify those key strategies and tactics under each game plan component that will increase the likelihood of successful change. It is also possible and helpful to identify critical incidents that will need to be made. A more successful game plan can be developed if the facilitator keeps in mind the overall change process, analyzes it, predicts problems, and plans ways to deal with potential obstacles. The Intervention Taxonomy offers one scheme for accomplishing these tasks.

Of course, modifications in the intervention game plan will be necessary as the change process unfolds. But these modifications can be made within the framework of the overall plan and, therefore, can be made with consistency and in relation to the larger picture rather than being more or less isolated mutations. As with athletic coaches, there are offensive and defensive dimensions to an intervention game plan. Offensive dimensions are developed when concerns-based change facilitators diagnose Stages of Concern, Levels of Use, and Innovation Configurations for those individuals asked to change. Defensive dimensions include consideration of how to accommodate the disadvantages of selected interventions, uncontrolled obstacles, mushrooms, and other happenings that can retard the change process. It is possible to decrease the number of surprises with some understanding, planning, and monitoring.

In some research sites, the game plan could only be identified after the fact because the manager(s) of the change process did not plan pro actively. In these cases, more of the incident interventions occurred in isolation, and fewer tactics and strategies could be identified. When incidents are not tied to or built into coherent tactics and strategies, the whole change process is uncoordinated and inconsistent.

In other cases, change facilitators have been observed doing an outstanding job of planning, but at only one intervention level. For example, one set of change facilitators planned at the strategy level only. They budgeted and scheduled a year-long series of workshops but did not share their expectations with participants or the other change facilitators, nor did they provide the necessary incident-level preparation and followup for each workshop. Other examples, of change facilitators planning only at the tactic level (one workshop at a time), can also be cited.

Advance planning can be done at all levels. We do not mean however, that change facilitators will have a cookbook to tell them precisely and unequivocally what will happen and what to do in all situations. The change process will have to be monitored closely, and the change facilitator will always have to be involved

Figure 29
Common Names for Selected Tactics and Strategies

Intervention	Description	Advantage	Disadvantage
Bootstraps Approach	Development and implementation of the innovation is added on top of already existing activities.	Additional personnel and resources are not required.	The staff usually have fulltime commitments already and the addition leads to overload and inefficiency.
Sabbatical Leave	A permanent staff member is sent for a period of time to another school or institution where they learn about use of the innovation.	Inhouse expertise is developed and there is a person on site with knowledge and experience with the innovation.	Frequently the person that is encouraged to take the sabbatical is not one who is apt to be most credible upon their return.
Superstar	One or more very prominent, energetic and able individuals are employed as innovation experts.	They bring to the institution advanced knowledge and recognition in relation to work with the innovation.	Superstars are not place bound and may leave after a short period of time. Also, when more than one are in a place their rivalry can end up in civil war.
Experimental Program	A special team or set of activities is set up to try out the innovation while the rest of the staff continues to use the regular way.	Everyone on the staff is not drawn through the traumas of initial implementation while local expertise and experience is being acquired.	Frequently the experimental program ends up being a parallel program and the two are not integrated into one.
Decree/ Mandate	Formal authorities announce that the innovation *will* be used.	Priorities are clear and the time to begin use is clear also.	Frequently the necessary development and implementation sup-

Figure 29 (Cont'd)
Common Names for Selected Tactics and Strategies

Intervention	Description	Advantage	Disadvantage
			port is not there and change is treated as an event.
Hit & Run Workshop	A recognized expert in use of the innovation conducts a multiple day introductory workshop, typically before school begins in the fall.	Initial training is offered by someone who knows about use of the innovation.	All to frequently the hit and run workshop turns out to be a "god bless you" workshop when the consultant leaves to never return. Then local availability of innovation expertise and followup implementation support is not available.
Good Time Workshop	A specialist does an entertaining and sometimes provocative presentation. No one expects changes in practice or behavior as a result of this experience. Though all are expected to have a good time.	There are times when the introduction of new ideas as a stimulus or as a change of pace can be very useful to morale and to creating a general awareness of the different options and activities that are available.	All too frequently, decision makers do not distinguish between good time workshops and other types of workshops where changes in practice are expected.
The Pennsylvania Contingent	A school district brings in an outside person (from Pennsylvania) to become the sup-	A critical mass of persons in leadership positions who have similar assump-	The contingent does not work at communicating with the rest of the members of

Figure 29 (Cont'd)
Common Names for Selected Tactics and Strategies

Intervention	Description	Advantage	Disadvantage
	erintendent or principal. This person upon arrival discovers that he needs more help and sends back to Pennsylvania for one or two key colleagues to join him. One of the colleagues becomes the assistant superintendent and her husband needs a job, so he becomes the school principal.	tions and expectations is established. Communication should be very effective and comfortable within this critical mass.	the organization. One consequence is that the permanent staff begin to say "Ha, we will be here long after they are gone." And usually they are right.
Multiple Adoption Design (Map)	A large number of innovations and innovation bundles are being adopted at one time. In some schools this number has been observed to range as high as 16 to 17 innovation bundles all requiring different staff resources, scheduling and staff development.	The school or school district is able to provide an impressive list of innovations that are being installed.	It is not possible for the staff to handle implementation of more than two or three innovation bundles at once. So little use of the different innovation bundles results and a great deal of staff fatigue and turn over can occur.
Wonder Woman/ Super Man	An innovation bundle is implemented and a	The person serves as a symbol of the prior-	The person selected for this position is typically one

Figure 29 (Cont'd)
Common Names for Selected Tactics and Strategies

Intervention	Description	Advantage	Disadvantage
	particular person is identified to have responsibility for facilitating its implementation. This person is given released time and a special title.	ity that is given to use of this innovation. The person is available to facilitate use.	who is not credible to all parts of the staff. In all too many instances un-tenured beginning teachers are given this assignment. Not only do they not have credibility with the more senior elements of the faculty, their future may be seriously endangered by having the responsibility to encourage more senior colleagues to use the innovation.

in ongoing analyses of the interventions, their effects, and the dynamics of the process. What is possible with the use of analytical tools such as the Intervention Taxonomy, Stages of Concern, Levels of Use, and Innovation Configurations is for change facilitators to have research-verified organizing structures and techniques for analyzing and charting their work. They can also have a set of procedures and frameworks for communicating with others about how the change process is advancing. In this way, the process of change can be more systematic than what was possible in the past. These approaches also make the role of the change facilitator more personalized, since their interventions are now based on teacher needs rather than on facilitator needs.

Having said all this, our research also indicates that characteristics of the change facilitator are important, and this topic will engage the next chapter.

Chapter **8**

What Kind of Change Facilitator Are You? Responder, Manager or Initiator

Responder

Herbert Johnson is a principal who is very pleasant. He speaks to students by name and inquires about family members of various faculty. He went to the first social studies inservice with the teachers but since that time he has not been engaged with the program. He tells his teachers that he doesn't know as much as they do and he trusts their judgment, but if they need anything to come to him and he will order it. He is interested in attending to their requests and keeping them satisfied. The district social studies coordinator has the "run" of the school and works a great deal with teachers to implement the social studies curriculum.

Manager

Helen James keeps the management systems and instructional programs of a well-oiled school humming smoothly. She is at school early and stays late seeing that all aspects of the newly adopted social studies curriculum are in place. She has put the resource teacher in charge of inventorying and managing the social studies materials and supplies for teachers. James telephoned the district coordinator and arranged for training for the teachers in the new curriculum. At a weekly meeting of her school's administrators James checks on progress of the implementation effort, solves problems with the other two administrators and plans for how to meet teacher needs. She stays in touch with teachers' efforts to change by reading their weekly lesson plans and having a conference when necessary.

215

Teachers report that James is helpful, responsive and understanding in that she does not impose too much on them at once.

Initiator

Aramintha Smith's teachers call her a "go-getter." They elaborate by saying that Smith will get anything they need in terms of resources, staff development or policy changes that will improve the school's new social studies program for students. Teachers also say that Smith will "get after" teachers herself if she thinks they are not delivering the social studies curriculum in ways that increase student learning. Smith wants students to be motivated and she wants teachers to do everything possible to infuse the social studies activities and lessons with excitement and stimulation. She visits classrooms to see if this is happening and to lend her own energy and enthusiasm to a lesson if it appears to be lacking.

In the first chapter of this book, a set of assumptions was introduced based on the premise that change is a process, not an event. In chapter 2 we provided a brief review of related research and theory about leadership and change. In chapters 3, 4 and 5, the diagnostic concepts of Stages of Concern, Levels of Use, and Innovation Configurations were described. In the previous two chapters, the concept of an intervention, levels of interventions, the development of intervention game plans, and the process of intervening were discussed. In this chapter, the focus is on the role and characteristics of change facilitators, the persons who deliver interventions. The main theme is that there are alternative change facilitator styles and that each style makes a unique contribution to implementation success.

The same intervention can be made quite differently and can have different effects, depending on the style the change facilitator uses. The tone of voice, the type of facilitator concern that is reflected, the facilitator's knowledge of clients' concerns,and the circumstances of the change process and local context affect the way an intervention is delivered and interpreted. To some degree, each change facilitator will have his/her particular style; however, some general patterns are found more frequently than others. Three in particular have been the subject of extensive research in our studies. These "change facilitator styles" are manifested in the responder, the manager, and the initiator.

In this chapter, the specific application of style to change facilitation will be explained, and the results of recent research and theory explored. Implications about the meaning of style are important not only for those interested in facilitating change, but also for those interested in training change facilitators. Although the most intensive research has been done with school principals, the concepts will be generally described here to apply to all change facilitators, for the idea of change facilitator styles is a universal one and can be applied to teachers, staff developers, curriculum coordinators, and others.

Style Versus Behavior

The idea of a leadership style is not new; however, when various bodies of literature were examined—particularly those regarding industrial/organizational leadership, the change process, and educational administration—it was surprising to discover that there has been no careful definition of style. Further, and more troubling, clear distinctions have not been drawn, either conceptually or methodologically, between leaders' behaviors and leadership style (Rutherford, Hord, Huling, and Hall 1983). The two concepts have been used interchangeably, and often the measures used apparently bear little relationship to the variables being described in the hypotheses.

The shortsightedness of many studies in their treatment of style was revealed by McCall and Lombardo (1978), who point out that "leadership researchers may see delegation activity as a leadership style and correlate it with group productivity, while, in many cases, delegation is a political tool used by leaders to create a desirable situation" (McCall and Lombardo 1978: 158). A particular behavior does not represent an overall style, in fact, one cannot accurately describe or understand any behavior without understanding the motivation behind it. The importance of motivation in understanding style has been emphasized by others, including Fiedler (1978) and Tannenbaum and Schmidt (1958). Fiedler contends that effective group interaction is dependent on

". . . leader personality attributes, reflecting his or her motivational structure . . ." (p. 60), and on the situational control and influence of the leader. Tannenbaum and Schmidt maintain that a manager must consider three forces or motivations when deciding how to manage, and one of these they term "forces operating within his own personality" (p. 98). In contrast, other researchers (Jago and Vroom 1977; Hill and Hughes 1974) seem to view style as a set of behaviors, without referring to motivation.

Besides being plagued by definitional and conceptual difficulties, the idea of style had another serious problem. Invariably, research on leadership styles has begun with the a priori identification and description of a style or elements of a style. Leaders were then observed or subordinates and leaders questioned to see if the leader exhibited the described style in different situations. To further complicate things, in many of these studies, followers were asked about the individual behaviors of leaders rather than being surveyed about a gestalt of the leaders' behaviors and motivations.

A more multivariate approach to defining leadership has emerged recently in several research studies (Thomas 1978; Hall, Rutherford, and Griffin 1982) and in a literature review (Leithwood and Montgomery 1982). The authors of these works have distinguished between individual behaviors and style, and have acknowledged the importance of an affective component. In Thomas' study (1978) of more than sixty schools, the focus was on the role of school principals in managing diverse educational programs. From this study, Thomas identified three patterns or classifications of principal behavior related to the facilitation of alternative programs: A principal acted either as a director, an administrator, or a facilitator.

Principals who were *directors* maintained an active interest in all aspects of the school, from curriculum and teaching to budgeting and scheduling. They also retained final decision-making authority in the school, although teachers contributed to decisions affecting the classroom. *Administrators* made decisions in areas affecting the school as a whole, leaving teachers much autonomy in their own classrooms. These principals tended to identify with district management rather than with their own faculties. *Facilitators*, on the other hand, thought of themselves as colleagues of the faculty. They perceived their primary role to be in supporting and assisting teachers in their work. One way they accomplished this task was to involve teachers in the decision-making process.

Thomas concluded that, although many factors affected implementation, the leadership of the principal appeared to be one of the most important factors in the success or demise of an alternative program. Schools under the leadership of a directive or facilitative principal had greater success in implementing alternative programs than did schools headed by an administrative principal. Furthermore, in those schools that had a single alternative program (versus multi-building programs), program offerings tended to drift toward something different from that originally intended and teachers within the program tended to follow disparate classroom practices when strong leadership was lacking. Finally, Thomas found that directive principals had more difficulty managing multi-building alternative programs than did administrators and facilitators.

Working independently of Thomas, researchers at RDCTE identified three change facilitator styles (Hall, Rutherford, and Griffin 1982) that are very similar to Thomas' styles. As a result of this research, we now have operational descriptions for the three types, which we call initiator, manager, and responder (Hall, Rutherford, Hord, and Huling-Austin 1984). These styles are described in more detail in the next section of this chapter. In a careful literature review by Leithwood and Montgomery (1982) that explored the behaviors of principals, including their roles in change and implementation, "effective" and "typical" principals were described. These findings are included, also, in this chapter's next section.

A More Complete Definition of Style

Until recently, as was suggested in the preceding section, when leadership style has been examined, a careful distinction has not been made between the individual behaviors leaders exhibit and the total combination of their behaviors. Further, the notion that style encompasses more than the total array of behavior was not explored. To illustrate a more comprehensive definition of style, a framework has been developed that incorporates key vectors of the gestalt of style. A simplified version of the framework is presented in figure 30. At its simplest, style can be considered to be a combination of motivations and intervention behaviors. To determine a person's style, therefore, a large number of behaviors must be considered, as well as the person's attitudes, perceptions, and orientation. When action is taken by the facilitator and received by the target (e.g., teachers), the target interprets the intervention, which leads to change (or no change) in the use of the innovation. This change, in turn, affects client (i.e., student) outcomes.

This framework takes into account much of the previous research and theory (see chapter 2) and also has some special emphases. Rather than examining all aspects of leadership style, the emphasis here is on describing and conceptualizing style in relation to the particular leadership role of facilitating change. Instead of dealing with the many aspects and roles of leadership behavior in general, therefore, one can concentrate on the "interventions" that facilitate the use of particular innovations.

Another element in this definition of style is the emphasis on the target's reception of an intervention. Teachers and others who are the targets of interventions make their own interpretations of each intervention. The same incident intervention can be interpreted quite differently by a person with intense Stage 2, Personal Concerns, and also by someone with intense Stage 4, Consequence, concerns. In the first case the facilitator's actions are examined using a self focus, that is, the targeted individuals analyze what implications the action holds for them personally. In the second case, however, the intervention is interpreted in terms of its implications for classroom practice and student effects. As the literature on attribution theory suggests (see chapter 2), variation in the interpretation of an intervention must be taken into account when asking teachers and others about the leadership behavior of administrators and others who are sources of interventions. Even the description of the intervention behaviors is apt to be colored by the receiver's interpretation. The most accurate assessment of the intervention behavior of a particular facilitator can probably be made by an independent observer who is not a participant in the change process. This independent inter-

Figure 30
A Framework for the Analysis of Style

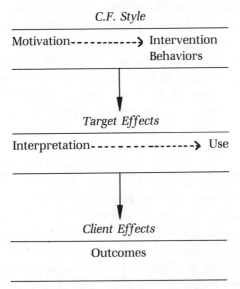

C.F. Style

Motivation----------> Intervention
　　　　　　　　　　　Behaviors

Target Effects

Interpretation--------------> Use

Client Effects

Outcomes

pretation should be less colored by personalized interpretation of the local conditions.

An expanded definition of style portrays a sequence of vectors, starting with change facilitator motivations and moving to change facilitator interventions, to interventions received by targets and interpreted by targets, and finally to change-related responses by clients. Using the concepts that have been developed in earlier chapters, it is possible to provide operational definitions and illustrations of each of these vectors. This more detailed picture of the definition of style is presented in figure 31. In summary, the interventions change facilitators make are based on their *knowledge* of what is happening and their *concerns* about it, which in sum equals their motivation. Facilitator knowledge and concerns lead to, and are affected by, the *behaviors* the facilitator exhibits. One method of describing the delivery of interventions in this definition of style is to use the concept of *tone*. The same action can be made in several different ways, and each way has a different affect to it. It "feels" or "sounds" different to the facilitator as well as to the targets. The tone of interventions plus the overall approach is what is usually referred to as style.

During research, the concerns cell in the style definition was studied more closely. Like teachers, college professors, and other "front line" users of an innovation, change facilitators also have Stages of Concern; however, change facilitators' concerns are focused on their facilitator role rather than on the use of the innovation. (Definitions of the change facilitator Stages of Concern are presented in figure 32.) One reason for including SoC as a vector in defining style is that the tone of interventions and the behaviors facilitators employ can be quite different depending on their concerns. Also, to some degree, their style may shift accordingly.

The target box of the framework outlined in figure 31 includes the target's *knowledge* of and *concerns* about the innovation and their use or nonuse of it (LoU plus IC). The targets' knowledge of the setting, understanding of the change facilitator's intentions, concerns about the innovation will also affect their interpretation of interventions. Interventions that are perceived to be positively related to concerns are likely to lead to changes that advocate LoU and lead to more complete configurations of the innovation. Interventions interpreted as not being relevant or threatening are likely to retard use and lead to decreased confidence. Subsequent assessments should show a change in the Level of Use of the innovation, the configuration of the innovation, and/or the Stages of Concern profile. In the ideal concerns-based change process, the change facilitator reflects upon this new pattern and uses this latest diagnostic information to adjust the type and tone of his/her next intervention(s). The ultimate effects of this systemic and adaptive intervention process should be positive affects on client (i.e., student) outcomes. When facilitators encourage the use of more advanced forms of an appropriate innovation and users develop impact concerns, increased gains by students should follow.

In summary, change facilitator style by definition comprises the interactive combination of the facilitator's knowledge about the change process, the change facilitator's Stages of Concern, the particular facilitator's behaviors, and the tone of the delivery of these interventions. The effects of interventions travel through the target's (e.g., teacher's) filters of knowledge and concerns. The intervention is interpreted and applied to advancing the use of the innovation, which in turn should lead to more positive client outcomes.

Figure 31
A Framework for Analyzing the Relationship of Style to Effects

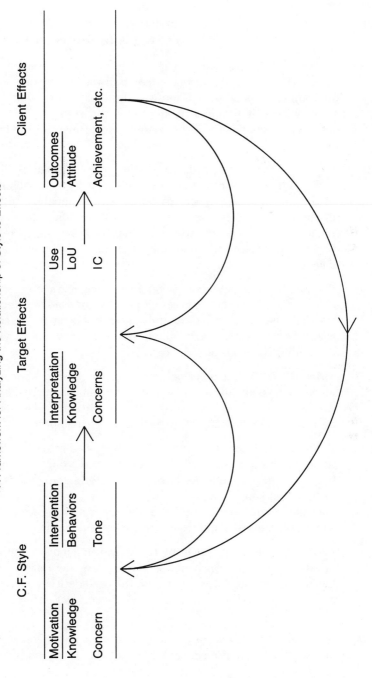

Figure 32
Definitions:
Change Facilitator Stages of Concern

6   *REFOCUSING:* Ideas about alternatives to the innovation are a focus. Thoughts and opinions oriented toward increasing benefits to clients are based on substantive questions about the maximum effectiveness of the present innovative thrust. Thought is being given to alternative forms or possible replacement of the innovation.

5   *COLLABORATION:* Coordinating with other change facilitators and/or administrators to increase one's capacity in facilitating use of the innovation is the focus. Increased coordination and communication for increased effectiveness of the innovation are the focus. Issues related to involving other leaders in support of and facilitating use of the innovation for increased impact are indicated.

4   *CONSEQUENCE:* Attention is on improving one's own style of change facilitation and increasing positive innovation effects. Increasing the effectiveness of users and analyzing the effects on clients are the foci. Expanding his/her facility and style for facilitating change is also the focus.

3   *MANAGEMENT:* The time, logistics, available resources and energy involved in facilitating others in use of the innovation are the focus. Attention is on the "how to do its" of change facilitation and decreasing the difficulty of managing the change process.

2   *PERSONAL:* Uncertainity about one's ability and role in facilitating use of the innovation is indicated. Doubts about one's adequacy in being able to be an effecive change facilitator and questions about institutional support and rewards for doing the job are included. Lack of confidence in oneself or in the support to be received from superiors, nonusers and users are a part of this stage.

1   *INFORMATIONAL:* There is interest in learning more about the innovation. The concern is not self-oriented or necessarily change facilitation oriented. The focus is on the need/desire to know more about the innovation in general, its characteristics, effects and requirements for use.

0   *AWARENESS:* Change facilitation in relation to the innovation is not an area of intense concern. The person's attention is focused elsewhere.

Obviously, the real world is more complex and subtle than is suggested by this framework. However, with this framework, it is possible to look at the gestalt of style and to include in the definition more than individual intervention behaviors. In addition, this framework shows the interrelationships between the characteristics of style, the state of the target, and the outcomes of clients. It is through this interactive and continually adaptive process that change facilitators function. More effective change facilitators appear to be more aware of the different vectors making up this framework and are more capable of fine-tuning the interventions they make.

The Research-Based Identification of Three Change Facilitator Styles

Defining style and distinguishing style from behaviors was a necessary step in preparing for studying principals. We and our colleagues had hypothesized that there were change facilitator style differences, and we began to speculate about them. The three change facilitator styles to be described here emerged out of the Principal Teacher Interaction Study and data that were collected as part of other studies. The initial clues regarding the existence of these styles appeared in a secondary analysis of nine schools, a subset of a larger sample that was studied systematically while implementing a revised science curriculum (Hall, Hord, and Griffin 1980). These schools were in a large suburban school district, where eighty elementary schools were implementing the revised curriculum. Twenty of the schools were selected for systematic study of the Stages of Concern and the Levels of Use of teachers and of the Innovation Configurations that were being implemented. Stages of Concern, Levels of Use, and Innovation Configuration data were collected from each teacher six weeks into the school year and six weeks before the end of the school year for three years. The original purposes of this study were to document the kinds of interventions, especially staff development experiences, that addressed the Stages of Concern and Levels of Use of teachers. Several findings from this study were presented in earlier chapters.

Following completion of the primary study, the data from nine schools were chosen for secondary analysis. For these schools, there was a large amount of quantitative and qualitative data about the implementation effort and a nearly complete set of data across the three years for all teachers. The analysis strategy entailed the development of nine mini case studies of school change (Hall, Hord, and Griffin 1980). The data afforded the opportunity to gain a deeper understanding of the implementation process as it unfolded within the nine different schools. An important consideration was that each school had the same districtwide resources, staff development experiences, and roughly similar demographic characteristics, such as kinds of teachers, students, community, and so on.

One immediate finding from the school-by-school analysis was that the implementation effort had not progressed at the same rate or with the same degree of quality in each of the nine schools. Rather, the schools clustered into three groups for which the implementation process varied dramatically in terms of teachers' Stages of Concern, Levels of Use, and Innovation Configurations.

The differences in the Stages of Concern data were particularly instructive. A summary of these SoC profiles is presented in figure 33. In one set of schools (A), the characteristic "W" concerns profile was observed. Teachers had high Stage 0 Awareness, Stage 3 Management, and Stage 6 Refocusing concerns. This profile is characteristic of teachers who have high management concerns, are dissatisfied with the way the implementation is going (high Stage 6 Refocusing), and are concentrating on other issues of concern to them (high Stage 0). The concerns of these teachers contrasted quite sharply with another set of schools (B) that had relatively low and flat SoC profiles. No particular Stage of Concern was in sharp focus for these faculties. The third grouping of schools (C) had a distinct peak in Stage 4 Consequence concerns, with relatively lower self and task concerns.

Although the nine schools had the same staff development and other resources, the concerns profiles of the teachers indicated that they were at quite different points of progress in implementation. The first set of schools still had high management concerns; another set of schools appeared to have resolved their

Figure 33
Patterns of Teacher Concerns after Two Years of
District Wide Implementation

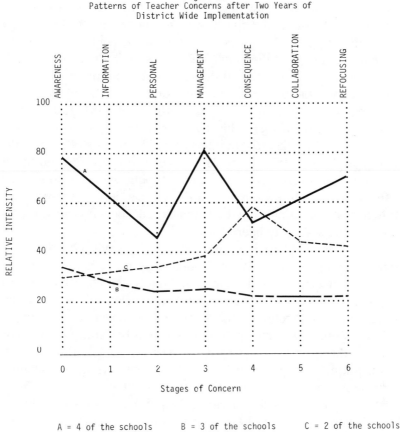

A = 4 of the schools   B = 3 of the schools   C = 2 of the schools

management concerns but had not developed any impact concerns. The third set of schools indicated impact concerns at Stage 4. How could these differences have resulted?

We, our colleagues, and the school district personnel came to identical conclusions. The principals in these schools had approached the role of change facilitator quite differently, and they had facilitated the implementation differently. They were demonstrating, what would now be called, different change facilitating styles. At the time, brief descriptions of how each group of principals worked were recorded, but there was hesitation to use the word "style" since the literature and experts in the field were discouraging the use of this term. Subsequent to the secondary analysis of the data from these nine schools, two other studies were conducted that examined more closely the change facilitating style of elementary school principals. Following development of the nine mini case studies (Hall, Hord, and Griffin 1980), a three-month pilot study was conducted that involved ten elementary schools in several communities, each implementing different curriculum innovations (Rutherford 1981; Hord 1981). In this study, the primary objective was to develop procedures for documenting the day-to-day intervention behaviors of principals. The principals in these schools appeared to represent the three styles. Based on the impressions and hypotheses from these two studies, composite profile descriptions were developed and used to select the principals for the Principal-Teacher Interaction (PTI) Study, as has already been described.

The Principal Teacher Interaction (PTI) Study was the most significant study. In this investigation, nine elementary school principals were selected for study. They were characterized as using one of the three change facilitator styles and, at the time, were tentatively referred to as initator, manager, or responder types. To select the principals, key central office administrators in each of three school districts were asked to review the working descriptions that had been developed of the three change facilitator styles. They were then asked to nominate school principals whom they believed closely approximated these styles in their dealings with teachers. Central office administrators were easily able to identify principals representing each of the styles. In each district, one principal of each style and their faculties agreed to participate in a year-long study. It must be emphasized that none of the principals were in "trouble" and that their schools were seen as satisfactory. The focus of the study was on the different approaches to facilitating change the principals and their schools took.

In the PTI Study, interventions made by the principals and other change facilitators were documented over a one-year period. The analysis procedures described in preceding chapters were used to document and analyze their interventions. In addition, the teachers' Stages of Concern, Levels of Use, and Innovation Configuration data were collected three times during the school year. A combination of on-site visits, telephone calls, and related procedures, such as subscribing to local newspapers, was used to maintain close contact with the change process as it unfolded in each of the study schools.

The study schools were in three different school districts in three different parts of the country, with each school district implementing a different educational innovation. One school district was in the first year of implementing a writing composition program, another was in the second year of implementing a mathematics program, and the third district was in the third year of implementing a revised science curriculum. Within each district, three principals judged to represent the different CF styles were studied. Using this design, impressions of how principals and intervention behavior varied across innovations and across years of implementation could be developed. Because the design was limited to one year of data collection, and since there was a confounding of year of implementation with the specific innovation being implemented, the interpretations needed to be done with caution, using careful cross-checkings. The collection of descriptive information and a review of documents, plus a triangulation of key events across interviewers, were completed to support interpretations. In addition, district office administrators were engaged in the data analysis activities and cross-checked the interpretations. This process helped confirm the findings.

Interpretations of the quantitative and qualitative data were consistent and clearly supported the existence of the three change facilitator styles. In addition, strong relationships were found between the change facilitator styles and implementation success at the classroom level. The earlier secondary analysis and the two studies of principals that followed resulted in a clear identification of three change facilitator styles, with supporting detail. Additional outcomes of these studies, included the development of a set of behavioral indicators for the styles and tentative conclusions about how the change facilitator style employed by the principal affects implementation success. These findings and their implications are the subject of the remainder of this chapter.

Initiators, Responders, Managers Defined

As part of the research, extensive descriptions of intervention behaviors and anecdotes about the characteristics of the change facilitators' styles were compiled. From this data, specific behavioral indicators of style were identified and refined, and paragraph definitions of each of the three change facilitator styles were developed. Descriptions of each of these styles follows.

Initiators

Initiators hold clear, decisive, long-range goals for their schools that transcend, but include, implementation of current innovations. They have a well-defined vision of what their school should be like and of what teachers, parents, students, and the principal should be doing to help the school move in that direction. They tend to have strong beliefs about what constitutes good schools and teaching. They listen to their teachers, then make decisions. The decisions are based on input from those who will be involved. Each decision is made in relation to the long-term goals they hold for the school and what they believe to be best for students. Initiators push; they have strong expectations for students, teachers, and themselves, and they push to see that all are moving in goal-oriented directions. They convey and monitor these high expectations through frequent contact with teachers and clear explication of how the school is to operate and how teachers are to teach. When they feel it is in the best interest of the school, particularly in the students' interest, initiators will seek changes in district programs or policies or they will reinterpret them to suit the needs of the school. They will be creative in interpreting policies at times and strive to capture as many resources and as much capability for their schools as possible. Initiators tend to be adamant, but not unkind.

Managers

Managers exhibit a different set of behaviors and orientation. They demonstrate responsive behaviors to situations or people, and they also initiate actions in support of a change process. Variations in their behavior seem to be linked to their rapport with teachers and the central office staff, as well as to how well they understand the purposes of a particular innovation. They are efficient in administering their schools and work without fanfare to provide basic support to teachers. They keep teachers informed about decisions and are sensitive to teacher needs. A particularly significant characteristic is that they protect their teachers from what they perceive as excessive demands. They question changes at the beginning and tend to dampen their entry. Once they understand that outsiders, such as the central office, want something to happen in their school, they become very involved with teachers in making it happen; yet, they do not typically initiate attempts to move beyond the basics of what is imposed. Managers try to do everything themselves. They try to do all the different tasks associated with the principal's role rather than delegating jobs and responsibilities. When they do assign jobs, they monitor very closely what the designated person is doing rather than work with him/her or letting go.

Responders

Responders emphasize the personal side of their relationship with teachers and others. They are concerned about how others will perceive decisions and the direction the school is taking. They therefore tend to delay decisions, to get as much input as possible, and to be sure that everyone has had a chance to express their feelings. They view teachers as strong professionals who are able to carry out instruction with little guidance from them. As a consequence, they will allow others to make decisions, if they wish. They believe their primary role is to maintain a smoothly running school by focusing on traditional administrative tasks, keeping teachers content, and treating students well. Another characteristic of responders is the tendency toward making decisions based on immediate circumstances rather than on longer range instructional or school goals. This tendency seems to be due in part to their desire to please others and to their more limited vision of how their school and staff should change in the future. As a consequence, decisions tend to be made one at a time and to be most heavily influenced by the last person(s) they talk to.

Another characteristic of responders is that, once a decision is made, it is set in concrete. A great deal of new information and extended discussion are required to bring about major modifications.

The behavioral indicators presented in figure 34 provide further detail about these three different change facilitator styles. The indicators allow the styles to become much more concrete and also provide possible content for training sessions. Another use of the indicators is in research studies, where there is interest in assigning styles to change facilitators. For example, Ruch (personal communication, 1984) is using the CF style indicators to develop a paper-pencil procedure for assessing CF styles. Also Van der Perre (1984) has used a questionnaire and interview procedure to assess the CF style of principals in a current research study. Using these indicators, it is easier to picture the gestalt of each style, whatever the application.

Clearly, these three styles represent stereotypes, and not many individual principals or other change facilitators will fit them exactly. They have, however, proved to be instructive for thinking about the change process and the differences in the approaches different change facilitators take. In addition to these three styles, other styles can be imagined. For example, if the change facilitator styles were placed on a continuum, as is illustrated in figure 35, to the right of the initiator style at some point would be a despot style. This style of change facilitator would not listen to teachers for input but would decree the directions and simply demand what should happen. At the other end of the continuum, to the left of the responder, would be such styles as the "laissez-faire," "covert-saboteur/gorilla," and "overt resister." To place persons on this "styles" continuum, scaled points representing initiator, manager, and responder styles have been set. If the scale runs from 0 to 100, the stereotypic responder is placed at the 30 point, the stereotypic manager at point 60, and the stereotypic initiator at point 90. It is then possible to represent blends of styles by placing persons at points between the stereotypes. This system is another way to incorporate the rich differences that exist. A summary of some of the findings from change facilitator styles research is presented in the next section.

Figure 34
Indicators of Change Facilitator Style

Dimensions/ Behaviors	Responder	Manager	Initiator
Vision and Goal Setting	Accepts district goals as school goals	Accepts district goals but makes adjustments at school level to accommodate particular needs of the school	Respects district goals but insists on goals for school that give priority to this school's student needs
	Allows others to generate the initiative for any school improvement that is needed	Engages others in regular review of school situation to avoid any reduction in school effectiveness	Identifies areas in need of improvement and initiates action for change
	Relies primarily on others for introduction of new ideas into the school	Open to new ideas and introduces some to faculty as well as allowing others in school to do so	Sorts through new ideas presented from within and outside the school and implements those deemed to have high promise for school improvement in designated priority areas
	Future goals/direction of school are determined in response to district level goals/priorities	Anticipates the instructional and management needs of school and plans for them	Takes the lead in identifying future goals and priorities for the school and for accomplishing them.

Figure 34 (Cont'd)
Indicators of Change Facilitator Style

Dimensions/ Behaviors	Responder	Manager	Initiator
	Responds to teachers', students' and parents' interest in terms of goals of school and district	Collaborates with others in reviewing and identifying school goals	Establishes framework of expectations for the school and involves others in setting goals within that framework
Structuring the School as a Work Place	Grants teachers much autonomy and independence and allows them to provide guidelines for students	Provides guidelines and expectations for teachers and parents to maintain effective operation of the school	Sets standards and expects high performance levels for teachers, students and self
	Ensures that school and district policies are followed and strives to see that disruptions in the school day are minimal	Works with teachers, students and parents to maintain effective operation of the school	Establishes instructional program as first priority; personal and collaborative efforts are directed at supporting that priority
	Responds to requests and needs as they arise in an effort to keep all involved persons comfortable and satisfied	Expects all involved to contribute to effective instruction and management	Insists that all persons involved give priority to teaching and learning

Figure 34 (Cont'd)
Indicators of Change Facilitator Style

Dimensions/ Behaviors	Responder	Manager	Initiator
	Indefinitely delays having staff do tasks if it is perceived staff are overloaded	Contends that staff are already very busy and paces request and task loads accordingly	Will knowingly sacrifice short term feelings of staff if doing a task now is necessary for the success of longer term school goals
	Allows school norms to evolve over time	Helps establish and clarify norms for the school	Establishes, clarifies and models norms for the school
Managing Change	Accepts district expectations for change	Meets district expectations for changes required	Accommodates district expectations for change and pushes adjustments and additions that will benefit his/her school
	Sanctions the change process and attempts to resolve conflicts when they arise	Maintains regular involvement in the change process sometimes with a focus on management and at other times with a focus on the impact of the change	Directs the change process in ways that aim toward effective innovation use by all teachers

Figure 34 (Cont'd)
Indicators of Change Facilitator Style

Dimensions/ Behaviors	Responder	Manager	Initiator
	Relies on information provided by other change facilitators, usually from outside the school for knowledge of the innovation	Uses information from a variety of sources for gaining knowledge of the innovation	Seeks out information from teachers, district personnel and others to gain an understanding of the innovation and its demands
	Develops minimal knowledge of what use of the innovation entails	Becomes knowledgeable about general use of the innovation and what is needed to support use	Develops sufficient knowledge about use to be able to make specific teaching suggestions and troubleshoot problems that may emerge
	Communicates expectations relative to change only in very general terms	Informs teachers that they are expected to use the innovation	Gives teachers specific expectations and steps regarding use of the innovation
	Monitors change effort primarily through brief, spontaneous conversations and unsolicited reports	Monitors the change effort through planned conversations with individuals and groups and informal observations of instruction	Closely monitors the change effort through classroom observation, review of lesson plans and student performance

Figure 34 (Cont'd)
Indicators of Change Facilitator Style

Dimensions/ Behaviors	Responder	Manager	Initiator
	Information gained through monitoring may or may not be discussed with a teacher	Information gained through monitoring is discussed with teachers and compared with expected behavior	Information gained through monitoring is fed back directly to teachers, compared with expected behavior and a plan for next steps including improvement is established
Collaborating and Delegating	Ideas are registered by every staff member with one or two most heavily influencing the ultimate flow	Ideas are offered by both staff and the principal and consensus is gradually developed	Ideas are sought from teachers as well as their reactions to principal's ideas, then priorities are set
	Allows others to assume responsibility for the change effort	Tends to do most of the intervening on the change effort but will share some responsibility	Will delegate to carefully chosen others some of the responsibility for the change effort
	Those who assume responsibility have considerable autonomy and independence	Coordinates responsibilities and stays informed about how others are handling their responsibilities	Establishes first which responsibilities will be delegated and how they are to be accomplished, then monitors closely the carrying out of tasks

Figure 34 (Cont'd)
Indicators of Change Facilitator Style

Dimensions/ Behaviors	Responder	Manager	Initiator
	Those who assume responsibility are more likely to be from outside the school e.g. district facilitators	Others who assume responsibility may come from within or from outside the school	Others who assume responsibility are likely to be from within the school
Decision Making	Accepts the rules of the district	Lives by the rules of the district, but goes beyond minimum requirements	Respects the rules of the district but determines behavior by what is required for maximum school effectiveness
	As the deadlines approach makes those decisions required for ongoing operation of the school	Actively involved in routine decision-making relative to instructional and administrative affairs	Routine decisions are handled through established procedures and assigned responsibilities. Non-routine decisions are handled with dispatch following solicitation of teacher ideas
	Decisions are influenced more by immediate circumstances of the situation and formal policies than longer term consequences	Decisions are based on the norms and expectations that guide the school and the management needs of the school	Decisions are based on the standards of high expectations and what is best for the school as a whole, particularly learning outcomes and the longer term goals

Figure 34 (Cont'd)
Indicators of Change Facilitator Style

Dimensions/ Behaviors	Responder	Manager	Initiator
	Allows all interested parties to participate in decision-making or to make decisions independently	Allows others to participate in decision making, but maintains control of the process through personal involvement	Allows others to participate in decision making and delegates decision making to others but within carefully established parameters related to goals and expectations
Guiding and Supporting	Believes teachers are professionals and leaves them alone to do their work unless they request assistance or support	Believes teachers are a part of total faculty and establishes guidelines for all teachers for involvement with the change effort	Believes teachers are responsible for developing the best possible instruction and establishes expectations consistent with this view
	When requests for assistance or support are received, attempts to respond in a way that is satisfying to one who made the request	Monitors the progress of the change effort and attempts to anticipate needed assistance and resources	Anticipates the need for assistance and resources and provides support as needed (whether or not requested) and sometimes in advance of potential blockages
	Relies on teachers to report how things are going and to	Maintains close contact with teachers and the change	Collects and uses information from a variety of sources to

Figure 34 (Cont'd)
Indicators of Change Facilitator Style

Dimensions/ Behaviors	Responder	Manager	Initiator
	share any major problems	effort in an attempt to identify things that might be done to assist teachers with the change	monitor the change effort and to plan interventions that will increase the probability of a successful, quality implementation
	Relies on whatever training is available with the innovation to develop teacher's knowledge and skills	In addition to the regularly provided assistance, seeks and uses sources within and outside the school to develop teacher knowledge and skills	Takes the lead in identifying when teachers have need for increased knowledge and skills and will see that it is provided, most likely using personnel and resources from within the building
	Provides general support for teachers as persons and as professionals	Support is directed to individuals and subgroups for specific purposes related to the change as well as to provide for their personal welfare	Provides direct programmatic support through interventions targeted to individuals and the staff as a whole

Figure 34 (Cont'd)
Indicators of Change Facilitator Style

Dimensions/ Behaviors	Responder	Manager	Initiator
	Tries to minimize the demands of the change effort on teachers	Modifies demands of the change effort to protect teachers from perceived overloads	Keeps ever present demands on teachers for effective implementation
Structuring their Leadership Role	Sees role as administrator	Sees role as avoiding or minimizing problems so instruction may occur	Sees role as one of ensuring school has strong instructional program and that teachers are teaching and students are learning
	Maintains low profile relative to day-to-day operation of school	Is very actively involved in day-to-day management	Directs the ongoing operation of school with emphasis on instruction through personal actions and clearly delegated responsibilities
	Identification and accomplishment of tasks are determined by the opinions and concerns presented	Is consistent in setting and accomplishing tasks and does much of it himself/herself	Identified and accomplished tasks are consistent with school priorities but responsibility may be delegated to others

Figure 34 (Cont'd)
Indicators of Change Facilitator Style

Dimensions/ Behaviors	Responder	Manager	Initiator
	Maintains a general sense of "where the school is" and how teachers are feeling about things	Is well informed about what is happening in the school and who is doing what	Maintains specific knowledge of all that is going on in the school including classrooms through direct contact with individual teachers and students
	Responds to others in a manner intended to please them	Responds to others in a way that will be supportive of the operation of the school	Responds to others with concern but places student priorities above all else

Figure 35
A Continuum of Change Facilitator Styles

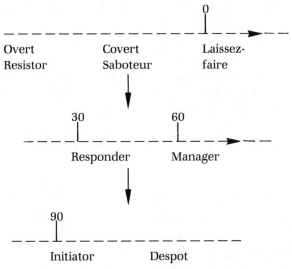

Findings from Research on Change Facilitator Style

The three change facilitator styles found in these studies are consistent with the findings from other studies. For example, the existence of principal types or styles was verified in the carefully designed literature review by Leithwood and Montgomery (1982), who characterized principals as "effective" and "typical." In their review of twenty-nine studies, the authors used a framework for planned change to investigate existing knowledge about principal behaviors as they related to effectiveness. One aspect of the review considered the role of the principal in general, while two other avenues considered the principal's roles in school change and innovation implementation and school effectiveness. Leithwood and Montgomery (1982) found that effective principals were active, particularly regarding instruction and student welfare. On the other hand, they found that, "rather than being pro-active as the effective principal appeared to be, the typical principal tended to be primarily responsive—responsive to district demands and the demands from the many other sources of problems encountered everyday" (p. 27). Rutherford (1985) reports similar findings that contrast the more-effective and less-effective principals.

The types found in Leithwood and Montgomery's review (1982), the styles identified by Thomas (1978), and the change facilitator styles hypothesized by Hall, Rutherford, and Griffin (1982), Hord (1981), and Rutherford (1981) have similarities. The director (Thomas), initiator (Hall et al.), and effective principals (Leithwood and Montgomery) have like characterizations. The administrator (Thomas), responder (Hall et al.), and typical principal (Leithwood and Montgomery) have some similar characteristics, while the facilitator (Thomas) and manager (Hall et al.) are also alike in many ways. Additional support for the initiator principal is also found in the effective schools studies by Edmonds (1979) and Venezky and Winfield (1979).

The Frequency of Principal Incident Interventions

One contribution of the PTI study came from closely examining the day-to-day behaviors of principals using each of these change facilitating styles. A major part of the PTI study was to document the incident interventions the principals made and to organize the findings by CF style. In the study, an attempt was made to associate each style with change process effects.

The distribution of incident interventions by principal style is summarized in table 7. A striking feature of the data displayed in table 7 is that so many incident interventions were made by principals during one school year to support implementation of relatively small-scale curriculum innovations. Each of these innovations involved only one curriculum area and no organizational changes, yet, on average, each principal made sixty-five incident interventions.

The data reflect a consistent pattern of differences in the number of principal interventions according to style. Responders made the lowest average number of interventions, manager style principals made the highest number of interventions, while the initiator style principal ranked in between. One of the generalizations that emerged from this finding is that manager style principals attempt to facilitate all by themselves.

There were no "isolated" incident interventions (interventions unrelated to other interventions) made by initiators, and a relatively small number, 2 to 3 percent (N = 11), made by

Table 7
Distribution (in percentages) of Principal Incident Interventions By Change Facilitator Style of the Principal and Incident Sublevels
Sublevels of Incident Interventions

Principal CF Style	Isolated	Simple	Complex	Chain	Rep'ted	Total (N)	Average (N)
Initiator N = 2 principals	0	62-	22	11	5	138	69
Manager N = 3 principals	2	82	10	5	2	241	80
Responder n = 4 principals	3	83	3-	8	2	204	51
Total (N)	11	452	60	43	16	583	65

±indicate cells that have values that are different from expected

responder and manager style principals. Of the identified incident interventions, then 97 to 100 percent were connected to other interventions, suggesting that each principal had internal continuity in the way they were facilitating the change process.

Style Similarities and Differences in Principal Interventions

Coding each intervention has provided more detail on how the study principals facilitated change. The SPSS cross–tab analyses (Brown 1974), the X^2 test, and the "cell search" procedure (Brown 1979) were used to determine statistically significant differences. The data from these analyses are presented in figures 36 and 37. Figure 36 is a summary of the similarities in interventions across all three styles, and figure 37 presents the differences identified in the analyses. For the convenience of the reader, the coding dimensions follow each statement. Keep in mind that although each difference in and of itself is interesting, it was the pattern of differences that led to the fuller description of each of the three change facilitator styles.

Figure 36
Similarities in Intervention Behavior Across
Principals' CF Style

There were no systematic differences in principals use of
   —chain incident interventions (average of 5 per principal)
   (Sublevel 4)
   —repeated incident interventions (average of 2) (Sublevel 5)
   —isolated incident interventions (average of 1) (Sublevel 1)
   —Interventions targeted beyond the district (target 9, average 1)
   (Target 7-11)
   —interventions for all functions except policy making (Function 1A)
   and reporting on monitoring and evaluating (Function 4C)
   —one way flow to interventions (Flow 1)
   —the office, classrooms, and the district as locations for interventions. (Location, 1A, 1B, 2A)

Initiators made more interventions in classrooms and made more rule and policy decisions. They tended to deliver the same intervention to different teachers individually. The fact that several teachers would then receive the same intervention (i.e., a chain) seems to reflect some advance thinking and continuity in the initiator principals' interventions.

Initiators made fewer than expected interventions for teachers as groups, (e.g., all third grade teachers); while managers' interventions were targeted toward subgroups of teachers more than would be expected. Teachers at a grade level would be addressed, or all the primary/intermediate teachers would be addressed. Field notes further confirm this managerial approach. The finding that managers did more than the expected number of interventions for monitoring and evaluation requires some explanation. The percentage of monitoring interventions done by one manager principal was almost twice as large as the percentage for the other two manager principals. This result may be due to that particular district's emphasis on monitoring rather than to some inherent characteristic of the principals' style. The probable influence of the district on the monitoring function should be even more pronounced among responders. In fact, the two principals in this district that were judged as using the responder style averaged 29 percent for interventions regarding monitoring and evaluation functions, while the average for the

Figure 37
Summary of Identified Cells in the Principal Incident Intervention Codings that Contributed Heavily to Significance of the X² Statistic

Principals using the initiator style did *more* than expected:
—interventions for global rule and policy decision making (Function 1A)
—interventions taking place in classrooms (Location IC)

Principals using the initiator style did *fewer* than expected:
—simple incident interventions (Sublevel 2)
—interventions aimed at individual teachers (Target 2)
—interventions aimed at central office innovation facilitators (Target 7)
—Interventions aimed at subsets of teachers as intact groups (e.g., all 3rd grade teachers) (Target 3C)
—interventions that were interactive (Flow 2)

Principals using the manager style did *more* than expected:
—interventions to subsets of teachers as groups (Target 3B)
—monitoring and evaluating to report findings (Function 4C)
—monitoring and evaluating that had to be specified by the coder (Function 4E)

Principals using the manager style did *fewer* than expected:
—interventions that were complex incidents (Sublevel 3)
—interventions that were aimed directly at students (Target 1)

In schools that were led by principals using the responder change facilitator style there were *more* interventions than expected that were:
—made by district innovation facilitators (Source 7)
—made by district resource people (Source 8B)
—aimed at an individual teacher (Target 2)
—aimed at teachers as whole subsets (Target 3C)
—aimed at the principals (Target 6A)
—that took place at the district central office (Location A)

In schools that were led by principals using the responder change facilitator style there were *fewer* interventions than expected that were:
—policy and major decision making (Function 1000A)
—information sharing about use (Function 3000A)
—consulting and reinforcing that had to be specified by the coder (Function 3000E)
—transferring of monitoring and evaluation data (Function 4000D)

other two responders was 5 percent. When the data for the three principals from that one district are removed, managers and initiators had almost identical percentages of monitoring and evaluation functions, while responders made far fewer interventions for this purpose. This case shows that interpretation of quantitative findings can be definitely influenced by the qualitative information at each site.

Principals using the responder style conducted fewer complex incident interventions (e.g., staff meetings, planning meetings, and workshops), and they targeted students less often. This latter finding is consistent with research staff observations and impressions that responder principals interacted less with students about nondiscipline-related topics. Although initiator and manager style principals interacted with students on discipline matters, they were also observed intervening with students about innovation-related matters.

Analyses of All Interventions for Each School by Principal CF Style

Principals are the formal leaders of their schools, and there are systemic consequences depending on whether they make one or many interventions. The interventions that occurred over the academic year in each school provided illustrations of how the principal's actions were complemented by the actions of others. Results from these analyses (table 8 and figure 38) contributed further to the descriptions of the three change facilitator styles.

There are wide differences in the frequencies of incident interventions shown in table 8. One obvious pattern is the dramatic increase in the average number of interventions moving from the responder-led to manager-led to initiator-led schools. The differences identified in figure 38 further illustrate this trend. In the schools with principals who used the initiator change facilitator style, there were more interventions than expected with a wider variety of sources, targets (including students), and functions. Much intervention activity occurred in the manager-led schools; however, it was made by fewer sources and with more limited targets and functions. In schools where principals used the

Table 8
Distribution (in percentages) of All School Related Incident Interventions Identified By Incident Sublevels and CF Style of the Principal

Principal CF Style (School)	Isolated	Simple	Complex	Chain	Rep'ted	Total (N)	Average (N)
Initiator N=2 schools	1	63	14	18 +	3	588	294
Manager N=3 schools	2	74	13	6-	6 +	584	195
Responder N=4 schools	3	71	13	10	3	683	171
Total (N)	40	1,285	247	213	69	1,855	

responder change facilitator style, there were fewer interventions in total, with more outside sources and the principal more frequently the target. Also, less decision making and less of certain types of consulting and reinforcing were done in those schools.

Apparently, once the principal defines his role, the responsibilities of others are configured accordingly (Hord, Stiegelbauer, and Hall 1984), although this interpretation moves beyond the data. For example, the responder principals made a smaller total number of interventions; consequently, other actors did more, including district-level change facilitators. The initiator principals did not, on the average, make as many interventions as did the manager style principals. However, in the initiator-led schools, more interventions occurred as a whole. In the responder-led schools, the principals did less, and the combined total of all facilitator interventions was also less.

Initiators made more interventions than did responders, but not as many as the manager style principals. Of course, in the initiator-led schools, many other actors were making many more

Figure 38
Summary of Identified Cells in the Total Set of Incident Interventions for Each School that Contributed Heavily to Significance of the X^2 Statistic

In schools that were led by principals using the initiator change facilitator style there were *more* interventions than expected that were:
—chain incident interventions (Sublevel 4)
—made by individual teachers (Source 2)
—made by unspecified others (Source 11)
—aimed at students (Target 1)
—aimed at all teachers as individuals (Target 4B)
—aimed at other specified people (Target 11)
—consulting and problem solving (Function 3000C)
—complimenting and praising (Function 8000A)
—occurred in classrooms (Location 1B)
—occurred in locations other than the office and classrooms (Location 1C)

In schools that were led by principals using the initiator change facilitator style there were *fewer* interventions than expected that were:
—made by district innovation facilitators (Source 7)
—aimed at district innovation facilitators (Target 7)
—done to manage and schedule (Function 1000C)
—done to acknowledge concerns (8000E)
—made via telephone (Medium 4)

In schools that were led by principals using the manager change facilitator style there were *more* interventions than expected that:
—were repeated (Sublevel 5)
—made by the CBAM research staff (Source 11A)
—aimed at subsets of teachers as individuals (Target 3A)
—aimed at the change efforts (Target 10)
—had the function of making major decisions (Function 1000A)
—had the general function of evaluation and monitoring (Function 4000)
—took place in the office (Location 1A)
—took place in the district offices (Location 2)
—took place in the surrounding area (Location 3)

In schools that were led by principals using the manager change facilitator style there were *fewer* interventions than expected that were:
—chain incidents (Sublevel 4)

Figure 38 (Cont'd)

—compliments and praise (Function 8000A)
—specifically focused on gathering information for monitoring and evaluation (Function 4000A)
—face-to-face (Medium 1)
—interactive (Flow 2)

In schools that were led by principals using the responder change facilitator style there were *more* interventions than expected that were:
—made by district innovation facilitators (Source 7)
—made by district resource people (Source 8B)
—aimed at an individual teacher (Target 2)
—aimed at teachers as whole subsets (Target 3C)
—aimed at the principal (Target 6A)
—that took place at the district central office (Location A)

In schools that were led by principals using the responder change facilitator style there were *fewer* interventions than expected that were;
—policy and major decision making (Function 1000A)
—information sharing about use (Function 3000A)
—consulting and reinforcing that had to be specified by the coder (Function 3000E)
—transferring of monitoring and evaluation data (Function 4000D)

interventions. Apparently manager style principals try to do everything themselves, while the responder style principal lets others take action and is more frequently targeted by the central office that wants to get things to happen. Simply put:

Initiators make it happen.

Managers help it happen.

Responders let it happen.

Finally, in the initiator-led schools, more of the action occurred within the site. There were fewer interventions targeted toward the school by district facilitators and fewer interventions from the school toward district facilitators. In the manager- and responder-led schools, more interventions originated or were targeted off campus. With a responder principal, off-campus actors were the sources of interventions significantly often. Most notable of such sources were innovation facilitators and district resource people.

The Relationship of Style to
Implementation Success

In a related set of data analyses (Huling, Hall, Hord, and Rutherford 1983), the intervention behaviors of principals by style was related to implementation success. Implementation success was defined from a concerns-based point of view. Principal effectiveness was judged in terms of change process variables; that is, the combination of teachers' Stages of Concern, Levels of Use, and Innovation Configurations data served as measures of implementation success. A school was considered to be more successful in implementation if its teachers' self and task concerns were quickly resolved and impact concerns were developing, if Levels of Use had moved from earlier to later levels, and if more acceptable configurations of the innovation were being implemented.

To make this judgment, research staff and key administrators from each school district met in a series of three, two-day meetings. At each meeting, the data from one dimension was reviewed and a consensus was reached regarding how successful implementation had been at each study school. The schools were then ranked in terms of implementation success on each of the dimensions and on a composite of all three dimensions. Finally, these rankings were compared with the change facilitator style of the principal, the total number of interventions that were being made, and other variables.

The key finding from these analyses was that principal change facilitator style was correlated .76 with overall implementation success, a statistically and clinically significant correlation. The suggestion, then, is that the change facilitator style of principals is directly related to implementation success at the classroom level.

The direction of the correlation is also significant. For different reasons, one might expect each of the styles to be the one most directly related to implementation success. There are leadership theories and philosophies of human development that advocate each one of these styles as the most appropriate one. Since each study school seemed to have achieved satisfactory implementation, the discussion focused on the degrees of implementation success rather than on comparing successful schools with nonsuccessful schools. The direction of the correlation indicated that schools with initiator style principals were most successful. Manager-led schools were next successful, and responder-led schools were least successful.

The PTI study data analyses indicated that the strong vision, push, consistent decision making, and priority setting of the initiator style principals resulted in teachers achieving more success in implementing the innovations. The manager style principals also appeared to provide effective leadership for facilitating implementation. Their rankings and placement are clearly second to that of initiator style principals, but implementation still progressed well. Managers' high level of activity and efficiency was effective. The teachers in responder-led schools, however, did not appear to progress at the same rate, especially in their Stages of Concern and Innovation Configurations. Self and task concerns were not resolved in responder-led schools, and the Innovation Configurations that were implemented tended to be less rigorous.

The Relationship of Style to School Climate

Policymakers and others are all too quick to draw conclusions about the effectiveness of principals and other change facilitators based on a single factor or index. To point out the danger of this tendency, the results of another analysis will be instructive.

When the criterion for effectiveness was changed from change implementation success to ratings of school climate, the rankings of the schools changed. As part of the PTI study, psychological climate (James and Jones 1974; Jones, James, Bruni, Hornick, and Sells 1979) was assessed. Traditional organizational climate variables such as relative autonomy, communication, job satisfaction, and role ambiguity were measured using especially developed questionnaires (Hall and Griffin, 1982). These climate factors were then related to the change facilitator styles of the principals. In this case, a curvelinear relationship appeared, with the manager style school having a slightly higher correlation with positive climate than did the initiator-led schools. Once again, the responder-led schools ran a distant third. Apparently, the fact that manager principals run smooth and efficient operations and protect their teachers results in more positive climate scores. The initiator principal's tendency to push may reduce some teachers' positive views; however, these scores were still positive in comparison to the climate scores in the responder-led schools. Ruch (personal communication, 1984) found similar results. In his study, the initiator principals out-ranked the manager style principals by a small amount, and the climate in responder-led schools was last again.

These findings indicate that change facilitator style can be an important descriptor and can be used in making various judgments about the effectiveness of change facilitators. The style that appears to be most effective can be different, however, depending on what criterion for effectiveness is used. In the PTI study, when implementation success was the criterion for effectiveness, the initiator style rated first. When psychological climate was used as the criterion, the manager style ranked first. Style is a multivariate phenomenon, and policymakers, trainers, and others would be wise to consider its multiple dimensions when preparing for change and when making judgments about the effectiveness of the change process. The facilitator's style must be placed within the larger picture of the total change process and all the various actors and conditions that apply; yet, the indicator certainly is an important one.

Some related points and other implications of change facilitator style are described in the final section of this chapter, and, in the next chapter, the significance of other change facilitators will be linked to the principal's CF styles.

Implications

Several implications from the research on change facilitator style were included in earlier discussions in this chapter. Some of the most salient points as well as some of the questions that remain unresolved are highlighted here.

1. HOW WELL WILL THE RESEARCH ON THE CHANGE FACILITATOR STYLE OF ELEMENTARY SCHOOL PRINCIPALS TRANSFER TO HIGH SCHOOL SETTINGS? The bulk of the research on the role of school principals and change facilitator style has been done in elementary schools. What is the potential for generalizing and applying this concept to

high school settings? The more recent research we and our colleagues are doing in high school settings suggests there is a surprising degree of transfer. Although the final answer to this question is still open to empirical testing, at this point it seems that the initiative, managerial, and responsive styles of facilitating change can also be identified in high school principals. This finding has led to serious questioning about the often-heard theme that high school principals do not have time to serve as instructional leaders. In our research studies in high schools, we have found an impressive array of high school principals who do find time to serve as instructional leaders and to be effective change facilitators (Hord and Rutherford, 1985; Murphy and Hord, 1985). They are not apt to have detailed and technical knowledge of all the innovations entering their high schools, but their role of change facilitator appears to be expressed in significant ways. It also appears that principals who use each of the styles can be found in high schools and that the behavioral indicators are similar to those identified for elementary school principals.

2. A NEW CONTENT FOR THE TRAINING OF PRINCIPALS AND OTHER CHANGE FACILITATORS IS SUGGESTED. Although there has been an extensive history of research on leadership and the role of the principal, and more recently on the characteristics of change facilitators, most of the research has emphasized the larger tactical- and strategic-level roles of these actors. Using the related research of others and the identification of the behavioral indicators presented in this chapter, it is now possible to think about specific content for the training and skill development principals and other change facilitators need. They do not appear to receive this type of skill development in the traditional education administration training, and in most districts the meetings principals and central office staff have do not deal directly with their leadership role or change facilitation. By using the ideas for content that have been suggested here, principals and other change facilitators can possibly receive more concrete practice and skills that they will be able to use on a day-to-day basis (Hord and Huling-Austin 1985; Hord and Thurber forthcoming). Since it is the daily incident interventions that make such a critical difference in implementation success, training for principals and others in providing these interventions in ways that have the most

supportive tone and relevance should pay off significantly.

3. HOW READILY CAN CHANGE FACILITATORS CHANGE THEIR STYLE? A great deal of theory and several attractive workshop packages suggest that change facilitators can readily change their style. At this point, we and our colleagues do not believe this assertion. We think it is possible to change individual behaviors, but even when placed in different contexts, one's overall style remains relatively stable. Style has a permanency that is not likely to change through participation in a two-day workshop or by simply being assigned to a different job location. Within different contexts, individual behaviors will change, but the tone, knowledge, concerns, and overall approach are likely to remain quite similar. This area needs further speculation and systematic research however. To what degree style is fixed and trait based versus readily adaptable and changeable is a critical question. Much more needs to be known about whether or not change facilitators will maintain the same style when different innovations are involved or when placed in different contexts. We also need to know how style changes over time. Based on the research and clinical experience to date, though, it does not seem that style is changed very easily.

4. POLICYMAKERS AND STAFF DEVELOPERS MUST STOP TALKING IN TERMS OF THE "AVERAGE" PRINCIPAL. The research on change facilitator style argues the case for individual differences. A widespread practice among policymakers, staff developers, and others has been to think of all principals as alike. Several major studies have been done that document average characteristics and practices of principals. If CF styles are real, then such studies and that perspective for policy and staff development are counterproductive. The different change facilitating styles of principals suggest that the needs, repertoire of skills, required supports, and so on will be quite different among principals. In game planning change efforts, it will be important to take these differences into account and to plan accordingly. Planning change processes as if all principals had the same intervention skills and style is another likely reason for the failure of so many change process attempts.

5. WHAT ARE SOME OTHER POTENTIAL IMPLICATIONS? One subject that has been in many of our conversations with principals has had to do with the implications of principals changing

assignments. What happens when one principal replaces another? Are certain transitions more desirable? Principals seem to agree that some matches are easier than others. For example, an initiator has usually accumulated a lot of success and attention. On the other hand, a manager or responder can follow an initiator and almost "coast" on the momentum left by the initiator. Following a responder can be a good opportunity, but all the strong individualistic teachers might not take well to a new principal who wants to get involved in instruction.

The questions raised here are but a few of the possibilities. This work on change facilitator style is a useful heuristic that can help us think more about what we and others are studying and what we might research next. Yet, principals do not facilitate change alone. Even initiators have help. The other change facilitator role is the topic of the next chapter.

Chapter 9

Principals Do Not Do It Alone: The Consigliere And Other Change Facilitators

A Consigliere

Is a special teacher on the faculty who is spending several class periods each day working with teachers individually to help them understand how to make the new program work. Typical activities include developing additional materials for teachers' use, calling volunteer parents to schedule their assistance, and correlating program materials with particular program objectives. The activities that teachers say they value most is the individualized problem-solving and consultation that this facilitator provides.

A Consigliere

Is the district level consultant who pops into classrooms regularly checking to see how things are going and how teachers are progressing in their use of the new approach. Do you understand what is meant by this procedure? Is the process beginning to have an effect? Would you like me to demonstrate with that student? What should be the focus of our next inservice day?

A Consigliere

Is the assistant principal who frequently co-teaches with various members of the faculty as they are learning to organize their teaching around the new instructional strategies. Who also models the new procedures in small group interaction and in teachers meetings. Who provides praising and constructive feedback to the teachers about their use of the innovative techniques.

259

The principal has been the focal point of attention in much of the writing on school change and educational improvement. The principal is seen as the key to what happens in schools, as the gate keeper of change, and as critical to the adoption and institutionalization of innovations in schools (Fullan 1982). School effectiveness studies have identified the principal as being an important variable in student achievement outcomes (Cohen 1982; Edmonds 1979; Stallings 1982). The hypothesized importance of the principal in school improvement was of primary consideration in designing the Principal-Teacher Interaction Study. The investigations led to the conclusion that the principal is the change facilitator of school improvement processes.

Our PTI study was designed with that premise in mind. Thus, the study design required close documentation of the principals' interventions. At the beginning of the PTI study, however, a new discovery was made. Researchers in each school quickly identified an additional person, or in some cases several additional persons, who were doing a large number of important interventions. Regardless of hypothesized style, the innovation, year of implementation, or the district, in each school there was more than one active change facilitator. Principals were not facilitating change by themselves; they had help. From our study design perspective, principals were the first CFs, but we discovered there were others involved. It became clear that the PTI study should not only focus the principal as an individual change facilitator, but should examine the interventions of other change facilitators as well.

In some schools, these facilitator teams developed as a result of the principal's initiative. In some schools, the momentum came from teachers, and in other cases, more initiative came from central office facilitators. Who these facilitators are, what they do, and how they interrelate provide important new insights about the change process. Understanding the role of the second change facilitator and the facilitator team can be useful for planners and trainers as well as for facilitators.

In this chapter, therefore, second change facilitators, or consiglieres, are described. What they do is compared with what the "typical" principal does. Further, their role is related to the change facilitator style of their principals. The chapter concludes with a discussion of the implications of the second facilitator role for training, planning, and facilitating the change process.

Who Is the Second Facilitator?

As was described in chapter 6, many persons were identified at the school level and beyond who were sources of interventions. For each school, there was one person who was nearly as active or, in some cases, more active than the principal. This discovery resulted in the identification of the second CF (if the principal is assumed to be the first CF). In some schools, this person was the assistant principal. In others, a special teacher such as a resource teacher was given added responsibilities for facilitating the change process. In still other schools, second CFs were individuals whose major role and responsibility were described as "facilitator of the innovation" being implemented. Some of these second CFs were based at the school and worked with their colleagues. Others were area-level or district level-specialists or curriculum coordinators who had responsibility for several schools but were more active in particular schools. Although the second CF functions were filled by persons at different levels and different organizational positions, a person with this role was identified in each school, and there were special characteristics to the role.

In two of the PTI study California schools, where there was no assistant principal, the district resource teacher was the likely candidate for the second CF position. The innovation had been designed by the district, and district individuals were trained to facilitate implementation. In one school, however, the principal chose two teaching members of his staff to act as second facilitators, one to work with lower grades and one to work with intermediate grades. Much of the day-to-day planning for the innovation was left to these individuals. The lower grade facilitator served much more actively and backed up facilitation in the middle grades. These facilitators discussed problems with teachers, developed materials and ideas to motivate teachers, and worked with teachers to review needs and progress. Both facilitators met regularly with the principal to plan and discuss progress.

In another school, the assistant principal did very little with the innovation, nor did teacher leadership emerge. In essence, the principal did not place much emphasis on using the innovation nor on utilizing the resources available to do so. In this setting, a central office curriculum consultant was identified as the most frequent intervenor, but implementation progressed very slowly.

Several of the schools in the study had assistant principals who became the second CFs. In many cases, these individuals were assigned roles specifically dealing with instruction and curriculum development. In one of the schools, the assistant principal made as many incident interventions as did the principal. In another school, the assistant principal in charge of curriculum worked closely with the principal, teachers, and students by meeting with grade-level chairpersons, visiting classrooms, and talking to individual teachers. The principal met with the assistant principal frequently for joint planning and decision making. In a similar school, the assistant principal, the principal, and a teacher facilitator worked as a team to facilitate use of the innovation. They met regularly to plan and divide tasks.

In summary, the second CF can be filled by a variety of persons. The important consideration is what they *do* rather than who they *are.* In each study school, at least one other person in addition to the principal was very active as a change facilitator, regardless of his/her formal job or location.

What Do Second Change Facilitators Do?

In the intervention data base described in chapter 6, the incident-level interventions made by the second CFs were isolated and examined as a group. Analysis of this data sheds light on the characteristics of the intervention process employed by second CFs. Tables 9–12 provide information about the frequencies and percentages of these interventions, organized by their sublevels (table 9), targets (table 10), functions (table 11), and medium/flow/location (table 12).

Table 9: Second CF Incidents by Sublevels

On the average, simple incidents were those most frequently

used by the second CFs. Again, simple incidents are single actions that typically involve one or a few people and take little time. One such simple incident involved the second CF at school 38, who sent a note to an individual teacher giving her feedback about her use of the innovation.

Chain incidents averaged the second most frequently used sublevel; however, this data may be skewed by the large numbers of chains at schools 12 and 25. A chain is a series of the same simple incident delivered to different targets, such as a facilitator moving through the school to each classroom to solicit examples of students' work.

Table 10: Second CF Incidents by Target

All targets in table 10 received some intervention activity by the second CFs. The second CFs targeted individual teacher-users most frequently. Nearly one out of every two interventions was targeted at an individual user (2 and 3A = 45 percent). Clearly, the second CF's job in aiding teachers' day-to-day use of the innovation was done by spending large amounts of time with individual teachers. The principal was a target of many second CF incidents. These incidents seemed especially frequent in the California (24, 25, 26) and Colorado (37, 38, 39) schools. These sites had a high number of district resource persons as second CFs, possibly resulting in more interaction with the principal about plans for the innovation.

Table 11: Second CF Incidents by Function

Approximately one-third of the second CF's functions were of the 1000 function, logistical/organizational and material arrangements. This frequency is higher than the researchers expected. Even though these functions are normally associated with the principal, possibly so much effort is needed to handle logistics, organization, and materials that help from the Second CF is needed. Alternatively, perhaps such a large part of what needs to be done to facilitate change is of the 1000 function that everyone must help out. The second CFs also did more monitoring, 4000 function, than was expected. This monitoring is most likely in the sense of checking progress rather than in the sense of evaluation. The 3000 "coaching" function (consultation and reinforcement)

Table 9: Second CF Incidents by Sublevels (in percentages) (Schools Grouped by District)

	California *Year 1			Florida Year 2			Colorado Year 3			Average	Frequency (N)
Site #	24	25	26	11	12	13	37	38	39		
Sublevels											
1. Students		2				2			7	1	5
2. Simple	68	51	67	66	10	79	60	83	89	64	347
3. Complex	23	14	30	19	10	6	22	6	1	13	70
4. Chain	9	31	3	12	79	10	13	3	2	19	103
5. Repeated											
6. Blank (Specify)		2		3		2	6	8		3	16
Total Number	22	128	33	32	48	48	79	66	85		541

*How many years the district had been involved in implementing the curriculum innovation that was being studied.

Table 10: Second CF Incidents by Target (in percentages) (Schools Grouped by District)

Targets / Site #	California *Year 1			Florida Year 2			Colorado Year 3			Average	Frequency (N)
	24	25	26	11	12	13	37	38	39		
1. Clients		6						2			9
2. An Individual User	5	19	6	28	6	27	32			1	5
3A. Subset-as Individuals		11	24	9	77	17	11	56	58	30	162
3B. Subset-as Groups	18	1				4		3	4	15	81
3C. Subset-as Whole Subset	18	1		6	4	25	8	8	7	2	11
4. All Users											
4A. All Users-as Individuals	9	21	3	6		4	1		2	11	60
4B. All Users-as Groups		2	3	6						5	27
4C. All Users-as a Whole	27	6	9	6	2	8	2	4	1	7	38
5. Imple. Site Resource People		4				6	4		6	2	11
6A. Principal	18	9	39	6	6	2	40	23	4	16	87

Table 10 (Cont'd)

Site #	California *Year 1			Florida Year 2			Colorado Year 3			Average	Frequency (N)
	24	25	26	11	12	13	37	38	39		
6B. Assistant Principal											
6C. Imple. Site Dec. Maker-Other					2				1		
7. Innovation Facilitators		2	3						12	2	11
8A. I.U.S.-Decision Makers		2	9			2		2		2	11
8B. I.U.S.-Resource People	4		3	19		4		2		4	22
8C. I.U.S.-Other (Specify)				9			1		2	1	5
9. Extended User System		2		6						1	5
10. Change Effort		6							4	1	5
11. Blank		3									
11A. Blank-CBAM		1		3							
11B. Blank-(Specify)		4			2						
Total Number	22	128	33	32	48	48	79	66	85		541

would logically be expected of second CFs and, indeed they did perform these types of interventions; but we also found principals coaching. As with principals, the first four functions received the most attention overall by second CFs. Such interventions must cover the most crucial functions in facilitating change processes.

Table 12: Second CF Incidents by Medium/Flow/Location

The overriding medium for intervening was face-to-face, although among the second CFs there was a lot of variation in this medium (56 to 100 percent). More use was made of the written and telephone mediums than the research staff had expected. Interactive flow between the second CF and the target was the predominant method; however, there was still a great deal of one-way flow, especially in the Colorado schools (37, 38, 39).

Logically, second CFs did the major portion of their interventions at the school site. A large portion were made in classrooms, with most of the others made in the school office and within the building or campus. Fourteen percent of the second CF interventions occurred outside the school but within the district, possibly because several second CFs were housed at the district level.

The Second CF with the "Typical" Principal

Another way to examine the second CF role is to contrast their interventions with what their principals are doing. Is the second CF a carbon copy of the principal, or is the second CF operating in a different sphere, intervening in ways quite different from principals? Do they complement each other? To investigate these questions and to understand more about the two roles, findings about the second CF were compared with the interventions of principals.

Principal and Second CF Incidents by Sublevels

The number of second CF incidents (N = 541) totals almost the same as that identified for the principals (N = 583). On the average, principals made simple incident interventions 78 percent of the time. The highest proportion of simple incidents for the second CF averaged 64 percent. For complex incidents, second CFs averaged 13 percent and principals, 10 percent. The second CF performed more chain incidents (19 percent), since only 7 percent of the

Table 11: Second CF Incidents by Function (in percentages)
(Schools Grouped by District)

Functions	California *Year 1			Florida Year 2			Colorado Year 3			Average	Frequency (N)
Site #	24	25	26	11	12	13	37	38	39		
1000. Dev. Supp./Org. Arrangements	54	31	58	69	8	38	34	20	32	34	182
2000. Training	23	2	24	9	8	2	6	3		6	30
3000. Consultation & Reinforcement	23	32	6	19	44	25	15	17	24	24	130
4000. Monitoring & Evaluating	23	32	6	3	40	36	42	41	34	30	162
5000. Communicating Externally		2						2			4
6000. Disseminating											
7000. Impeding Use											
8000. Expressing/ Resp. to Concerns	6	6					1	18	11	6	30
9000. Blank (Specify)	2	2					1	1			3
Total Number	22	128	33	32	48	48	79	66	85		541

Table 12: Second CF Incidents by Medium/Flow/Location (in percentages) (Schools Grouped by District)

Site #	California *Year 1			Florida Year 2			Colorado Year 3			Average	Frequency (N)
	24	25	26	11	12	13	37	38	39		
Medium											
1. Face-to-Face	91	88	70	56	100	90	68	82	73	80	433
2. Written	9	9	12	19		10	10	14	20	11	60
3. Audio Visual		1	3	25			22			1	5
4. Telephone		2	15					3	5	7	38
6. None/Other								2	2	1	5
Flow											
1. One-Way	18	20	12	53		6	27	33	41	24	131
2. Interactive	82	80	88	47	100	90	73	65	56	75	404
3. None/Other		1				4		2	2	1	6
Location											
1. Implementation Site	41	13	70	22		23	14	9	20	19	101
1A. Imple. Site-Office	18	7	9	31	12	38	5	17	34	17	94
1B. Imple. Site-Classroom	9	42		12	35	35	29	35	36	32	171

Table 12 (Cont'd)

Site #	California *Year 1			Florida Year 2			Colorado Year 3			Average	Frequency (N)
	24	25	26	11	12	13	37	38	39		
1C. Imple. Site- Other	27	34	3		46	4	5	15	1	16	89
2. Immediate User System	4	2	18	25	4		44	21	7	14	75
3. Extended User System		2		9	2		2	3		2	10
4. Blank (Specify)									1	1	1
Total Number	22	128	33	32	48	48	79	66	85		541

principals' interventions were of this sublevel. The use of repeated incidents was the same, 3 percent for both the principal and second CF. In summary, the principal experienced a higher percentage of simple incidents; the second CF performed a higher percentage (35 to 20 percent) of the more involved incidents (complex +chain +repeated). These percentages indicate that the principals' interventions were smaller in duration and tended to be less involved than those made by the second CF—a logical result. It would be interesting to know something about their relative impact, potency, and saliency.

Principal and Second CF Incidents by Target

Like the second CF, the principals' greatest number of targets was the individual teacher (code 2); an equal percentage of the two facilitators' interventions were targeted there (30 percent each). When all teacher target categories (codes 2–4C) are lumped, the percentages of interventions targeted at users were the same, 67 percent and 70 percent.

Second CFs targeted their principal with 16 percent of their interventions. When the possible codings of second CFs as targets are added together $(5 +6B +7 +8B = 7 +4 +8 +2)$, it shows that the principals targeted the second CF with 21 percent of their interventions. These two figures seem to be fairly close, suggesting a degree of give and take between these facilitators.

Principal and Second CF Incidents by Function

On the average, the principals did a higher percentage of the function 1000 intervening to develop supportive arrangements and manage logistics (41 percent to 34 percent), while the second CFs were doing more consultation (24 percent to 16 percent) and slightly more monitoring (30 percent to 28 percent). The second CF did twice as much training; however, the amounts for both the principals (3 percent) and the second CFs (6 percent) were quite small. The principals were more involved in expressing and responding to concerns (10 percent to 6 percent)—the "affective" function.

Overall, the second CFs seemed to have less involvement in 1000 functions, more involvement in 2000 and 3000 functions, and about equal involvement in 4000 functions when compared to the principals; however, the differences are not very great. In terms of averages, the function tasks had surprisingly similar proportions in both role groups. Both change facilitators were active and doing similar things.

The similarity in overall function distribution between the principals and the second CFs may be related to researcher observations that the principals took a more directive planning approach and the second CF a more action-oriented approach to the same tasks. In other words, for function 1000, the principal would budget and order the supplies, and the second CF would organize and distribute them or inform teachers about them. In 3000 functions, the principal would support and give general reinforcement to teachers at a staff meeting, and the second CF would discuss problems and consult with individual teachers. Still, in general, there was a great deal of similarity in the functions of their incident interventions.

Principal and Second CF Incidents by Medium/Flow/Location

On the average for the two facilitators, their medium of delivering interventions was the same, 80 to 82 percent face-to-face, 11 to 11 percent written. For the flow of interventions, more of the principals were directive or one way in their interventions (32 to 24 percent), while the second CFs conducted a heavier percentage of interactive incidents (75 to 60 percent). The principals intervened in the office twice as often as the second CFs, and the second CFs intervened in classrooms almost three times as often as the principals. Some of the general patterns in the overall relationship between principal and second CF incident interventions are summarized in figure 39. The two facilitators are almost identical in terms of who they targeted in their interventions and the frequency of those targeted interventions. How they delivered the facilitations was also alike in terms of the medium, but the flow had a slightly different balance. Principals were more likely to be directive, have one-way flow, and be less interactive with their targets than were the second CFs.

When the interventions were examined for their simplicity or complexity (sublevels), the principals' ratio was tipped more heavily toward simple interventions, while the second CFs had a lower percentage of simple and a higher percentage of complex interactions.

Figure 39
General Comparisons Between Second CFs' and Principals' Incident Interventions

—The total number of identified Second CF incident interventions, 541, is close to the number identified for the principals, 583.

—Principals did more simple interventions while the Second CF had a higher proportion of more complex interventions.

—The distribution of the Second CFs' intervention targets is parallel to those of their principal.

—In general Second CFs made fewer interventions to develop support and organizational arrangements (Function 1), more formal training (Function 2), more consultation and reinforcement (Function 3), the same amount of monitoring and evaluating (Function 4), less communicating externally (function 5) and half as much responding to concerns (Function 8).

—Second CFs had similar proportions as principals in their use of medium but the flow of Second CFs was more interactive and less one-way.

—Half as many of the Second CFs' interventions occurred in the office and nearly three times as many took place in the classroom.

Function-wise, the two facilitators were almost alike in monitoring teachers' implementations. The second CFs did as many monitoring and evaluation interventions as the principals did. There were some differences in other functions: the principals were more active in developing support and organizational arrangements, and the second CFs had higher percentages in training and in consultation/reinforcement interventions. Apparently, the second CF can provide assistance and, at the same time, monitor and interpret the implementation effort. In theory, this double function seems reasonable; however, in practice, there is much discussion of the need to separate evaluation from "coaching" so that teachers will not feel threatened.

There is an affective domain of interventions, and the principal was more active here in expressing and responding to concerns. This result is interesting since the expectation would be that the second CFs would have the responsibility for responding to purely affective, innovation-related concerns.

These comparisons and interpretations have been made by

"reading" the averages from the principal and second CF data. A cursory examination of the data, however, reveals wide variation in almost every row. To look within the schools and understand how principals and second CFs related on a case-by-case basis is also instructive. In general, the type of interactions between an individual principal and their second CF appears to be as much a factor of the principals' "change facilitator style" as of any other single variable. Regrouping the data around this factor and making further interpretations around this hypothesis are the next subject.

The Second CF and Principal Style

To examine the relationship between the second CF and their principals, the intervention data were organized according to the change facilitator style (i.e., responder, manager, and initiator, chapter 8) each principal apparently used during the year of the study. It seemed reasonable to expect that the role of the second CF would vary in systematic ways that interfaced with the change facilitating style their principal used. When the interventions each performed were compared, some predictable and rather surprising patterns were identified. Some patterns were readily understandable, while others were less clear but seemed logical when the descriptive information about each school was referred to.

A sumary of the comparisons between the role of the second CF and the change facilitator style of their principal is included as figure 40. In general, these similarities and differences reinforce the argument that the change facilitating style of the principal affects the implementation process.

In schools with principals using the initiator style, the second CF was active, used more chain interventions, targeted the principal rarely, and did proportionately fewer interventions for developing supportive/organizational arrangements (function 1000) than did their principals. In these schools, the role of the second CF appears to have been previously charted with sufficient structure and planning so that he/she could regularly pro-

Figure 40
Similarities and Differences of Second CFs' Incident Interventions to the Change Facilitator Style of the Principal

In comparison with their principals, Second CFs with principals using the *Initiator CF style*

—did proportionately more chain interventions (Sublevel 4)

—did proportionately more consultation and reinforcement (Function 3)

—did proportionately more monitoring and evaluating (Function 4)

—had the same distribution of targets as did their principals

—targeted the principal infrequently (1 to 10 times)

—did slightly fewer interventions proportionately that were for developing supportive/organizational arrangements (Function 1)

In comparison with their principals, Second CFs with principals using the *Manager CF style*

—in ⅔ of schools did proportionately more interventions for developing supportive/organizational arrangements (Function 1)

—had half as many interventions as their principals

—did proportionately more formal training (Function 2)

—targeted the principal occasionally (2-15 times)

In comparison with their principals, Second CFs with principals using the *Responder CF style*

—had on the average 20% more incident interventions identified than their principals

—did proportionately more complex and chain interventions

—tended to target the principal more frequently (3-31 times)

—in functions 1, 2, 3 and 4 their interventions appear to balance the functions of the principals' interventions, where one is higher then the other is lower.

vide the same intervention to different teachers individually (i.e., chain incident interventions) and intervene less in issues of support/organizational arrangements.

In schools with principals using the manager style, the second CFs performed, on average, the fewest number of interventions. This finding is consistent with our understanding of the manager change facilitator style, characterized by the principal trying to accomplish everything alone.

The second CFs in schools with principals that used the responder CF style were, on the average, more active than the principal. They performed proportionately more complex and chain interventions. For the functions of the interventions the second CFs did, the principal and the second CF appeared to complement each other. The proportions were different in each school; however, for those functions where the principal conducted a lower proportion of interventions, the second CF counterbalanced with a higher proportion (and vice versa). Second CFs with principals using the responder style also tended to target more interventions at the principal.

For all nine principals and nine second CFs, there appeared to be a complementarity to their intervention behavior. The dynamics of this relationship are most clearly observed in the responder-led schools, and the data displayed in table 13 illustrate this pattern. For most functions, when the principal did more, the second CF did less, and vice versa.

Apparently, the most balanced and complementary intervening occurred when the principal used the initiator style. When the manager style was used by the principal, the second CF was less active. At the other end, in the responder-led schools, the second CF seemed to be in the position of having to make up for what the principal did not do. At the same time, the second CF was constantly checking with the principal or prodding the principal to carry out his/her end of the work. We propose that some of the functions of interventions can be done by any of several actors, but that there is a critical subset that must be done by the line administrator (i.e., the principal).

Beyond the Front Line: Other Resources

Researchers in the PTI study had no difficulty identifying a second facilitator important to the implementation process. The discovery of this role was discussed at the beginning of this chapter. For most PTI study schools, the research staff could also easily identify a third person significantly involved in some way with facilitation, and in a few schools a fourth person was identified. In most cases, the "third CF" was a regular classroom

Table 13
Comparison of Incident Functions for the Second CF and Their Principals Who Used the Responder CF Style (in percentages)

Site	12		26		37		39	
		2nd		2nd		2nd		2nd
Function	P	CF	P	CF	P	CF	P	CF
1000	61	8	28	58	52	34	39	32
2000	3	8		24	2	6	6	
3000	24	44	56	6	8	15	8	24
4000	6	40	4	12	30	42	28	34
TOTAL	31	48	22	33	56	77	69	76

teacher who had either prior experience with the innovation or was an "expert" in the area, who was well respected by other teachers, and who was appointed by the principal to aid facilitation. The following are examples.

In one of the schools, the researcher identified a first grade teacher who had been selected by the principal as a third CF to facilitate the use of the innovation in the kindergarten and first grades. The assistant principal took responsibility for the other grades and was identified as the second facilitator for this school. Both worked on materials development and helped with problem solving and training for teachers. They met weekly with the principal at a regularly scheduled lunch hour to discuss problems and procedures. In all, they saw themselves as a team. In the same district, another school developed a similar kind of change facilitator team that included the principal, the assistant principal, and a third CF fourth grade teacher who was reassigned at midyear as an in-house consultant for the innovation. The latter's role was to work with teachers in grades three through six.

A sixth grade teacher in one of the schools in another district was very experienced with the innovation, was assertive, and was respected by other members of the staff. The principal consulted with her about the innovation, as did the district resource person who was the second CF. This third CF was asked to lead workshops about the innovation for other teachers.

In another example, a fifth grade science teacher acted as an in-house resource for teachers, district resource personnel, and the principal. She was highly respected by teachers and had long been involved with the innovation. She helped the district science department consultants teach in-service programs and had even helped develop the science program.

A sixth grade teacher in another school was identified by the principal to work with the second CF in planning and interpreting the innovation to other teachers. This teacher was very dynamic and worked with the second CF as part of a team in the lower grades. This school had another facilitator, an on-site resource person like the second CF, who worked with the upper grades.

All of these third CFs shared a number of characteristics. First, they were all school based. The second CFs were sometimes on-site resource persons, sometimes district resource personnel, and sometimes assistant principals. Second CF roles varied with other duties but were usually separate from the teacher group in some way, either by role (i.e., resource teacher) or distance from the school (i.e., district based). In contrast, the third CFs were based in the school and were a part of the corpus of teachers. As such, they could act as peer interpreters of information for teachers, as disseminators, and as models. The third CFs were usually respected by their peers as leaders because of their prior knowledge and experience with the innovation. Involving these individuals in the facilitation process, especially in the early stages of implementation, gave both primary facilitators and teachers a means of responding to the process.

As mentioned earlier, a "configuration" of facilitation took shape in different schools. For some schools, facilitation was a "team" approach including the principal, the second CF, and perhaps a third CF—a teacher interpreter/model. In calling this group a "team," the assumption is made that there is some degree of planning and group interaction. Another configuration was more hierarchical, with the principal working with or directing the second CF, the second CF, in turn, working with the teacher model who, in turn, worked with others.

While these variations and their implications have yet to be explored in depth, the role of other facilitation resources and especially of a teacher interpreter/representative/model for the school appears to be important. In cases where the second CF is appointed to this role from the teacher group, a third CF may not be as strongly needed, but in schools where the second CF comes from an administrative position or is an outside district resource teacher, an in-house interpreter becomes a special aid to the success of the change process. Regardless of how they were assigned, the fact that several persons served in the change facilitator role in every study school was a reality.

Discussion

The main concept discussed in this chapter adds new insight to studies about the change process in schools and provides a clue to more effective facilitation of change in the future. Contrary to the much publicized position of superintendents, state and national policymakers, and theoreticians that the principal is singularly important, the PTI study documents that principals do not facilitate change alone. In these study schools, a second change facilitator was identified who was as active as the principal or, in some cases, more active. This finding has important implications for planning, training, and facilitating the change process. The following highlights regarding this role and its implications illustrate this point.

1. THE SECOND CF IS NOT ALWAYS THE ASSISTANT PRINCIPAL. In some sites, the assistant principal did serve as the second CF; however, in several sites the second CF was a teacher, and in other sites the second CF was a curriculum consultant from the central office. In general, it appears that the second CF role is not necessarily an administrative duty; rather, the second CF tends to be a staff person. This assignment is no accident. The kinds of consulting and reinforcing interventions second CFs tend to do are not typically characteristic of administrators, perhaps why the second CF role is not always carried out by the assistant principal. Assistant principals are aspiring to be principals. Their role models and the typical training they experience do not include extensive training about innovation-specific consulting, coaching, and responding to the concerns of teachers relative to implementation. Persons who become second CFs have to know and understand the details of innovation use as well as having basic, facilitator clinical skills.

2. THERE IS A DIVISION OF THE CHANGE FACILITATING TASKS BETWEEN THE PRINCIPAL AND THE SECOND CF. These two facilitators do not do the

same things. Principals provide more of the overall guidance and direction setting, and the second CFs do more of the day-to-day, individualized coaching. In those schools where the second CF was not the assistant principal, it appeared that the principal and assistant principal shared the principals' CF role. The second CF in those schools did different and complementary interventions to those done in combination by the principal and assistant principal.

3. There is a Difference in the Types of Interventions the Second CF and the "Typical" Principal Do. A larger percentage of principal interventions are of the simple type—briefer and less involved substantively. By contrast, the second CFs' interventions are more likely to be of the complex, chain, or repeated type, that is, interventions involving more than a single action. Consequently, the second CF's interventions with teachers are longer and contain multiactions. An additional tendency is for the second CF interventions to be more frequently of an interactive nature, unlike the principal who is more often direct and one way. This finding relates to the one above; that is, the principal intervenes quickly, simply, and in a direct manner; the second CF intervenes more interactively with more complex and involved interventions.

4. There Appear to be Some Systematic Relationships Between the Principals' Change Facilitator Style and the Second CF Role. In manager-led schools, the second CFs did one-half as many interventions as did the principal. In responder-led schools, they did more, and in initiator-led schools, they both performed approximately equal numbers. The functions of the interventions made by the second CF and the principal were complementary. An interdependence or a coordination of activity to address the array of facilitation requirements was observed.

5. The Location of the Second CF Seems to be Related to the Change Facilitator Style of the Principal. In schools with principals who used the initiator or manager CF style, the second CF was located in the school. In the schools that had principals using the responder style, the second CF was located in the central office. Apparently, initiators and managers organize and utilize their own staff and resources to facilitate implementation, while the responder waits for someone in the central office to initiate action and keep the implementation process going. Although there was

central office administrative pressure regarding implementation, the central office second CFs were curriculum staff and made their interventions with limited formal authority at the school and classroom level.

6. THERE IS A NEW UNDERSTANDING CONCERNING PERSONNEL RESOURCES. Regardless of the location of the second CF, there appeared to be a teacher representative acting as a third CF and member of the "change facilitator team." This person was sometimes appointed by the principal, whereas at other times was the "obvious choice." The role and importance of these teacher representatives are yet to be fully understood, but they appear to be quite important as intermediaries, interpreters, and models for other teachers.

7. SECOND CFs SHOULD RECEIVE EARLY TRAINING WITH THEIR PRINCIPALS. In the future, the preimplementation training principals receive should also include their second CFs. Consequently the second CF must be identified early, and the concept of a change facilitating team should be built into the intervention game plan. The innovation-related leadership training conducted for principals should be arranged for the entire CF team in the future.

8. THE SECOND CF AND THIRD CF VARY WITH THE INNOVATION. The persons who become second and third CFs bring background knowledge and interest in the innovation to their roles. As a consequence, for different innovations, different persons become likely candidates for CF roles. For technology innovations, this person would be the computer buff, for language arts, the facilitator would be the teacher who loves literature, and for some other innovation, the logical choice is the teacher who is extremely creative with materials. This approach serves to share leadership among a number of people and to increase status and recognition for those who go the extra mile. Furthermore, the role is already being used and needs to be made legitimate.

In Conclusion

Further study is needed to see if the second change facilitator role commonly found in implementation efforts in elementary schools is found in high schools as well (Hord and Murphy 1985). Our high school studies (Hall, Hord, Guzman, Huling-Austin,

Rutherford, and Stiegelbauer 1984) lead us to hypothesize that, in leadership and facilitation processes, high schools are more similar to elementary schools than different. Clearly, future studies should take into account the change facilitator style of the principal and the location of the second CF, since these factors appear to be key variables.

In future research, it would be instructive to study principals at all levels and their second CFs when they were brought together in the early planning and training process. With some common, and some specialized, training and clarifying of their mutually supportive roles, facilitation effectiveness and implementation success could be greatly enhanced.

In addition to research needs, there are policy and practice implications surrounding the second CF role. Superintendents and policymakers who are interested in the success of school improvement efforts should alter their perspectives to consider this role. Instead of assuming that the principal is the only key to school improvement, thereby implying that the principal is the single target accountable for bringing about school improvement, these authorities must consider the change facilitator team and the significance of the second CF. They are likely to see more impact by directing their priorities to the principal *and* the second CF. Both should receive the advance training that in the past was sometimes done for principals.

Principals, as well as policymakers, should formally consider factors related to the identification, training, placement, and role of the second CF when they are planning a change process. At present, the second CF role emerges out of necessity. The role carries with it little formal recognition and no training. In the future, there needs to be formal recognition and conscious attempts to optimize the second CF's work and their membership in the change facilitating team.

The second CF role also has relevance for teacher career ladder schemes. Since by definition second CFs are leaders who assist other teachers with their work, the role provides a way for teachers to take on additional, formalized responsibility, a key to defining the upper rungs of the career ladder. The role exists, has been discovered by change process researchers, and needs to be made legitimate and recognized through options such as steps in the professional career path of teachers.

The concept of the second CF is powerful and has direct implications for the management of the change process, implications that have already been summarized. Responding to the needs for facilitating change is a vital mission for second CFs. We view this role as important and critical, and we encourage giving it the significant attention it warrants.

Chapter 10

How Does The Concerns-Based Approach Really Work? A Case Study

Upper level official in state education agency
We have never done longitudinal studies before, why should we start now?!

An exasperated assistant superintendent for instruction
What do you mean, there needs to be more inservice sessions? We gave them the books in the August workshop, can't they read?

An innovation facilitator
We have been using it for three years and only now are most teachers beginning to see the subtle beauties of this approach.

First year teacher
When she (the principal) told me that she could see the improvement I had made, I couldn't decide whether to laugh or cry.

High school English teacher
I thought I knew all about the program. After all, I had been using it for four years. But that consultant, who did the follow up in my classroom after the staff development institute, showed me some ways to work with under-achieving high school students that were, as the kids would say, "awesome."

In each of the preceding chapters, a key concept, its related research and theory, and some suggestions for applications were presented. The three diagnostic dimensions of the Concerns-Based Adoption Model (CBAM), the significance of incident interventions, intervention game plans, and the different styles change facilitators use were described. Also, the discovery of the key role of the second change facilitator and the role's significant function in the change process was examined. Throughout the chapters, the personal side of change and the importance of viewing change as a process have been emphasized.

In many ways, this chapter is a mirror image of the preceding chapters, however it is assumed that the reader now has a working knowledge of the concepts and assessment procedures in the Concerns-Based Adoption Model and understands the dynamics of the model's different components. Here, we put these interactive concepts together and explore their application as a totality.

A case study of change involving an entire school district will be used for this purpose. Sample data from research studies and anecdotes from field experiences have been organized into this districtwide case. The case includes an exploration of several particular schools, their individual teachers, and their experiences throughout a five-year change process. One objective for presenting the case is to increase the reader's understanding of how the concepts and procedures of the CBAM can be applied. A second objective is to increase the reader's appreciation of the subtlety inherent in the change process. The process of change is not simple, thus additionally organizing and classifying examples of the phenomena can be useful and instructive. Increased understanding and sensitivity of the dynamics of the change process by change facilitators can contribute to more successful and more personalized efforts.

It is possible to deal with systemwide change, treat schools as unique, while at the same time attend to individuals. In one case, however, we can not illustrate all the different events and dynamics. The case study should help the reader in developing a wider perspective, though, and at the same time aid in developing additional insights about the interrelationships among the concepts that have been introduced.

The Case:
Mathematics Curriculum Reform in the Prairie School District

This story is of a large school district that undertook a change from individual classroom autonomy in curriculum to a district-wide, uniform curriculum for the teaching of mathematics. This fictitious case is comprised of real data that were extracted from several in-depth, longitudinal studies. The data are real, but the names have been changed to protect the . . .

The Prairie School District is located adjacent to a large urban area. The district is diverse in the socioeconomic status of its patrons and their length of residency within the district. Most of the eighty schools involved in the change are "typical" elementary schools with an enrollment of three hundred to six hundred students, the district enrollment totaling approximately eighty-five thousand students. The superintendent, Dr. Allan, has pushed for stronger central office instructional leadership, and there is a large central office staff including a cadre of subject matter coordinators, a staff development academy, and an array of special education and compensatory education staff. The district is divided into five areas, each being administered by an area superintendent.

Dr. Allan has been with the district seven years and has consistently had the support of the school board in developing his instructional policies. As a consequence, policies have been implemented in the district regarding curriculum development and curriculum implementation. These policies include a seven-year cycle for reviewing subject matter areas. Each cycle begins with an internal review and needs assessment. An advisory group of lay and professional personnel examines possible alternatives that might strengthen the subject matter area under scrutiny. The advisory group reviews current practices, student outcomes, and explores alternative curriculum materials and other modifications. It then makes recommendations to the board. The board, in turn, charges the subject area staff in the central office to chair a task force of teachers, administrators, and parents who will become involved in the selection and/or development of refined curriculum materials for use in the subject area. These curriculum materials are then field tested in three to five schools, and, following acceptable revision of the materials, a recommendation is made to the board for implementation districtwide.

The experiences of the district have demonstrated that their districtwide implementation should be phased, with approximately a third of the schools starting implementation at a time. It had not been possible to provide sufficient facilitator support, related staff development experiences, materials, and other needs when the entire district was involved in implementing a curriculum change simultaneously. In this and other ways, the district's implementation policies and practices are based on the premise that change is a process, not an event.

During the past several years, the district administrators, most of the building principals, staff developers, curriculum coordinators, and even some school board members have experienced orientation and training in CBAM concepts. As a result, they have a working knowledge of how to use CBAM variables to develop strategic plans for change, as well as for monitoring and facilitating implementation. This supportive background does not mean no problems will arise, as the story will reveal; however, the change facilitators do have basic understandings and skills in using the concerns-based approach.

The Innovation: Prairie Unified Mathematics Curriculum

For a period of years, Superintendent Allan had been concerned about the variability he had observed in classroom instruction in the elementary schools. Historically, the school district had allowed each school to adopt the textbooks of its choice, and in many schools, individual teachers at the same grade level used texts from different publishers. More recently, regional and national interests in testing and evaluating schools had been escalating, and assessing pupils through achievement on standardized tests was increasing in popularity. The scores on the standardized achievement tests by students in the Prairie School District were far from acceptable to parents and district staff. As a result, mathematics was selected as the priority subject for review and revision in the curriculum improvement cycle.

The district mathematics curriculum coordinator, Reg Wilson, was very knowledgeable about mathematics curriculum design. He was a contributor to one of the mathematics texts that was commercially published and had been involved in the development of "modern" mathematics curriculum materials during the 1960s. Wilson was skilled as a mathematics supervisor and most willing to take advantage of the "opportunity" offered by the superintendent and the board's policy decision to move towards a unified K–12 curriculum in mathematics.

Following the submission and the board's acceptance of the parent/teacher task force report on mathematics, a curriculum development team was established. This team was chaired by Reg Wilson. A new position for an elementary mathematics consultant was created and became a key resource for Wilson. This position was temporary, to be filled by a teacher on leave. The teacher selected for this position was Delores Gonzales, an outstanding sixth grade mathematics teacher who had been in the district for the past ten years. Working with an outside team of consultants from the local university, Wilson and Gonzales generated a game plan for the development of new curriculum materials for mathematics in the Prairie School District.

Part of this development effort included support from the district for the involvement of teachers representing the different grade levels and schools in curriculum writing teams during the summer. The following fall, the writing team members piloted the curriculum materials in their own classrooms. The curriculum materials were revised the next summer and, during the following school year, a more systematic field test was carried out in five schools. Although we do not have quantitative Stages of Concern, Levels of Use, and Innovation Configuration data from that five-school field test, there is sufficient anecdotal data to infer some of the concerns and some of the issues from the field test that seem relevant to plans for the large-scale, districtwide implementation.

Word about the development of the Prairie Unified Mathematics Curriculum was in the district rumor mill. The teachers involved in the summer writing assignments were sharing information with their friends and colleagues. The project had been before the school board at various decision points, and there had been a few, brief references to it in the local newspaper and in the district staff newsletter. Teachers as a whole, however, paid little attention to it, since it did not affect them right then. Some attention and interest did begin to appear as the materials went into the field test year. By this time, the curriculum had become labeled by the development team as the Prairie Unified Mathematics Curriculum, or P.U.M.C. program.

Although such a frequent problem that it seemingly could have been avoided, the first major problem as the field test year began was logistical. Following the end of the summer writing team's work, the P.U.M.C. materials were typed, printed, and distributed on a very short time line. Consequently, all the materials were not arriving in the schools by the time they were needed. There were major "typos" and omissions in the materials, and it was not too far into the school year before the curriculum was being referred to as the "P.U." curriculum. As the year progressed, some of the problems in the draft versions of the materials were addressed, but word still spread from colleague to colleague across the district, arousing concerns regarding whether the materials really were satisfactory and potentially of use to all teachers (i.e., a mushroom was emerging). Throughout the district, teachers were beginning to focus on the imminent implementation mandated to begin the following school year.

Initial CBAM Diagnosis

The initial assessment of Stages of Concern and Levels of Use was done in May of the field test year for use in systematically guiding plans for the change process and to monitor its progress. In hindsight, it would have been wise to have had Stages of Concern data earlier—from the pilot techers. The open-ended interview data from that period clearly indicated that there was some "tailing up" on refocusing concerns. It also seems reasonable to predict that other teachers might tend towards increased personal and informational concerns as they approached the due date for using the P.U.M.C. curriculum and materials.

The field test data are summarized in figure 41, and this time period will be referred to as Year "0." The data summarized in figure 41 are from teachers in phase 1 of a representative sample that included twenty of the district's eighty elementary schools. This sample was picked in advance to be followed longitudinally for monitoring overall implementation across the district. These schools were considered to be representative of all eighty and also to be representative of the projected different phases of implementation. By this point, an Innovation Configuration Component Checklist had been developed by the writing team and Wilson and Gonzales, which took into account what they considered to be the essential components and acceptable variations of use of each of the P.U.M.C. program components (figure 42). IC data were collected in May also.

Interpretation of Initial Diagnostic Data

The composite information provided through analysis of Stages of Concern, Levels of Use, and Innovation Configurations data were presented to Wilson and Gonzales by the evaluation department in the middle of May. The mathematics facilitators immediately went to work with these data, using them as a basis for planning the overall intervention game plan. As part of the planning process, they invited Marge Shelby, a CBAM consultant to work with them.

The diagnostic data were interesting from several points of view. Clearly, the Levels of Use data illustrated that most teachers were not yet very knowledgeable about or active in relation to the upcoming implementation of the P.U.M.C. Twenty-one percent were taking some action to learn more about the program, and 6 percent had prepared somewhat in anticipation of beginning use in the fall; thus, apparently the majority of the teachers at that point were inactive in the implementation of P.U.M.C. Most likely, those teachers who were classified as "users" (6 percent) were the teachers involved in initial materials development and field testing. As expected, since so few teachers were using the program, the Innovation Configurations checklist summary confirmed that initial program use was very rudimentary, with few teachers significantly engaged with the components of the program.

Clearly, the Stages of Concern profile represented a warning signal to the change facilitators. The overall profile was that of the

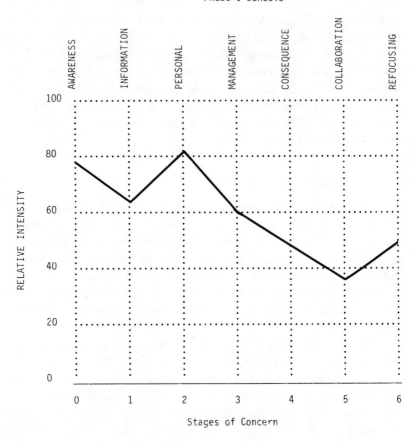

Figure 41
Stages of Concern and Levels of Use Data for Year 0
Phase I Schools

Levels of Use Distribution
(in percentages)

	0	I	II	III	IVA	IVB	V	VI
May, Year 0 Field Test of Materials	67	21	6	6	0	0	0	0

nonuser, with Stage 0 Awareness, Stage 1 informational, Stage 2 Personal concerns as the highest stages and other stages being much lower in intensity. In addition, personal concerns were higher than the informational concerns and, in combination with the "tail up" on refocusing concerns, suggested that there were many teachers at this point who were questioning the P.U.M.C. and not particularly pleased about the approaching implementation time.

There were several jokes floating around the district that characterized the new curriculum in various odiferous ways. There definitely was a mushroom growing across the district regarding the "P.U." materials. Reg and Delores were quick to explain to Marge their hypotheses about why the concerns profile had such negative indications. One of their ideas was that two of the three schools selected for piloting the materials had many teachers who tended to be more dissatisfied in general and were known around the district as less innovative in their teaching. This general attitude, in combination with lack of knowledge and the logistical problems encountered in getting out the pilot test materials, had resulted in an immediate districtwide rumor about teachers' dissatisfactions. Clearly, something would have to be done to address the "P.U." mushroom of growing teacher complaints. These complaints in part were based on real problems with the initial curriculum development and in part on lack of correct information. Using the results of the field test and the guidance of Marge Shelby, the change facilitators began developing their intervention game plan.

One of the first questions Marge asked Reg and Delores was about the overall goal for their game plan. Did they want all teachers using the P.U.M.C. at a minimum level, or did they want some teachers using the program at higher Levels of Use? Marge emphasized that the initial intervention game plan would be different in design and emphasis depending upon their goal for the implementation effort. If the goal was to have all teachers using the innovation, then emphasis would have to be on reaching out to those with personal concerns and those more resistant to change, which would necessitate providing them with additional support. On the other hand, if there was less interest in everyone using the program and more interest in helping users use it well, then the intervention game plan would emphasize drawing in strong teachers and principals and supporting those who were more openly disposed to use of the new materials.

Reg Wilson's answer was quick and to the point. He wanted all teachers in the district teaching the P.U.M.C. and assurances that all children within the district were receiving instruction in

Figure 42
PUMC Checklist

School Name _____

I.D. (Last 4 digits of SS#) __ __ __ __

Please check the category(s) that is most descriptive of the math instruction.

1. *Objectives Used for Planning*

   _____Teaches PUMC Resource Guide objectives

   _____Teaches Heath text objectives

   _____Teaches other objectives

*2. *Objectives*

   _____Uses PUMC objectives largely in sequence within the clusters

   _____Uses PUMC objectives largely out of sequence

   _____Does not use PUMC objectives

3. *Instructional Resources* (Check all that apply)

   _____Activity Kits

   _____Heath text

   _____Teacher generated materials

   _____Other commercial materials

   _____Games

   _____Manipulatives

   _____Math learning centers/lab

*4. *Testing* (Check all that apply)

   _____Uses Heath textbook tests

   _____Uses teacher made tests

   _____Uses PUMC Mastery Test at recommended times

   _____Uses teacher observation/judgment

*5. *Grouping*

   _____Grouping based on test results

   _____Individualized

   _____3 or more small frequently changing groups

   _____3 or more small stable seldom changing groups

   _____2 groups at generally same objectives

   _____Whole class at generally same objective

Figure 42 (Cont'd)

6. *Use of Test Results*
   _____Each student's instruction is *individualized on basis of test results*
   _____*Group(s) change; students are reassigned frequently*
   _____*Group(s) remain intact; students receive extra help as needed*
   _____*Group(s) remain intact; any review is done by group*

mathematics. "It is only through doing this that we will have any chance at all of increasing scores on achievement tests. And if we don't do that, then we won't really be successful."

Following further discussions and analysis of the characteristics of the district, some of the resources that could be available were identified. For example, school board policy provided for three released-time, in-service days to support implementation. There were also other resources available to support implementation, and the three facilitators proceeded with outlining the intervention game plan.

A summary of some of the key strategies and tactics they planned in relation to the Game Plan Components is presented in figure 43. This excerpt from the overall intervention game plan highlights some of the kinds of strategies and tactics that were launched over the summer and during that first school year.

One topic that received a great deal of discussion by the change facilitators was how to address the emerging anti-P.U.M.C mushroom. The "P.U." theme had regularly shown up around the district during the spring, and the change facilitators realized that if something were not done quickly to bring this mushroom under control, it could undermine the entire districtwide implementation effort before it even began. The strategy developed to address the "P.U." mushroom was a series of interventions that included a positive affective element and reflected optimism and en-

Figure 43
Example Key Strategies and Tactics: Year One

GPC 1

Strategy: Materials, games and visuals are provided to each school on a bi weekly basis.

Tactic: A Materials Center is organized at each school.

Tactic: A scheme is collaboratively developed by teachers and school's Materials Resource Teachers for checking materials in and out of the center.

GPC 2

Strategy: Training is provided to each building principal and their facilitator team.

Tactic: A two-day workshop on classroom observation and feedback techniques is held in early September.

Tactic: A weekend retreat in mid August is used to develop the facilitating skills of the teams.

GPC 3

Strategy: A teacher program promotion campaign is initiated.

Tactic: A bi-weekly *PUM is Fun* newsletter is established for distribution to teachers, parents and administrators.

Tactic: A campaign to solicit successful teaching tips of the program to publish in the newsletter is launched in the fall.

Tactic: A contest is arranged to select students' drawings about math for publication in the newsletter.

GPC 4

Strategy: Central office monitors each school's progress.

Tactic: A monthly meeting of all the schools' facilitator teams is held to obtain feedback on program use.

Tactic: A central office "comfort and caring" team calls on each teacher during October to ascertain how they can help the teacher in their new use of the program.

thusiasm about the P.U.M.C. materials. They also decided to change the pronunciation of the acronym from spelling out the letters P-U-M-C to PUM (as in fun). They hoped that changing the pronounciation of the innovation name would immediately draw emphasis away from the negative mushroom that was beginning to develop, and that through positive advertising, a positive orientation would replace it. A tactic created within this strategy was the "PUM is Fun" newsletter, which would go out twice a month to teachers, parents, and administrators. The "Pum is Fun" newsletter included descriptions of students' and teachers' comments, reflected enthusiasm about the materials, provided up-to-date information about printing and other logistics, suggested teaching tips, and in general attempted to standardize and facilitate communication regarding use and districtwide progress.

Progress Check, October Year 1

In October, an assessment of Stages of Concern, Levels of Use, and Innovation Configurations was made in each of the sample schools used to monitor the implementation effort. A summary of the data collected at this point for the phase I schools is presented in figure 44. These data clearly indicate that implementation had begun. There was a definite shift in the Levels of Use data toward preparation for using the innovation. Most teachers were at a Level of Use I, Orientation, or a Level of Use II, Preparation. Only 9 percent had actually begun use, and, as would be expected, these teachers were at a Mechanical Level of Use.

The Stages of Concern data were equally encouraging. Informational and personal concerns were down 15 to 25 points, with personal concerns having shifted from being more intense to being only slightly more intense than the informational concerns. There was still a noticeable "tail up" on Stage 6, Refocusing; however, its intensity had decreased as well. By this point, apparently the "PUM is Fun" strategy had had an effect. It also would appear that the organized delivery of materials and the various training and consultation tactics and incidents that had been put into place were making a difference. The Innovation Configurations data of the 9 percent who were users indicated

Figure 44
Stages of Concern and Levels of Use Data for October,
Year One, Phase I Schools

Levels of Use Distribution
(in percentages)

	0	I	II	III	IVA	IVB	V	VI
May, Year 0 Field Test of Materials	67	21	6	6	0	0	0	0
October Year one	3	16	72	9	0	0	0	0

that teachers were relying heavily on the commercial text for "component one—objectives used for planning." They were using the PUM objectives largely out of sequence and were teaching with predominately small, stable, groups.

Altogether, these data provided the change facilitators with valuable information to use in planning what to do during the late fall and winter to best facilitate implementation. As one step, Reg Wilson, Delores Gonzeles, and Marge Shelby met with a sample of principals, teacher leaders, and teachers to discuss possible ways to address concerns and facilitate implementation. In this meeting, it became clear that many teachers did not perceive that the use of the PUM materials was *really* a district priority. Several other programs were being implemented at the same time, and there appeared to be mixed signals coming from the district office regarding what actually were the priorities for that fall. This revelation led to a critical intervention, made by the district superintendent.

At the monthly board meeting during the first week of November, Dr. Allan announced that implementation of the PUM materials was underway but that there was concern over the amount of progress that had been made. At this point, one of the more conservative members of the board launched an extensive discourse about the importance of achievement in mathematics to the future well-being of the district and to the economic success of the community. "After all, how can we succeed in having high tech companies move to this area if our students are achieving below the national norms on mathematics tests?" A vigorous discussion led to the board's unanimous vote to direct the superintendent to make implementation of the PUM materials his number one priority, and if need be, the board would direct that further resources be assigned to this end.

Dr. Allan assured the board that there was no need for further resources at this time but that, since change is a process and not an event, he was confident implementation would continue as the year unfolded. He did point out, however, that there would be need for support over the next two to three years for further staff development and monitoring of implementation. He explained that indeed there would be progress, but that there would be a need for continuity in policies and continued support in facilitating teacher mastery of the new resources. The local news reporter's impression of the board, as stated in the paper the next day, was that it was willing to accept "change as a process, not an event," *as long as* they received regular reports indicating that progress was being made. Superintendent Allan made a mental note at this point that, before the spring CBAM diagnostic data was collected, he would bring in Marge Shelby to do a half-day workshop with the board to help the members learn how to interpret Stages of Concern, Levels of Use, and Innovation Configurations data.

Meanwhile, the PUM change facilitators had developed further plans for their facilitation work for the fall and winter months. They felt that the second staff development day (the first staff development day had occurred in the third week of September) should focus on using the teachers' PUM Teacher Resource Guide. From one-legged conferences with teachers and principals, it appeared that teachers were primarily using the commercial text, although the program developers had viewed it more as a resource. The PUM Teacher Resource Guide had been developed within the district and was meant to be used as the primary source of instruction. The change facilitators believed that the teaching of objectives in sequence would occur if the PUM guides were used rather than the commercial text. The change facilitators made a conscious decision to push teachers' use of the guides but not to concentrate on how students were grouped. They decided that the latter intervention should wait until the second or perhaps even the third year of implementation.

The Stages of Concern data had indicated that progress was being made but that personal and informational concerns were still high. It was thus felt that the "PUM is Fun" newsletter should continue to emphasize the positive aspects of the P.U.M.C. materials, that the change facilitators should be heavily involved on a personal basis in each of the schools, and that, in the next workshop for principals and their second CFs, the emphasis should again be on how to address and attend to personal and informational concerns. The facilitators also thought it was important to plan other interventions to anticipate the arousal of management concerns as more and more teachers became involved in using the PUM materials.

The winter months of this first year unfolded as planned and highlighted here. Because of the board's critical incident intervention, teachers and principals understood that use of the PUM curriculum was a priority. The staff development and consulting interventions were carried out with a great deal of success across the district. The results of these interventions could be observed in the diagnostic data that were systematically collected in the twenty monitoring sites during May at the end of Year 1. These data are shown in figure 45.

Interpretation of May, Year 1, Diagnostic Data

Clearly, phase I schools made progress during Year 1. Phasing the implementation had kept the change facilitators from being spread too thin. They had been able to concentrate on the early implementation problems that turned up in the fall in several of the schools and to further refine their techniques so that implementation for the last groups of schools could be accomplished quite smoothly.

Phase I teachers' Levels of Use dramatically shifted from a heavy majority of nonusers toward a large proportion using PUM curriculum materials. The Stages of Concern data reflected progress, with personal and informational concerns dramatically lower than they had been in the previous two assessment periods. Stage 3 Management concerns were increased, given the fact that teachers were using the curriculum for the first time. It is interesting to note that Stage 4 Consequence concerns appeared to be on the rise. Tailing down on the Stage 6 Refocusing concerns was a good indicator that the implementation was progressing well.

The change facilitators suspected that one reason for the increase in consequence concerns had to do with the enjoyment and success the children were experiencing with the new math curriculum. They really were finding that PUM was Fun. The students' enthusiasm was being reflected in the teachers' increasing enthusiasm for teaching mathematics. The earlier fears of math and the potential resistance to the use of the materials had been, for all purposes, eliminated.

The Innovation Configurations data reflected the emphasis of the late fall and winter interventions. More teachers were using their PUM Teacher Resource Guide and the PUM objectives, *and* they were using the objectives in sequence. Still, most teachers were teaching in three small, relatively stable groups, and students were receiving little extra help or being left on their own

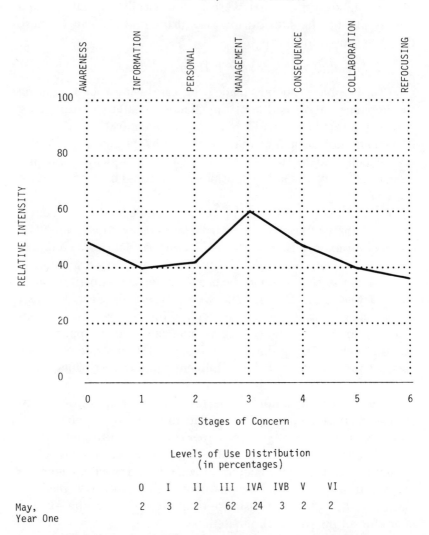

Figure 45
Stages of Concern and Levels of Use Data for May,
Year One, Phase I Schools

Levels of Use Distribution
(in percentages)

	0	I	II	III	IVA	IVB	V	VI
May, Year One	2	3	2	62	24	3	2	2

under the assumption that they would pick up missed material in subsequent years (due to the "spiraling" nature of the PUM curriculum).

In a June planning meeting, the change facilitators, including Marge Shelby, examined the diagnostic data to determine the kinds of interventions that would be most useful during the second year of use. Clearly, further support was needed, since many of the teachers were at Level III, Mechanical, use, understandable at this point in relation to CBAM theory. Facilitating support and continuity would be needed.

During the spring, superintendent Allan's reports to the school board had been well received. He had followed up on his idea for the board's winter weekend retreat. Marge Shelby had done an overview presentation of the three CBAM diagnostic dimensions, and members had developed sufficient skill to interpret rudimentarily the May, Year 1, monitoring data when it was presented to them. They, too, could see the need for further support, and they developed a policy position that sanctioned the continued involvement of the change facilitators and the maintenance of PUM implementation as a priority for the next two years.

The change facilitators decided that the PUM configuration component on grouping had to be addressed. The philosophy of the PUM curriculum encouraged individualization, if not with each student moving at their own pace, at least with flexible groupings. The facilitators were somewhat at a loss as to how to accomplish this goal with teachers. Clearly, some sort of staff development program would be needed. They decided that the grouping component could be tied to the use of test results, or, perhaps, the testing could be made into a more meaningful part of the curriculum. It was thought that if a special record keeping form could be created, the form could be used as a way to trigger teachers' thinking about testing and the placement of students as a result of testing. So over the summer, a select group of teachers and the math facilitators developed the PUM Record Card, which became Component 7 on the PUM configuration checklist.

The intervention plan, then, for the second year was to emphasize grouping. They would emphasize testing, the use of test results, and record keeping as a basis for grouping students. One-half of an August in-service day was allocated to PUM to introduce these ideas. Another major portion of the day was spent in question and answer sessions regarding various PUM materials and in building enthusiasm for second-year use of the curriculum.

End of Second Year CBAM Monitoring

During May of the second year, Stages of Concern, Levels of Use, and Innovation Configurations data were again collected. These data are summarized in figure 46. The Stages of Concern data from Year 2 depict a group concerns profile relatively low in intensity in all stages! There was some indication of remaining management concerns, probably relating to the logistics of organizing students by groups and handling the testing and record keeping procedures that had been introduced; however, those concerns did not appear to be overly intense. In conjunction with the Levels of Use data, one could conclude that the implementation effort was well along the way toward becoming a successful one. There was still a large proportion of teachers at a Level III, Mechanical, use (33 percent); however, a significant proportion of the users were at Level of Use IVA, Routine (43 percent).

Some teachers were at a Level of Use 0 because of teacher reassignments made during the course of the longitudinal study. These teachers had taken on other assignments and were not in positions to use PUM math. Thus, the number of "nonusers" who should be users was not as high as it appeared.

The Innovation Configurations data provided further information about classroom practices. PUM resource materials were continuing to be used, objectives were being taught largely in sequence in most classrooms, and the PUM mastery tests were being used as a basis for individualizing instruction. Much of the grouping being done made use of more frequent and flexible groups, and a noticeable number of teachers were beginning to individualize their instruction. A large amount of change had been accomplished in two years. A more typical time frame for obtaining the results shown by this set of data would be three to four years. Because of the careful attention and concerted efforts by knowledgeable facilitators, teachers had been able to progress with relative efficiency.

Year 3 and Beyond

From the research studies that have been done using the Concerns-Based Adoption Model, Year 3, and especially the end of Year 3 is a critical point in the life of a change process. At this

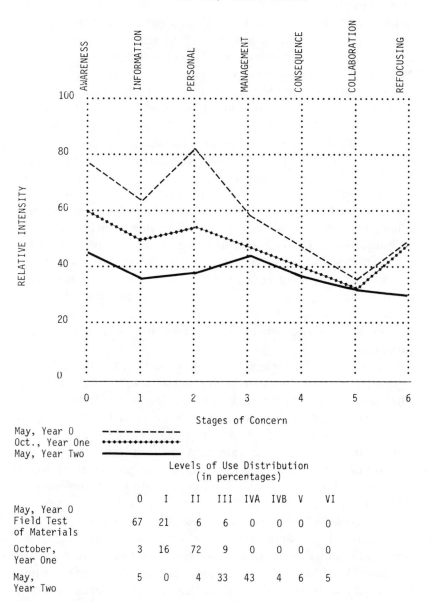

Figure 46
Stages of Concern and Levels of Use Data for May,
Year Two, Phase I Schools

May, Year 0 — — — — — —
Oct., Year One ◆◆◆◆◆◆◆◆◆◆◆◆◆
May, Year Two ▬▬▬▬

Levels of Use Distribution
(in percentages)

	0	I	II	III	IVA	IVB	V	VI
May, Year 0 Field Test of Materials	67	21	6	6	0	0	0	0
October, Year One	3	16	72	9	0	0	0	0
May, Year Two	5	0	4	33	43	4	6	5

point, the implementation effort is at a critical juncture. Typically, informational, personal, and management concerns have been reduced in intensity, and most users are beyond a Mechanical Level of Use. However, this progress does not lead to automatic arousal of impact concerns, to the Refinement Level of Use, or to implementation of more advanced configurations of the innovation. Various research studies show that a new intervention game plan is required in the third year. This plan should encourage the arousal of impact concerns, movement towards Refinement Levels of Use, and implementation of more advanced configurations of the innovation. If nothing is done after the third year, then use of the innovation is apt to wander. A few more reflective teachers might continue to advance, however many go into a form of routine use and equilibrium that amounts to a gradual trailing off of use. Some may regress to using only favorite components.

In intervening for refinement use, CBAM research has demonstrated that the unit or focus for intervention should be the school. For a move from nonuse to districtwide implementation of an innovation, it is possible to work across schools using common interventions and resources, as was described in the case study. To develop movement above the Routine Level of Use, however, or to generate arousal of impact concerns in many teachers, individual schools must be the units of intervention. The central office facilitators and others must, therefore, treat each school uniquely.

In the case of Prairie School District during the third year, a new intervention game plan addressed a concern of the district. That concern involved principal instructional leadership. There was increasing interest in the local press, as well as in various national commissions and reports, in principals becoming the instructional leaders in their schools. A decision was made that the intervention game plan for the next several years would add a new "innovation"—principals serving as monitors of implementation at the classroom level.

Principals in Prairie School District were sensitive to the concern about school leadership, but, as is typical of many principals, they had minimal training and few developed skills for carrying out the role of instructional leader. The new intervention game plan thus called for Wilson, Gonzales, and the district working with individual schools and the principals in the schools. This plan necessitated the creation of a series of workshops for principals and attendance to and development of strategies for coaching principals as they became more involved in monitoring implementation. Principals were also trained in how to facilitate refinement of teachers' use of the PUM materials.

To start, principals were trained in using the PUM Innovation Configurations Checklist. Also, through a series of workshops and consultation sessions, they worked toward understanding what was going on in the classrooms, the dynamics of concerns of their teachers, and planning and implementing interventions that would facilitate teacher movement toward higher Levels of Use and would support the arousal of impact concerns. The second intervention game plan, then, entailed helping principals develop skills in monitoring and facilitating implementation by giving them training in monitoring and coaching techniques. The ultimate goal was to further advance the configurations of PUM that were being used, to encourage teachers to move toward impact concerns (especially toward Stage 4, Consequence), and to support advancement to Refinement Level of Use.

One implication of encouraging Refinement Level of Use is that various adaptations in the PUM materials would result. LoU IVB is defined in large part by the teacher making outcome-oriented adaptations. Wilson and the other developers of the materials felt that teacher creativity was certainly desirable, once basic implementation had been accomplished. They expected most teachers to adapt and refine the instructional resources and some of their teaching behaviors in ways that would further enhance the quality of mathematics instruction in their classrooms.

As will be discussed more in chapter 11, the arousal of impact concerns does not necessarily come about as a direct consequence of the provision of time. Further, there is no known set of interventions that will guarantee that all teachers on a staff will develop impact concerns. The potential for the arousal of impact concerns appears to be, in part, related to inner characteristics of teachers. It does appear, however, that principals can make a difference in the proportion of teachers that arouse impact concerns, as will be demonstrated by the case of Prairie School District.

In some of the schools, there was a shift toward Stage 4 Consequence concerns, in part attributable to interventions the principals made. In other cases, teachers continued to have management concerns; in still other cases, teachers' Stages of Concern profiles remained relatively low in intensity on all stages. Some brief illustrations of the differences and the effects principals made are summarized in the three school-level cases that follow.

Three School-Level Case Studies of PUM Implementation

Washington School: Where It All Happens

> When "new math" came in twelve years ago, I was a new principal in a small school. Because I did not understand what new math was all about and that was my concern, I talked a teacher into letting me teach side-by-side with her for a year every afternoon. We would both prepare for the lessons, both presented and alternated with each other. I began to tune into the "new math" curriculum. (Interview with Mike Johnson)

WASHINGTON SCHOOL AND ITS PRINCIPAL. Washington School is an older campus consisting of four, one-story buildings with three to four classrooms per building and a two-story building that houses the gymnasium and the cafeteria. The school is located in a declining part of a lower socioeconomic status community that has a high proportion of Mexican-American students, with a sprinkling of blacks, Asians, and "half-whites." Forty teachers, thirty teacher aides, twenty-two lay assistants, four custodians, and two and a half secretaries are included in the 120 persons listed as faculty and staff in the school. There is also a media specialist and an assistant principal. As you probably have guessed, this facility is a Chapter I school.

Although the buildings are old, the classrooms are very lively and colorful. A great deal of student work is displayed in all parts of the campus, and there is a sense of high energy and enthusiasm wherever one goes. Principal Johnson was interested in PUM from the very beginning. As might be expected due to his earlier experiences with math, he was involved at various points as the principal representative when the PUM materials were being developed. Math was not his only interest though. He was actively involved in the introduction of other curricula, and he had a particular interest in activities that provided additional outdoor science and environmental experiences for his students.

In a conversation relative to the principal's role in the math curriculum implementation, Johnson revealed his ideas about implementation in general. The factor that helped encourage implementation the most, he felt, was his being told by the district and his telling teachers, "We're going to implement it! You're going to teach it. I'm going to help you." In addition to the mandate from the central office to implement, he reported, "I need more help as a principal than just being told to implement. I need information."

After "putting their feet [his staff] to the fire," he described the importance of his support role. In staff sessions, he typically talked with his teachers about implemention—how it could be done, problems that might be encountered—and asked for their ideas. He solicited their nominations for potential problems and used a problem-solving approach, rather than saying, "This is the way we will do it."

As an example of his response to problems, when a teacher came to him and reported she could not teach science because she had no microscopes, the next day there were six microscopes on her desk. Johnson felt he should work with his staff to resolve any problem areas with the innovation so that criticisms of the innovation would not build and slow down implementation. He recorded teachers' feedback so that corrections could be made and the task of implementation could move ahead "quickly."

Another factor Johnson feels is important is building staff cohesiveness—"If you don't have that kind of staff, you don't have anything." Building unity into a staff is a stimulating undertaking for him as a principal. To do it, he utilized activities such as the *We Agree Workshop*, which is based on building a philosophy of education around statements the faculty agree upon. Johnson summarized his position, "To operationalize your philosophy and your leadership style, you use human relations theory/training; however, you add another key dimension. You help teachers take the lead. You haven't abdicated your authority; the buck still stops with 'you.' You always have the final decision making authority, and at the same time, you are backing your people, with high-dollar equipment and support. . . . My friends say, 'There is a clear feeling that you know where you are going and the staff knows where you are going. There are no hidden agendas; there is a clear plan of what is happening.' " Teachers address this principal by his first name, Mike.

Mike was observed to be constantly out of his office—in classrooms attending to details. He believed himself to be an effective teacher and was regularly observed in consultation with his teachers about some lesson they were teaching. They were as apt to ask him about teaching tips as he was to ask them about instructional techniques or processes being used in their classrooms. He regularly visited their classes and provided teachers with written feedback about what they were doing. Clearly, he represented the initiator style of principal in terms of change facilitation.

THE TEACHERS. The teachers in this school had the typical range of educational experience, with many veteran teachers on the staff and several first-year teachers. They were observed by Reg Wilson and Delores Gonzales early in the implementation effort as being, "old pros, no concerns, friendly, open staff, and all is going well. This is probably a model school for math." Under Mr. Johnson's leadership, all teachers were expected to teach math and were doing so.

THE SECOND CHANGE FACILITATOR. It is interesting to note that, in this school, the second change facilitator role was carried out by teachers within the school, not by the assistant principal (who had intended to back up Johnson). The second change facilitator role was, in fact, carried out by two teachers. One was a resource specialist, Rhonda Ford, who was also an in-service leader for the PUM training workshops. Being in this school made it possible for her to answer questions as they came up and to be a regular, ongoing resource to teachers relative to the PUM materials. Other teachers highly respected her and saw her as being a key spokesperson for PUM. She was of particular assistance to some of the teachers who were not well organized and knowledgeable about individualizing instruction.

Another PUM in-service leader and the other second change facilitator was Linda Lorens, who was transferred to Washington School in the second year of implementation. This transfer was a result of a shift in attendance populations at other schools. In Levels of Use interviews with teachers, Linda was regularly cited as a source of information and help in Washington School, although she was relatively new to the building.

CBAM DIAGNOSTIC DATA. A summary of the Stages of Concern and Levels of Use data for Washington School are presented in figure 47. These data reflect the "ideal progression" as suggested in CBAM theory. At the beginning of the implementation effort, teachers tended to have higher informational and personal concerns and relatively low impact concerns, except for a small emphasis on consequence. Over time, the informational/personal concerns decreased in intensity. The group profile moved to higher concerns—to Stage 4 Consequence and some refocusing concerns.

The Levels of Use data also reflect movement from nonuse to use. Clearly, a high level of implementation was occurring in this school. It is of particular interest to note that the Stage 3 Management concerns were never very intense in the concerns profiles for the staff as a whole. This result must be attributed, in part, to the activities of Principal Johnson; but, one would suspect that having two persons serve as consiglieres also made a significant difference.

SOME CRITICAL INCIDENTS AND TACTICS. Clearly, many interventions were occurring in Washington School during the first several years of implementation of the PUM materials. Only a couple will be highlighted here to illustrate the intervention game plan.

One set of interventions, a tactic, occurred during the second year of implementation. Rhonda Ford and one of the sixth grade teachers went to a weekend professional conference on teaching mathematics. One of the presenters at this conference was a classroom teacher from another district, who shared creative materials and activities that could be used in math interest centers. These materials had very similar objectives to those that had been identified for the PUM curriculum. Rhonda Ford and the teacher returned from this conference believing that a presentation by this teacher would be very effective in encouraging teachers to use the PUM materials. They individually approached Johnson about the possibility of such a presentation at an afternoon in-service session for teachers in Washington School. Johnson encouraged them to check out the availability of the teacher and the cost for leading this in-service session. Meanwhile, Johnson confessed to the researchers that he had already used all his allocated release time monies and that the only way he could finance the in-service day would be to combine the special monies set aside for Chapter I and bilingual education in-services.

The two teachers contacted the presenter who agreed to do

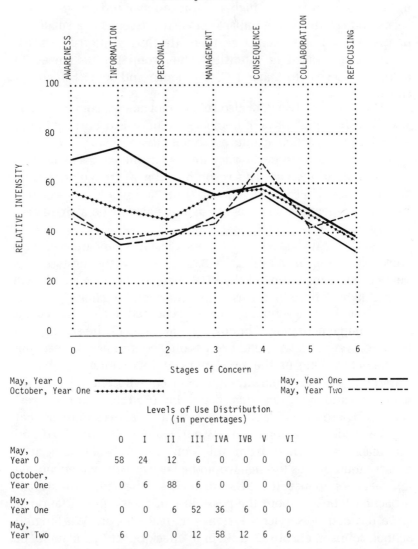

Figure 47
Summary of Stages of Concern and Levels of Use Data:
Washington School

Levels of Use Distribution
(in percentages)

	0	I	II	III	IVA	IVB	V	VI
May, Year 0	58	24	12	6	0	0	0	0
October, Year One	0	6	88	6	0	0	0	0
May, Year One	0	0	6	52	36	6	0	0
May, Year Two	6	0	0	12	58	12	6	6

the afternoon in-service session. A series of discussions was held
with the entire school staff about their potential interest and the
quality of the presentation given at the professional conference.
The principal encouraged all to be involved in the in-service session.

Meanwhile, the principal filed a request through the superintendent for permission to have the in-service session. He knew he was out of allocated in-service hours for that school year; however, he ran the request through channels in the routine way. No one noticed the discrepancy, the superintendent and the board approved the in-service, the teacher came, and the in-service was a major success.

This illustration is an example of the initiator's philosophy, "It is easier to seek forgiveness than it is prior approval." It should be noted that the principal not only scheduled the workshop and encouraged all teachers to be there, but also creatively interpreted district policies by deciding that teacher aides should attend and that their attendance could be counted as part of their hourly work within the school, not actually part of the agreement with them. He attended, as he did all workshops, and organized how he and the second CFs would follow up with the teachers.

There are other interesting anecdotes surrounding this particular event that evidence how this principal and staff worked together, constantly looking for resources and not hesitating in promoting and organizing the resources that would help them best meet the instructional needs of their students. Unfortunately, we do not have space to elaborate on them here.

Another illustrative intervention was a *repeated* incident, a part of the monitoring Game Plan Component. Johnson and the two second change facilitators developed a plan to collect samples of students' work from each classroom. These samples were collected each Friday by the two second CFs, who were released from their other responsibilities to collect student work classroom by classroom. Several effects occurred from this repeated intervention. First of all, it provided a regular contact by the second change facilitators with each of the teachers. They were able to discuss problems and ideas on a weekly basis. The plan also encouraged students to produce their finest work, since the work would be displayed in the teachers' lounge and the school cafeteria. Further, it provided a procedure to monitor implementation of the PUM curriculum. The second change facilitators and the principal were able to know more about pacing, use of materials, grouping, and the extent of activity through these regular, task-related contacts. At the same time, the message to the teachers was that using the PUM curriculum was a priority, that help was immediately available, and that people were interested in talking to them about what they were doing.

INSTITUTIONALIZATION AND BEYOND. The concept of institutionalization has been given insufficient attention in this volume; however, institutionalization has not been the subject of extensive research or theory development. Few studies have focused on how institutionalization can be most effectively achieved or on how to move beyond institutionalization to a phase of fine-tuning and refinement. From the point of view of the Concerns-Based Adoption Model, a system has attained institutionalization when nearly all individuals' Stage 1 Informational, Stage 2 Personal, and Stage 3 Management concerns have been reduced in intensity and they are using an "acceptable" configuration of the innovation at a Routine Level of Use, LoU IVA. These are the criteria and standards for minimum institutionalization. Once this state is reached, a second intervention game plan is needed to move beyond minimum institutionalization. One example of what can happen when this second intervention game plan is launched is reflected in the activities and data at Washington School.

During the third year of implementation, Johnson became interested in arousing more impact concerns on the part of his teachers. Clearly, arousal had already occurred, but he became particularly interested in "pushing things further." At the same time, the district PUM math facilitators were encouraging greater principal involvement in expanding the quality of use of the PUM materials.

The refinement initiative in Washington School was based upon the use of cooperative pupil groups. Principal Johnson felt that if cooperative grouping was emphasized, it would not only be useful in the teaching of mathematics but could spill over into other curriculum areas. He also saw it as a way to encourage his teachers in their own collaborative efforts and to stimulate the team teaching he was interested in establishing as a norm in his school.

In the third and fourth years of implementation of the PUM materials, the "innovation" of cooperative grouping was thus introduced. This introduction did not interfere with the teaching of mathematics, but was complementary to it and moved teachers of math to higher, more refined Levels of Use. The effects in terms of the Stages of Concern and Levels of Use data are reflected in figure 48. The key interventions included bringing in the developers of the cooperative grouping materials (Johnson and Johnson 1975) and involving others from the Central Office Staff Development Academy who were interested in seeing whether these materials could be expanded to districtwide use. Again, Washington became a pioneer school for what eventually became another districtwide initiative.

One note is in order at this point. The Innovation Configuration Component Checklist has not been emphasized in this case description. This omission is due, in part, to the limitations of space in elaborating all three of the CBAM diagnostic dimensions. Another reason is that, in this school, teachers' Innovation Configuration components on the PUM checklist did not vary a great deal. All teachers were involved in implementing the PUM curriculum and used component variations that fell toward the acceptable and ideal end. At the time of the push toward cooperative grouping, the variations of grouping that were occurring were not easily assessed by using the PUM checklist as it was originally designed. One consequence of this inability was that the principal and staff, in conjunction with the cooperative grouping developers, worked out a new component checklist, specifically targeted toward the kinds of grouping activities being established in Washington School. We could easily talk more about this school, but it is time to look at another facility.

Grove Street School: Steady Progress

> I'm concerned as a principal both about the tasks that my faculty and I need to accomplish, but also, there are times when I feel I must protect my staff from undue pressures from "downtown." There are so many demands made of the teachers that I have on a few occasions told my superintendent that we need more time here before we get involved in the district's programs. I also promise that we will give it our very best shot when we get started. We have very good teacher/administrator relationships within our school and between our school and the central office, and I'm generally able to work out agreements with the superintendent's staff. In the case of math, the superintendent and I agreed that my school would implement with the second phase. (Remarks by Shawna Knowles)

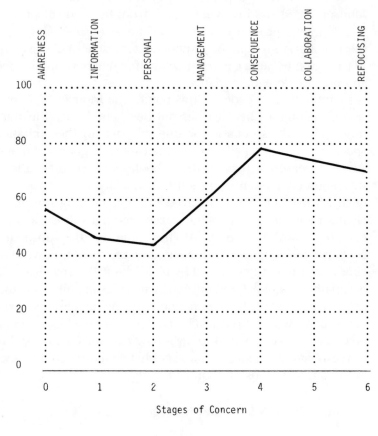

Figure 48
Summary of Stages of Concern and Levels of Use Data for Year Three:
Washington School

Levels of Use Distribution
(in percentages)

	0	I	II	III	IVA	IVB	V	VI
May, Year Three	0	0	0	9	28	28	32	3

GROVE STREET SCHOOL. This school is fairly new, having been built less than ten years prior to the beginning of the PUM implementation. It is a modern structure, originally built in a completely open-classroom style; however, during the previous few years, several walls were erected that gave the building a modified, open-building atmosphere. The school could comfortably house seven hundred students, but its enrollment was nearer to six hundred students in Year 1. Enrollment had been declining because of boundary changes in the school district and because of changing neighborhood patterns. There were approximately thirty full-time faculty members and approximately thirty support staff. There was also an assistant principal and a special class of exceptional students.

The school is located in a middle-class neighborhood that had undergone some changes—the more wealthy families had moved away while families of more modest means had moved in. Apparently, the previous principal had established close, open, and cooperative relations with parents in the community, and these ties continued to exist. The school was sometimes referred to as "the school to visit" because of the teachers' concern for their students and the cooperative reputation of the principal with parents. It was also known for its efficiently run math program and the use of an in-school math specialist, George Eby. Eby's ability to keep the materials and ideas for teaching math well organized and readily available to all teachers was an important factor in the success of the math implementation.

THE PRINCIPAL. The principal, Shawna Knowles, and the teachers in general had a very positive attitude towards the PUM curriculum. Much of this positiveness was due to the principal's attitude, style, and personality. Mrs. Knowles was approximately forty five years of age and married with two grown children. She had been principal of the school for about six years. In her role as principal, she tended to be more "administrative" than "instructional." She did not spend much time in classrooms. Seemingly, she felt comfortable delegating responsibilities to capable and reliable persons. As a person, she was mild mannered, a fairly conservative dresser, supportive, openly friendly, and seemingly content with her work. Knowles had been very supportive of the PUM implementation process. She attended preparatory and in-service sessions along with her teachers as often as time permitted. She believed that her teachers should attend in-services because they might not always have a math specialist to help them teach math and that they should experience the model in-services that had been designed.

The principal seemed pleased and genuinely proud of her school's participation and response to the PUM curriculum. She was pleased about the manner in which the math specialist assisted teachers, and she kept very close tabs on how Mr. Eby went about his work. When certain PUM curriculum materials were not properly coordinated, the principal tried to help her teachers downplay program weaknesses and focus on learning.

Some of the principal's concerns about the administrative aspects of the curriculum were about the constantly disappearing manipulative materials and about the need for additional aide support for teachers in individualizing instruction. The principal was concerned about the involvement of parents in the math program, and emphasized the importance of keeping parents up-to-date with the math program through take-home letters. The principal considered teacher-student interaction the most important aspect in evaluating the math implementation process.

Knowles' method of dealing with teacher/staff relations was to sit down with individuals, plan with them, and show them that the principal was there to assist and support their efforts. She felt that, as a principal, she could make things easier for teachers and staff if she knew what the problems were. She also felt she could get better performance and cooperation from teachers and other staff through positive reinforcement.

THE SECOND CHANGE FACILITATOR. Eby is a "true believer" in the importance of mathematics, in the ability of every teacher to teach mathematics, and in the ability of every child to learn mathematics. He has boundless energy and spends a great deal of time before and after school in discussion and consultation with teachers about teaching mathematics. Although Principal Knowles was interested in and emphasized math, it was Eby who provided the detailed assistance to teachers and the coaching so important to implementation in this school. Many teachers identified Eby as the person who had first made them understand the importance of using the PUM objectives in teaching mathematics and had shown them "how it could be done."

Eby thought it important to involve Knowles in much of his teacher support activities. He decided that if he did not involve her from the beginning, she would be checking with him to find out what he was doing, and that would cost him even more time. The two of them thus spent a great deal of time discussing and planning what had been done to facilitate implementation. One of

Eby's concerns was to assure Knowles' continuing support for his special position, which was reviewed annually. There was always some concern that, as enrollment further declined, Eby would not be able to have release time from his regular classes to work with other teachers. Over the first three years of implementation, his work with teachers clearly resulted in their more effective use of the PUM materials.

CBAM DIAGNOSTIC DATA. The Stages of Concern and Levels of Use data for Grove Street School are summarized in figure 49. The Stages of Concern data are particularly interesting here. Informational and personal concerns begin high, and there does not appear to be any dramatic arousal of management or impact concerns as implementation unfolds. In fact, management concerns stayed relatively low throughout the entire period. This result is most definitely linked to the role Mr. Eby played. Any logistical problems were quickly handled, and he was readily available to field any how-to-do-it questions.

The Levels of Use data are also interesting. Movement occurred from Level of Use 0 to Level of Use IVA, Routine, in the time interval provided, and the period ended with a complete absence of teachers at higher Levels of Use or at the Mechanical Level of Use. Apparently, teachers implemented the program to the "minimum" institutionalization, and there they stayed.

This outcome appears to be consistent with Knowles' philosophy, for she often pointed out there were many other areas of priority for the school and that the district was constantly "laying on" other changes that needed to be implemented. She strongly believed that teachers should not constantly be expected to do more and more and that she had a responsibility to "average out" some of these pressures so that teachers had a chance to teach their students.

SOME CRITICAL INCIDENTS AND TACTICS. The district plan was to deliver new supplies of math materials at the beginning of Year 2. These materials incorporated teachers' suggestions for revisions and cleaned up errors and omissions. Grove Street School placed its order for materials in midsummer. School opened in September, and the promised materials did not come. Knowles assured her teachers that the needed resources would arrive. When they did not she telephoned the president of the principals'

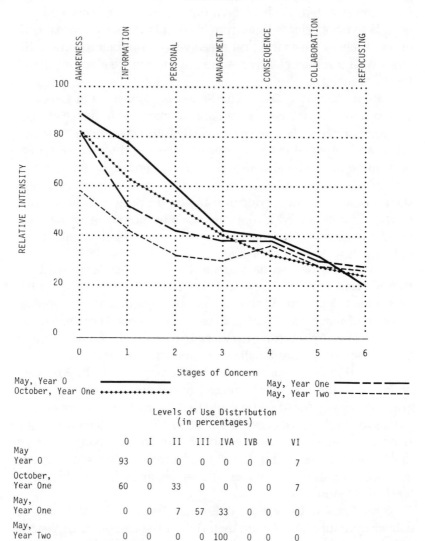

Figure 49
Summary of Stages of Concern and Levels of Use Data:
Grove School

May, Year 0 ————————   May, Year One — — — —
October, Year One •••••••••••••   May, Year Two — — — — — —

Levels of Use Distribution
(in percentages)

	0	I	II	III	IVA	IVB	V	VI
May Year 0	93	0	0	0	0	0	0	7
October, Year One	60	0	33	0	0	0	0	7
May, Year One	0	0	7	57	33	0	0	0
May, Year Two	0	0	0	0	100	0	0	0

association, who then telephoned the assistant superintendent. Knowles had established connections by serving on various districtwide committees. These interventions stimulated action.

In her review of the available materials, Knowles discovered that few of her teachers were using the game kits supplied for use in small group instruction. With Eby, she devised a series of long-term objectives—the kits were to be prepared for use and teachers were to be trained in how to use them. These objectives were addressed through shorter-term interventions. For instance, a three-session series of metric math workshops were planned, a consultant sought and scheduled, and other necessary arrangements made so that all teachers could attend and learn to use the metric games in the kit.

Another tactic used was for Eby to train one teacher per grade level in the use of the kit materials. This teacher then taught the other teachers at that grade level. Parents and permanent substitutes were organized to provide release time for the teachers to receive this training. Put simply, Knowles viewed the kits as important resources for the teachers' use of the math program, and she took action.

Parents were involved in another set of interventions. The kits were delivered still in need of cutting, coloring, laminating, and organizing by unit. Parents were scheduled for meetings, briefed on finishing the kits, and contributed their time and effort.

As these examples illustrate, Knowles's interventions typically focused on the first Game Plan Component—developing support and organizational arrangements. She provided space, personnel, materials, and other logistics for teachers' use of the new curriculum. She also provided training and in-service opportunities—Game Plan Component 2—evidenced by the planned interventions for learning to use the game kits in the classroom. In addition, Knowles supported districtwide in-service by reminding teachers of the dates, scheduling teachers to attend, and making sure that all teachers had every opportunity to go. At the same time, Knowles did not demonstrate much intervention activity in the other Game Plan Components, and Eby tended to focus on short-term consultation and reinforcement (GPC 3).

INSTITUTIONALIZATION AND BEYOND. As a result of the focus on game kits during Year 2, Knowles and Eby became satisfied that the kits had become a part of the teachers' mathematics classroom instruction. Knowles viewed the implementation of this set of materials as successful and as a concrete achievement by the teachers regarding the math curriculum.

At the outset of the third year, a small scandal broke in the local media regarding drug suppliers and several parents and children in Grove Street School. This event stimulated the school—teachers, students, and administrators—parents, and the school community to focus on substance abuse. Immediately, a school and community committee developed plans, selected and made arrangements for a drug abuse program, and implemented the program schoolwide with every person involved. This diversion precluded attention to refining PUM math. The innovation was assumed, without any real data or considerations, to have been institutionalized.

Pheasant Run School: Keeps Trying

> My teachers know their job. They are strong professionals and that's the way I treat them. They don't tell me how to do the principaling and I don't tell them how to teach. Behind the classroom door they handle the instruction. If they have problems, they know I'm ready to support them. We're all quite comfortable and satisfied with the way we work together to provide a safe and supportive environment for our children. (a conversation with C. T. Hancock)

PHEASANT RUN SCHOOL. Pheasant Run School is on the side of a hill in a well-to-do, suburban neighborhood. There is a significant proportion of Asian students, numerous expensive cars on the streets, and a preponderance of very expensive houses in the neighborhood. Pheasant Run School itself is approximately eight years old and has had the same principal since it opened. There are twenty five teachers, five hundred and fifty students, a principal, assistant principal, an array of teacher aides, and two to three parent volunteers in each classroom at all times. The school has a history of doing very well in academic areas. Students tend to "blow the top off" standardized achievement tests, and the school has been involved in an array of instructional programs and staffing arrangements.

THE PRINCIPAL. "C. T." Hancock is well known in the community and among the other district principals. His experience as a bass fisherman far exceed the normal-sized fish stories. He is seen as friendly, approachable, and a conversational philosopher with faculty and peers. He assumes a laissez-faire stance with faculty, allowing the capable and motivated teachers to assume leadership roles and be innovative. This same stance allows others to maintain the status quo, whether desirable or undesirable.

The principal tends to resist problem solving by default. He does not focus on problems or allocate time or energy in engaging them, unless confronted by public demand or by those perceived to be in a place of authority. When pressured to see that mandates from the central administration are carried out, he listens to those with expertise in the area, welcomes input, and makes an effort to see that his faculty cooperates and that the necessary changes are made. There is little indication, however, that Hancock follows through and monitors implementation. He feels he has "strong" teachers and that they know a great deal more about instruction than he does. He feels that to be "checking up on them" would undercut his support for them and make them doubt that he has confidence in them. A nondirective position and style are his norm; he tends to be more reactive than proactive when faced with problems. Hancock's outgoing, pleasant way of interacting with people is also characteristic of how he spends his time daily. It is quite typical to find him leaning over the office counter joking with a teacher or talking in a personable manner with a student. At other times, he will be in the faculty lounge having coffee with teachers or checking with his head secretary or assistant principal regarding some request that has just arrived from the central office or elsewhere.

THE SECOND CHANGE FACILITATOR. Leadership for the implementation of PUM did not develop within Pheasant Run School. In fact, Reg Wilson and Delores Gonzales determined from their initial visits that the teachers were not even getting the "word" about the imminent need to implement the PUM materials. As the Levels of Use data indicate, only 11 percent, or two of the teachers, had begun use of the PUM materials by October of Year 1. At this point, Wilson turned to the area superintendent and registered his concerns about the absence of PUM implementation at Pheasant Run School. The area superintendent then met with Hancock and advised him he was making a "career decision" if the PUM materials were not implemented in his school. At that time, Delores Gonzales decided to take on Pheasant Run School as her own personal "project." She, in effect, became the second change facilitator for that school.

CBAM Diagnostic Data. The diagnostic data for Pheasant Run School are summarized in figure 50. As can be seen, informational and personal concerns did drop over time with regard to implementation of the PUM materials, but, in general, the concerns profile is a "big W," with relatively intense informational and management concerns and a tail up on refocusing. During the years PUM was to be implemented, Hancock experimented with several staffing patterns, therefore, teachers' assignments were changing annually and they did not teach the same PUM materials each year. In addition, Hancock used a staffing pattern that allowed grade-level team leaders extra release time to work as "instructional supervisors" for the other teachers at their grade level. This pattern was a shift from the earlier teaming pattern, in which the primary grade teachers and the intermediate grade teachers worked in vertical teams with the same group of students moving across them. There were several other changes each year with regard to how the school was organized and what the instructional priorities were. This instability, in part, explains much of the "W-shape" of the concerns profile.

The Levels of Use data reflect the introduction of the PUM materials; however, the extended period of time teachers remained at the Mechanical Level of Use was disheartening. In spite of her efforts, Gonzales was not able to provide much coaching and facilitation for the teachers within the building. Some teachers were not receptive to her presence in the building and saw her as an evaluative invader, representing the authority of the central office. At other times, she would arrive to find that the schedule for the day had been changed and that her observations and meeting times were canceled. When she tried to pass information and materials through Mr. Hancock, there was a fifty-fifty chance they would be delayed or lost in transfer. The Stages of Concern and Levels of Use data thus reflect the school as it was seen by others—as succeeding in only a limited implementation of PUM. As would be expected, the Innovation Configurations data reflected minimal use of the materials as well.

Some Cricital Incidents and Tactics. Clearly, the pressure put upon the principal by the area superintendent was a critical intervention. The principal promptly returned to the school and announced that math was a priority and that all teachers should

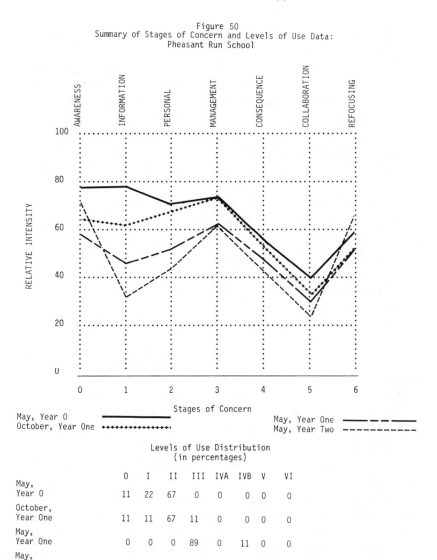

Figure 50
Summary of Stages of Concern and Levels of Use Data:
Pheasant Run School

	0	I	II	III	IVA	IVB	V	VI
May, Year 0	11	22	67	0	0	0	0	0
October, Year One	11	11	67	11	0	0	0	0
May, Year One	0	0	0	89	0	11	0	0
May, Year Two	13	0	0	63	25	0	0	0

begin using the PUM materials. Hancock was quick to point out, however, that his decision was not a personal one, rather it was being placed on him by the district—he was helpless to oppose it. He therefore respectfully requested that teachers put more emphasis on using the PUM math. These announcements were made in a hastily called staff meeting, several teachers being absent. No other record of Hancock's having referred to the use of PUM materials as a priority exists, and there is no indication of it having affected his day-to-day practice.

Another critical intervention was the mushroom that developed around the involvement of Delores Gonzales in the second CF role. Seemingly, no matter what she did nor how she tried to do it, teachers immediately interpreted her actions as being dictatorial about how they should approach their jobs. At other times, they would engage Gonzales in a "gripe session" about how the materials were poorly organized, how they would hurt the children, and how the students at Pheasant Run School had special needs not addressed by the materials. When Gonzales could get to the bottom of each complaint, however, she determined that the PUM materials were poorly understood and hardly used by Pheasant Run teachers. She was unable to come up with any approach that reduced the mushroom, and her "project" school had decreasing priority in subsequent years.

INSTITUTIONALIZATION AND REFINEMENT. There is not much to describe for this section. Mr. Hancock felt the PUM materials were implemented and that no further work needed to be done with them. During the third year of supposed implementation, parents in the community became very upset with what was happening in reading instruction for non-English-speaking students, and Hancock's energies were siphoned off responding to this new crisis. Thus, there were no documented activities associated with institutionalization and refinement of PUM math.

It would not have been possible to launch a game plan for refinement in Pheasant Run at this point anyway, since the CBAM definition of institutionalization (low SoC 1, 2, and 3; LoU IVA or above, with an acceptable configuration) had not been met. Refinement is not possible until use advances beyond the implementation phase, which clearly had not occurred at this school.

Summary

In the district and school examples that made up this case study, change was accomplished. It took time, involved many actors, and necessitated many interventions. There were schools in which the principal and/or the second CF/consigliere made a difference. The case descriptions could have included more detail, other mushrooms could have been described, and the experiences of individual teachers analyzed; however, the reader must know and be familiar with districts and schools like the ones described here.

What is the "moral" of the story? If the reader has responsibility for school improvement and facilitating the change process, we can suggest the following. Learn how to use the CBAM concepts and procedures, analyze your situation, and do something. Stages of Concern, Levels of Use, and Innovation Configurations can be useful for diagnosis, monitoring, and facilitation. Further, when change facilitators, policymakers, and evaluators use the same language, everyone is able to communicate and assess progress or lack thereof in the change process. Even though change is a highly complex, multivariate phenomenon, there are ways to think about, talk about, and influence the process.

A second suggestion focuses on contributing to the research base and to theory development. There is no shortage of innovations, but there is a shortage of usable theories, of reliable and valid concepts, and of procedures for understanding and facilitating the change process. Contributions are encouraged. Meanwhile, some promising topics that might contribute to further research and theory development are presented in the next chapter. Add your thoughts and questions to the list.

Chapter 11

So What Else is There To CBAM? Explorations Of Additional Theory, Practice, and Research

In this chapter, additional conceptual notions, subtle questions, and practical issues about facilitating change from a concerns-based perspective will be explored. Many intriguing questions can be asked of concerns theory and of the practice applications that can be considered from this perspective. For many of these questions, the answers we now have are not complete. The CBAM model does not address all the complexities of the change process. There are many additional directions to pursue and concepts to be discovered. In this chapter, we present a few of the next steps we see as possible, and we raise some enticing issues for others to consider also.

This short chapter starts with a review of the key dimensions of the Concerns-Based Adoption Model. This discussion will not just be a review though—new illustrations and descriptions will be used to interrelate the components that were separated as individual topics in each of the preceding chapters. The descriptions presented are an attempt to "push" the present limits of theory and our current understandings of the change process. This first section is followed by an exploration of more pragmatic and operational issues. Fittingly, some proposals for a research agenda are placed at the end.

Further Thoughts of a Theoretical Nature

Change is a Process, Not an Event

That change takes time has been recognized for several decades by theoreticians; philosophers have known it throughout the ages. The ancient Chinese curse, "May you live in a time of change," summarizes both the expectation that change takes time and that there is inherent stress for persons involved in it. Two keys to understanding change are that it is a process and therefore has a time dimension, and that there is a personal side to it.

Much recent research and theory has been devoted to identifying mileposts and other ways of measuring the time dimension of change. One of the most popular and successful approaches has been to describe the various phases that occur during the change process. A typical set of these phases is defined in figure 51. Note that these phases use the innovation as the frame of reference rather than the users or goals. What is happening to the innovation is the basis of phase differentiation. Some of these phases have received more concentrated emphasis and study, particularly the development, diffusion, and adoption phases. Other phases, such as institutionalization and refinement, have yet to be fully recognized and developed in the literature.

Earlier studies by rural sociologists concentrated heavily on the adoption and diffusion phases. There have been some instructive diffusion studies in education (e.g., Mort 1953; House 1974) as well. Development was the focus in the 1960s, the obvious example being the heavy federal investment in systematic curriculum development. One of the most fascinating fallacies of the development emphasis in the 1960s was the suggestion that one could develop a "teacher proof" curriculum. It was assumed that the curriculum would be so up-to-date, so well field tested, and so appropriate (having been based on learning theory) that teachers could just plug it in and use it. As was discovered by many, and as was documented in the unfortunately neglected study of Gallagher (1967), teachers used these "teacher proof" materials in surprisingly varied ways. The concept of Innovation Configurations could have been put to good use if it has existed at that time.

In the 1970s, implementation was brought to center stage. The Levels of Use work (Hall and Loucks 1977), the classic syn-

Figure 51
Phases of the Change Process
(when the innovation is the frame of reference)

Research:
> The findings of quantitative and qualitative studies lead to the suggestion that certain previously unidentified or underutilized practices or materials will be more effective.

Development:
> New approaches or materials are created, packaged and evaluated to achieve a particular objective.

Diffusion:
> The natural spread of awareness and use of an innovation across a social system.

Dissemination:
> The deliberate marketing of an innovation and encouragement of its adoption.

Adoption:
> The decision making process or conversely the decision point that leads to selection of an innovation and commitment to implementation.

Implementation:
> The initial and early use of an innovation involving negotiation between the user system and the innovation to arrive at an amicable match.

Institutionalization:
> The incorporation of routine use in a state of equilibrium.

Refinement:
> Fine tuning of innovation use to maximize outcomes in the local setting.

Abandonment:
> Discontinuance of use.

thesis by Fullan and Pomfret (1977), and the Rand Change Agent Study (Rand Study 1974–1978, vols. 1–8) all discussed implementation. The Rand Change Agent Study suggested that "mutual adaptation" was vital. For successful change, the innovation needed to be adapted to the local setting, and the local setting needed to be adapted to match the innovation. This premise was questioned by

Datta (1980), who suggested that the finding was a consequence of which innovations were studied and not a matter of mutual adaptation being an inherent part of all change processes.

By the end of the 1970s, the emphasis in curriculum development had shifted from national development to local problem solving. Federal policy, as reflected in the Joint Dissemination Review Panel and the National Diffusion Network, supported cottage industries by individual teachers and schools, who developed and validated their own programs. Studies of the NDN, including the DESSI studies conducted by Crandall and associates (1982) and the earlier Emrick and Peterson (1978) study, indicated that this approach can work too.

Apparently, one emphasis for the last decade of the twentieth century will be on the institutionalization phase, although accountability mandates may drive attention back toward the development of new solutions. Regardless of the orientation of policymakers and researchers, though, it is clear that school change is continuing through the phases cited in figure 51 and that it can succeed or fail at any of these points. The people involved is what makes the difference in particular initiatives—the style of the change facilitators, the interventions they make, and the characteristics of the teachers as users and nonusers. Regardless of the source of the innovation and the intervention game plan, change process participants will experience Stages of Concern and Levels of Use, and there will be variations in Innovation Configurations; additionally, each situation will have its own characteristics and critical incidents.

The Change Process When Viewed from the Users Perspective

The CBAM model emphasizes change as a process, and it includes a set of dimensions for describing the personal side of change. One key dimension is the Stages of Concern about an innovation (SoC). The Concerns-Based Adoption Model is significantly more than Stages of Concern, however. SoC is only one of three diagnostic dimensions that have been the subject of extensive research and application. The three diagnostic dimensions are independent of each other, but in combination, they can inform the policymaker, evaluator, and practicing change facilitator about their client's status in a particular change process and can provide clues for planned intervention. The three diagnostic dimensions are designed to answer three different questions:

1. How do you feel about it?
2. Are you using it?
3. What is IT?

Until recently, the status of individuals in the change process was not systematically conceptualized. Success in making a change was typically summarized in the form of declarative statements made by principals and others—teachers were using the program because they had been through a training experience or because the materials had been delivered to classrooms. With these three questions, however, it is possible to more carefully and systematically assess the state of change for individuals and an organization as a whole.

One advantage of using Stages of Concern, Levels of Use, and Innovation Configurations (in other words, of answering the three questions) is that teachers and others can be assessed with regard to these three dimensions at any point throughout all the phases of change. Consequently, it is possible to get standardized, individualized data that can be aggregated and used to facilitate, monitor, plan, and communicate about a change process. Another strength of these diagnostic variables is that two of them are "innovation free." Stages of Concern and Levels of Use are generic scales; they are not tied to particular innovations. A person at a Mechanical Level of Use for any innovation is always described as LoU III, Mechanical use. The same is true for the concept of Stages of Concern. With these generic scales, innovations, sites, and change efforts can be contrasted and compared using the same measurement procedures.

The Innovation Configurations concept is in part generic and, in part, innovation specific. The uniqueness and special emphasis of a particular innovation can be addressed through the component and variation descriptions. At the same time, the essential and related components and component variations can be described for different innovations. Although particular components will be unique to particular innovations, it is still possible to use the latter components and component variations to develop cross-innovation and cross-site analysis schemes when desired.

The important point is that these three diagnostic dimensions provide a way to assess movement or nonmovement in a change process across time. They provide standardized and generalized scales for understanding and communicating the rate of movement in a change process, and they can guide the planning of interventions needed to attain implementation success.

Arousal and Resolution of Concerns

Arousing and resolving concerns is a complex dynamic that is little understood. Proposing interventions to address aroused concerns (e.g., how-to-do-it help for teachers with intense management concerns) is relatively easy. It is much more difficult to characterize the effects of the interventions on the arousal and resolution of concerns.

From a theoretical point of view, a number of critical questions can be explored. For example, what are the critical factors that lead to the arousal of particular Stages of Concern and what are the critical factors that lead to the resolution of Stages of Concern? Are these factors the same regardless of the Stage of Concern? Fuller (1973) hypothesized that affective experiences are needed to arouse concerns and that cognitive experiences are related to concerns resolution. Even this picture becomes more complex, however, when one thinks about the internal, personal dynamics of concerns. For example, Fuller suggested that "resolution of concerns seems to be important not only so students can develop more mature concerns, but to prevent their slipping back to less mature concerns" (p. 11). If, for example, task concerns remain for an extended period of time, self concerns may become intense because of the continued inability to resolve the task concerns. Absence of interventions, then, may be associated with moving backward. This point may be particularly important in relation to institutionalization. If self and task concerns are not resolved, the innovation will not be permanent, at least, not in its present configuration.

A related issue has to do with the awareness of concerns. Awareness of particular concerns can be visualized with the use of a matrix (adapted from Fuller 1973).

TEACHER

		KNOWN TO TEACHER	UNKNOWN TO TEACHER
	KNOWN TO CF	PUBLIC	INCONGRUENT
CHANGE FACILITATOR			
	UNKNOWN TO CF	PRIVATE	UNCONSCIOUS

The skilled change facilitator is sensitive to the different cells in this matrix. Frequently, a "public" concern can become the basis of open and common understanding between the individual and a facilitator, although the intervention will still depend upon which Stage(s) of Concern is aroused. For example, if both parties recognize the client has intense personal concerns, some open discussion of concerns might be appropriate, but to suggest casually that the concerns will go away with time is likely to have effects similar to those produced by informing one's teenage son that he is simply going through a phase. This evasive statement is not what the client wants to hear.

A more problematical cell for the change facilitator is the one wherein incongruent concerns are found. These concerns are those that the facilitator perceives but that the client does not recognize. Careful thought is necessary before intervening in these cases. Quite often, the effective facilitator can describe and interpret his/her observations and perceptions of the client in ways that crystalize the concerns for the client. If so, they can then be dealt with openly.

Similar kinds of questions can be raised regarding Levels of Use. For example, must a person move through each of the levels sequentially, or can levels be skipped? Secondary analysis of data from our studies indicate that if use continues, then the sequence of steps is fairly sequential from Levels of Use 0, Nonuse, to Level

of Use IVA, Routine. At that point, a number of different branching options are possible. These branches include continuing use
of the innovation at a Level of Use IVA, Routine, moving to a Level
of Use IVB, Refinement or moving through a cycle of IVA-IVB-III-
IVA (in which refinements are added that trigger a return to
mechanical use and then, in time, back to routine use again). Of
course, it is quite conceivable that, with some innovations and
under certain conditions, a person will move away from use
altogether. A related point, alluded to previously, is that if LoU III,
Mechanical, Use problems are not resolved in time, it is highly
likely that users will mutate or abandon the innovation, since LoU
III Mechanical use is not a very comfortable and secure place
from which to operate continually.

Relationships Between SoC, LoU, and IC

Interactive questions can be explored also, such as: What is
the relationship between Stages of Concern and Levels of Use? Do
concerns and use move parallel to each other? Does one lead to
the other, and does it matter? How do each relate to the Innovation Configurations that are and are not used? In figure 52, some
possible relationships between Stages of Concern and levels of
Use are charted. At the simplest level, one would expect a linear
relationship between Levels of Use and Stages of Concern illustrated with line A in figure 52. With this relationship, as levels
of Use increase, so do Stages of Concern, with the most intense
concern being in a one-to-one correspondence with the parallel
Level of Use. Thus, a person at a Mechanical Level of Use would
be expected to have high Stage 3 management concerns. A person
with Stage 4 Consequence concerns would be expected to be at
LoU IVB, Refinement, and so forth.

But what happens when the data are examined? The dashed
lines marked B in figure 52 illustrate this analysis. One-to-one correspondence is most true at the ends of the dimensions. Persons
at LoU 0, I, and II have more intense self concerns, and persons at
levels of Use V and VI have more intense impact concerns. In a
statistical sense, it is possible to predict one from the other with
good accuracy; however, the closer one moves to Level of Use
IVA, the less accurate are the predictions. At a Level of Use IVA,
Routine, use, there is little likelihood of accurately predicting
what the most intense concerns will be, for a large variety of concerns profiles seem to be possible. Teachers at LoU IVA are

Figure 52
Possible Relationships between Stages of Concern and Levels of Use

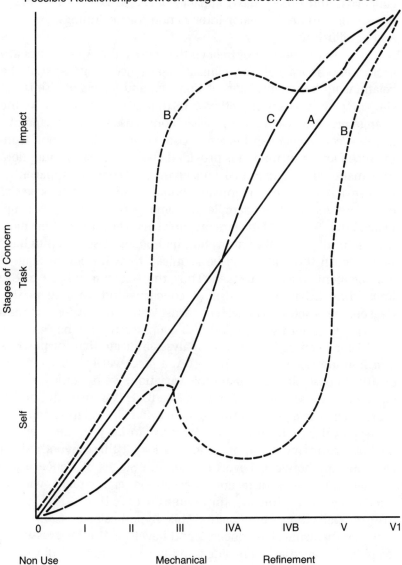

A───────Logical prediction

B─ ─ ─ ─ ─Boundaries for statistical prediction of individuals using group data

C━ ━ ━ ━Hypothesized relationship based on field observations

regularly found with few concerns, others still have task or self concerns, and others have impact concerns. LoU IVA in many ways seems to be the major intersection for beginnings, endings, and equilibrium.

At present, we do not believe that either the A or B lines are accurate. Theoretical and clinical experiences suggest that the relationship between Stages of Concern and Levels of Use is not simple. Our current hypothesis is that at early points in the change process, use tends to "drive" concerns, and at later points, aroused concerns push Levels of Use. When an innovation is introduced and information is provided about its possible adoption, informational and personal concerns are aroused. Apparently, the use activities (i.e., the introduction of information) arouse self concerns. As another example, in some of our field work it appeared that Stage 3 Management concerns were not at their most intense until use of the innovation had begun. Users had to have their feet in the water and be required to swim before Stage 3 Management concerns peaked. Thus, the Mechanical Level of Use apparently drives the arousal of concerns and, to a surprising degree, the resolution of self concerns. With more experience and knowledge about use, self and task concerns tend to be resolved.

As has been described, our analyses indicate that for persons at a Routine Level of Use, LoU IVA, a large variety of concerns profiles is possible. To explain this variation, we hypothesize that movement toward higher Levels of Use (LoU IVB through LoU VI) is driven by the arousal of impact concerns. This relationship may in part explain why interventions need to be very different to facilitate refinement use of an innovation. If these hypothesized relationships between Levels of Use and Stages of Concern are verified then very different intervention game plans will be necessary for initial implementation than for post-institutionalization refinement. This hypothesized relationship between the arousal of concerns and Levels of Use progression is graphically represented by line C in figure 52. At early points, use leads to concerns arousal. As crossover occurs at LoU IVA, the arousal of impact concerns triggers activities characteristic of higher Levels of Use.

The picture is further enriched when the third diagnostic dimension, Innovation Configurations, is included. In the few studies where sufficient data were available, some configurations appeared to be more frequently found in association with particular Levels of Use (Reidy and Hord 1979). In one study (Pedulla and Reidy 1980), 86 percent of the more "casual" or less rigorous innovation configurations were found with teachers at a Mechanical Level of Use, while more rigorous configurations were only found with teachers at Levels of Use IVA or higher. In conclusion, the three CBAM diagnostic dimensions, in combination, provide a set of tools that can be very useful in developing rich descriptions of the personal side of change and the operational use of the innovation at all points throughout the change process. To understand the change process from the point of view of the individual requires understanding of what is occurring personally as well as understanding the inherent chracteristics of a particular innovation and its use.

The Larger CBAM Picture

This extensive discussion of the dynamics and relationships of the three diagnostic dimensions should not undermine the importance of the context in which the change process is occurring, of the characteristics of change facilitators, nor of the relation of interventions to concerns-based diagnoses. As is reflected in the CBAM model (figure 53), change facilitators need to probe consistently to collect diagnostic information within the user system context and to plan for and deliver interventions related to the diagnostic base. The process is an ongoing, systemic, and adaptive one, wherein new diagnostic information is regularly collected through formal and informal means and the intervention behaviors of the change facilitators are adjusted accordingly.

There are general classes of interventions that have been most relevant for addressing particular diagnostic profiles; however, the interventions can not be used in a cookbook fashion. Replacing the diagnostic genius of the more effective change facilitator with some sort of calculator or computerized prescriptive process will never be possible. Rather, change facilitators must become more skilled in understanding the dynamics of the Stages of Concern, and Levels of Use and the requirements and potential of a particular innovation, and in bringing this knowledge to bear when planning and delivering needed in-

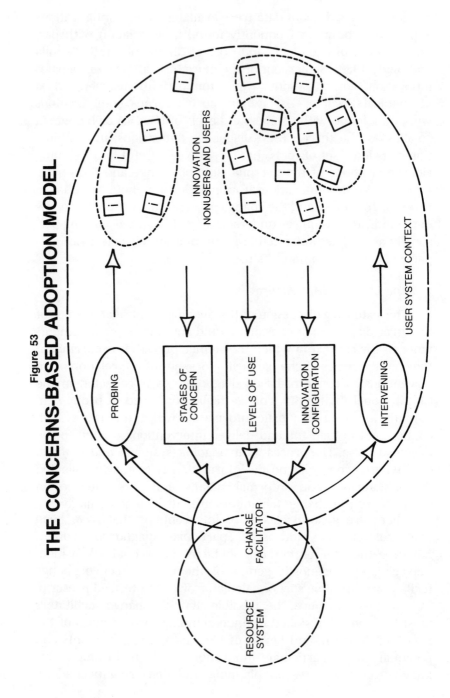

Figure 53
THE CONCERNS-BASED ADOPTION MODEL

terventions. The sample interventions provided in Appendix B may be of further guidance to change facilitators when thinking about possible interventions for particulr concerns. Similar lists can be created for Levels of Use and for components of particular innovations. Still, the actual intervention used at any moment in time will have to be tailored to the concerns-based diagnosis, the particular context, and the style of the facilitator.

Some Practical Considerations

In this section some "how-to-do-it" questions are discussed, and additional issues related to practice are addressed.

Monitoring and Evaluating the Change Process

Throughout this book, procedures and techniques for monitoring the change process have been proposed. Some of these techniques are informal and clinical in orientation and can be used by change facilitators on a day-to-day basis. Other techniques are more rigorous and more suitable for research and evaluation studies.

One important use of data systematically collected by these techniques is in preparing progress reports that can be understood by program directors, school boards, and other policy groups (for examples, see Roecks and Andrews [1980] and Roecks and Noonan [1981]). With the regular collection of Stages of Concern, Levels of Use, and Innovation Configurations data, it is possible to provide tangible mileposts that policy groups can use to judge and plan progress. Benchmarks of this type allow these individuals to acknowledge that change is a process and also to attend to needs for accountability. Decision makers can see progress without having to make final judgments about success, and decision making can center on developing the needed support and resources to further advance the change process. At subsequent reporting points, further change, or lack thereof, can be related to the supporting activities that have taken place in the interim.

Frequently, we are asked how often CBAM diagnostic data should be collected and when they should first be collected. There is no better time than right now to collect the first round of diagnostic data. The CBAM concepts apply to preadoption decisions as well as to all other decision making during the change process—from before inception of an innovation to long after institutionalization. Data collected at the very beginning can serve as a base line against which comparisons of future data can be made. Base line data are useful when making a case for decision makers. The latter can see where the change process is beginning and can make reasoned decisions between needs and requests for resources.

One monitoring approach is to collect Stages of Concern, Levels of Use, and Innovation Configurations data for the current practice, before an innovation is identified and developed. The CBAM data on the "old" way can be used to assess perceptions and potential readiness for the "new" innovation. In many instances, this early assessment has led to the discovery that key IC component variations of an innovation were already in use. When such use is observed, it is possible to decrease the perception that the "new" innovation is drastically different by grounding the new innovation into present practice. In many cases, this approach reduces the potential for high personal concerns and tailing up on refocusing concerns, often a problem when innovations are introduced.

How often should CBAM diagnostic data be collected? During the first year of implementation, it is probably wise to collect data early in the school year and once again late in the year. In subsequent years, once a year may be sufficient. In our research studies, SoC, LoU, and IC are normally assessed twice yearly. In some instances, the data have been systematically collected as frequently as three times a year. More frequent data collection has not led to problems with reliability and validity; however, teachers have become rather frustrated with answering "the same question over and over." A combination of formal research data collection twice a year with more frequent use of the open-ended and clinical procedures seems to work best.

These diagnostic variables can be assessed during implementation and early institutionalization, as has already been illustrated. The process can also be done with programs that have long been in place. Frequently, collecting these data has led to new awareness and interest in the innovation; and quite often, central office personnel are surprised at how much remains (or more frequently, how little remains) of the innovation as it was originally conceived. "Drastic mutations" are made in the innovation as it continues over long periods of use, and key components are glossed over. By collecting data over extended periods and monitoring implementation, it is possible to focus staff development and to stimulate renewal when and where excessive slips or new needs are identified.

Criteria for Success

An area of increasing interest is in selecting criteria to judge the success of change efforts. In earlier times, criteria were simpler. Evaluations of use were based on the act of purchasing materials and on testimonies by central office personnel that the innovation was being used. In more recent times, criteria for judging success have shifted to student outcomes. This process can be problematic if prior determination is not made about innovation implementation. As we noted when we described Levels of Use (chapter 4), probably one of the main reasons evaluation reports in the 1960s and 1970s so frequently indicated "no signiicant differences" between the old and the new program was the failure of the evaluators to first document implementation. It is rather difficult to associate student outcomes with a program if the program has been only partially implemented or not implemented at all.

From the change process point of view, it is essential to document that implementation of the innovation has occurred prior to instituting other criteria for judging success. There is no problem with selecting other variables, such as student outcomes, teacher happiness, student attendance, or whatever, as criteria for measuring innovation success or effectiveness; however, if implementation is not first documented, then interpreting any outcome data is extremely risky.

As was described in chapter 8, one way to document innovation implementation is through a set of effectiveness criteria (Huling, Hall, Hord, and Rutherford 1983). In this definition, implementation success is a function of Stages of Concern, Levels of Use, and Innovation Configurations. The more *effective* change process occurs when users more quickly and easily resolve self and task concerns, implement the innovation to LoU IVA or higher, and use more acceptable configurations of the innovation. Less successful implementation efforts take longer to achieve these ends and do so at lower levels.

Careful attention should be given to the criteria selected and the judgments made. In this multivariate world, changing the criteria changes the outcomes and, therefore, the judgments that result. For example, as reported in chapter 8, when the criterion of psychological climate (James and Jones 1974; Hall and Griffin 1982) was used, a rank ordering of the effectiveness of principals' change facilitator styles was different from the order derived from the criterion of implementation success. The manager and initiator styles reverse in the ranking, although they are still clustered closely together. The implications, therefore, for making judgments about "principal effectiveness" could be quite different, depending on which criterion is used.

Judging effectiveness becomes even more complex when student outcomes are the criterion variables. As pointed out in chapter 4, Loucks (1975) found that different innovations had different relationships between student outcomes and Levels of Use. For individualized instruction in reading, there tended to be a linear relationship between Levels of Use and student achievement. Teachers who were using individualized reading at higher Levels of Use had students with higher achievement scores. However, the same teachers and students did not produce the same results in individualized instruction in mathematics. In this case, there was a curvilinear relationship, with teachers at the Mechanical level of Use being associated with higher student outcomes. More research is needed in this area before broad-based conclusions can be stated, but this example is another illustration of the difficulties and risks in making judgments about relationships between particular predictive factors, such as student outcomes, and particular innovations or teacher or principal characteristics.

Characteristics of the Innovation

With few exceptions in this book, the assumption has been that "good" innovations were being implemented. What happens during the change process whan a "bad" innovation is being implemented? Most likely, in such cases the Stages of Concern, Levels of Use, and Innovation Configurations data will be quite different. The first issue here, however, has to do with defining a "bad" innovation. Perhaps the best method for addressing this question is to return to earlier work by Rogers and Shoemaker (1971) in which they describe five perceived attributes of innovations (relative advantage, observability, trialability, complexity, and compatibility). Note that their emphasis is placed on *perceived* characteristics. This approach is helpful in interpreting the good/bad phenomena. In many instances, innovations are probably perceived as being good or bad regardless of their actual effects on reality, especially in the educational environment. It is quite unlikely that any education innovation developer would deliberately create a malicious innovation; rather, there probably are perceptual problems with the innovation, the developer, the facilitator, or the intervention game plan. In some cases, the innovation may not fit the context or is being implemented for the wrong reasons. These cases will be perceived in a general sense as bad innovations too.

When an innovation is perceived as bad, indications of such will be manifested in the Stages of Concern data. At the beginning of implementation, the general pattern will be that of the nonuser, but there will be a tendency toward higher Stage 2 Personal concerns and possibly a tailing up on Stage 6 Refocusing. Stage 1 Informational concerns will typically be lower than the Stage 2 Personal concerns. One implication of this profile is that descriptive information about the innovation will not be accurately heard nor understood. The personal concerns will act as a filter that distorts the intent and meaning of the information provided.

For example, in one study, Emrick and Peterson (1978) found that teachers with concerns profiles that were not positively disposed toward an innovation had students with lower achievement than did teachers with more positive concerns profiles. This finding certainly points to the seriousness of attending to self and task concerns as well as to the potential for creating self-fulfilling prophesies. If the innovation is perceived as inappropriate, it is likely to be used with less commitment.

Related scenarios can be predicted for Levels of Use and Innovation Configurations data when an innovation is inappropriate for some reason. Levels of Use will not progress as rapidly. There have been indications in some studies that movement from Level of Use I to Level of Use II, and from Level of Use II to Level of Use III is not as rapid. A longer period of time will be spent at the Mechanical Level of Use. Innovation Configurations data will likely reflect more drastic mutations and alterations of the innovation and less use of the ideal components and variations.

The concerns-based diagnostic dimensions become useful again in this context. With data, it is possible to determine the intensity of personal concerns, and regular monitoring indicates when Levels of Use and Innovation Configurations are not progressing at expected rates. Change facilitators can then adjust their interventions, shift their expectation of rate of implementation, address the personal concerns, and strive to change perceptions with regard to the innovation and its use.

The Role of Context

One area of the Concerns-Based Adoption Model that has not been systematically addressed in this volume regards context. A great deal of speculation and work has been done in the area of context by others (e.g., James and Jones 1974, 1979; Brophy and Evertson 1978), and it is constantly nominated as an issue by policymakers, theorists, researchers, and practitioners. We and our colleagues acknowledge its importance but have tended to place priority for research in other areas.

One reason for not addressing context in more detail has to do with our position that context does not have to be *the* driving force. As we have observed principals and other change facilitators, we have come to the opinion that, rather than context determining the effectiveness of change facilitators, some change facilitators are skilled at interpreting context and functioning effectively in spite of it. In other words, some change facilitators appear to be more effective in accomplishing their objectives than others within a similar context. How do they do this? As you might guess, the more effective individuals have many of the attributes and skills of the manager and initiator style change facilitators. Rather than being victims of context, they are more apt to become users of the context, whatever it may be.

It is instructive to watch skilled change facilitators, whether they are high school principals in inner-city Philadelphia or elementary school principals in a barrio in Los Angeles. Although these contexts are such that others bemoan their inability to get anything done, these principals have made meaningful differences for students, teachers, and the community. Their effects show up in implementation success as well as in scores on standardized achievement tests. Others in the same context accomplish little. Ironically, district office administrators seem to see the more effective principals as the exception and accept as understandable the pronouncements of those in less successful schools that the context is the problem. Clearly, much more needs to be done in systematic research and theory development around context.

Additional work is also needed in the area of psychological climate, which, in spite of its long history of research in education, has not yielded consistent findings (James and Jones 1974; Jones, James et al. 1979). The measures tend to lack reliability and estimates of validity. The findings appear to be inconsistent; the concepts appear to be ill defined and, in too many cases, undefined. The instruments do not appear to measure the variables that are suggested, and the findings do not seem to add up. At some point, definitions and frameworks for understanding context will be better developed. In the meantime, it appears that some change facilitators within a given context prove themselves to be more effective than do other change facilitators. The "how and why" of this difference needs much closer examination.

The Change Facilitator Team

The importance of the roles, dimensions, and dynamics of the change facilitator team cannot be overemphasized. It is typically assumed that the principal is *the* key to successful school improvement. The change facilitator styles research supports this assumption and also reveals the role of the second change facilitator/consigliere and that of third and perhaps fourth change facilitators. This change facilitator team is the key to successful school improvement.

Regardless of the style of the principal, additional change facilitators in schools are needed. How these change facilitators work together and in combination, and how they address the various tasks, functions, and dimensions of the intervention game plan, is critical. Careful attention to the team's identification, training, and development will contribute significantly to how well these individuals work together. With different innovations, the second and third change facilitators are likely to be different persons, which provides opportunities for many members of a staff to participate in leadership roles.

The principal is not always the first change facilitator. Frequently, someone else in the school or in the district serves in this role. This phenomenon leads to an additional question: How does the role of the principal change as he or she shifts attention from one innovation to another innovation? We do not know the answer to this question. At some point, systematic study of how the principal functions in different situations and whether or not his or her style is maintained must be done.

When selecting persons to be change facilitators, the characteristics of people and the composite CF team should be thought out. Once they are selected, all facilitators should have training in change facilitation as well as advanced knowledge in the use of the innovation. To help in developing CF teams, we and our colleagues have begun to think about the characteristics of each team member. The characteristics and functions that appear to be optimal for each role are summarized in figures 54 and 55. Ideally, the first CF would represent all the descriptors listed under that role, and the same would be true for the second and third CF roles. An additional factor is the interactive nature of CF teams. The different CFs must complement each other so that the team in its totality covers all the necessary functions. If one person does not have certain characteristics or do certain things, then ideally someone else on the team will do these things. It is our best guess that, for optimal change process success, certain characteristics and functions will be associated with each CF role as outlined in figures 54 and 55.

Figure 54
Optimal Charactistics of Successful Change Facilitating Teams for School-Wide Change

Innovation Related Characteristics	First CF (principal)	Second CF (necessary)	Third CF (optional)	External CF's
Primary Assignment	Not in classroom.	In school, but not in classroom with special CF role.	In classroom	External to school.
Time Allocation	Spends much time.	Has as major part of job.	Spends small part of their time on CF role.	Full time or part time.
Authority	Has formal authority in line or staff position.	Has less authority than first CF.	Little or no formal authority.	Heavy responsibility with varying authority.
Orientation	Sees use of innovation as being important.	Truly believes that the innovation is good and should be used.	Is enthusiastic but not blind to the less practical parts.	Concerned about overall picture.
Role	Push for use, leads CF team.	Day-to-day coach, helper.	Supportive, backup to 1st and 2nd CF, opinion leader among user colleagues.	Fills in on key functions.
Innovation Expertise	Knolwegeable of and skilled in manipulating resources to support the innovation.	Expert in technical details of innovation use.	Knowledgeable of details in use and sensitive to local conditions that affect use.	Detail or general.

Figure 54 (Cont'd)
Optimal Charactistics of Successful Change Facilitating
Teams for School-Wide Change

Innovation Related Characteristics	First CF (principal)	Second CF (necessary)	Third CF (optional)	External CF's
Time Perspective and Tone	Impatient to have results so can get on to other things.	Has patience to do day-to-day problem-solving, hand-holding, cajoling and coaching.	Calm and comfortable about innovation use; willing to take time to help others.	Longer term with desire for major success.
Recognition	Success comes from having implementation and successful outcomes.	More internally oriented, not so interested in extra recognition or glory, but wants ongoing support to do what s/he believes has to be done to help users.	Gets recognition from their regular role, but willing to help out when asked.	Implementation and outcomes are important.
Relationship Between Team Members	Leads, listens, decides.	Communicates, shares, supports.	Listens, suggests, follows through.	Drops in and out.
Team Dynamics	Ongoing cross member exchange, mutual support and complementarity of emphases, characteristics and functions.			

The Concerns-Based Approach

One last point for the practical section of this chapter. An implicit set of assumptions about people and change undergirds the CBAM model and the research described in this book. We have a definite belief in the worth of people and in their potential to grow. Stages of Concern and Levels of Use represent pathways people move through as they develop. Our organizations and change processes can achieve their nomothetic goals and still

Figure 55
The Importance of Who Does What
For Successful Change

Change Facilitating Team Members

	First CF (principal)	Second CF	Third CF	External CFs
C.F. FUNCTIONS				
1. Sanctioning continued back up	xxxx	xx		xx
2. Providing resources	xxx	xx		x
3. Technical coaching	x	xx	x	x
4. Monitoring/ follow up	xx	xx	x	
5. Training	x	x		xx
6. Reinforcing	xx	xxx	x	x
7. Pushing	xx	xx	x	x
8. Telling others	xx	x		x
9. Approving adaptations	xx	x		x

Legend:

x, xx, xxx, xxxx = Degree of importance

acknowledge the humanness of the participants, if the personal side of change is attended to. In fact, we see this idiographic side as being just as important to successful change as is attendance to the technology and processes of the innovation. The human side includes the facilitators as participants as well as the innovation users.

For facilitators, the concerns-based approach means understanding the clients' point of view (e.g., teachers' concerns). Intervening solely from the point of view of the change facilitator is not appropriate from a concerns-based perspective. There are many examples of change facilitators—not only principals and central office personnel but managers in industry and elsewhere—making inappropriate interventions by basing them solely on their own points of view. The facilitator's point of view is important, but interventions should be matched to the present state of the client, the objective being a shared image of growth and increased quality of practice. One reason change is often so difficult is that the targets of interventions are not understood or addressed; rather, interventions are made based on what the change facilitator thinks *should be* happening. Without attendance to the individuals involved in the process, it is difficult to imagine how change can be successful.

Some Suggestions for Research

The CBAM research base is accumulating, and it provides some suggestions on how to facilitate change more effectively. The various research studies we and others have done have begun to clarify the role change facilitators can play and some of the aspects of interventions that make a difference. The picture is not at all complete, however, especially given the complexity of the change process. In past CBAM research, there has been heavy emphasis on understanding the personal side of change for nonusers, users, and change facilitators. In the remaining pages of this chapter, speculations about some of the implications of that work and what they mean for future research and theory development are described. Hopefully, some of these issues will be addressed in the near future.

CHANGING CF STYLE. There is no known, two-day workshop that will bring about a change in style, although changes in individual behaviors are clearly possible and immediately achievable. The question of whether or not principals and other change facilitators can change their style is more complex. We do not believe such a change is easily done. Change facilitator style seems to be more stable and enduring. Even in different situations, the "way" we do things is similar and usually predictable by colleagues. If style were more flexible, predictions would not be as accurate. We do not mean to suggest that our leadership behaviors are always the same. Individual behaviors will likely be different, but the gestalt of the overall style will still be there.

A related question regards whether principals and other change facilitators maintain the same change facilitator style across innovations. Do they systematically use one particular change facilitator style with one innovation and a different change facilitator style when working with a different change facilitating team or a different innovation? Again, we do not think so, although a formal study has not been done.

There is some indication that change facilitator styles can be depressed. For example, it seems reasonable to predict that an initiator style principal who reports to an area superintendent of the responder style could be depressed into a manager or perhaps even a responder as a result of inconsistent signals and negative feedback. It is more difficult to imagine the conditions under which a responder style principal can be "pushed" to use the manager style or the initiator style, assuming, of course, that movement in that direction is desirable (also an interesting question for study). Whether or how change facilitator styles are amenable and adaptable is a highly complex question and a needed area of research.

CRITICAL INTERVENTIONS. In most change processes, a small number of interventions apparently carry extra weight and, in some cases, make or break the effort. It should be possible to identify the characteristics and timing of these critical interventions. Perhaps there are ways to build into partially completed game plan maps specifications for these key interventions. They could be tied to the CBAM diagnostic variables, and their timing and characteristics anticipated. If successful, these "prescriptions" could be used in the future as training and coaching models or placed into computer simulations to help change facilitators plan and monitor the incident level.

CONCERNS DYNAMICS. Another area in need of systematic research is in understanding more about the dynamics of arousal and resolution of concerns. What are the characteristics of the interventions that lead to arousal? How are these different from interventions that aid resolution? How do arousal and resolution relate to Levels of Use, past experience, practice, intelligence, motivation, dogmatism, internality, and externality? One retarder in learning more in this area is that the nature of the questions requires longitudinal research designs. Unfortunately, these designs are more expensive in time and resources. Hopefully, at some time, there will be more support and opportunity to conduct longitudinal studies that focus directly on understanding the dynamics of arousal and resolution of concerns.

ELEMENTARY/SECONDARY SIMILARITIES/DIFFERENCES. In this book, descriptions of elementary and high school change processes have been blended. Clearly, there are some similarities, but there are some differences too. Research is needed to understand more about what similarities and differences occur between elementary and high school change. What about the dynamics and composition of change facilitator teams, the types of critical interventions, and the characteristics of innovations that are more or less easily implemented in elementary and high school settings? There also need to be studies in institutions of higher education where the organizational structures are again different. The concepts of Stages of Concern, Levels of Use, and Innovation Configurations exist in these settings. It even appears that deans can use the responder, manager, and initiator styles; yet, there is less clarity about the characteristics of successful change facilitating teams and how the change process unfolds in these settings—another promising area for research.

PERSONNEL CHANGES. What happens when there are changes in school leadership? Imagine what it is like when an initiator style principal follows a responder style principal, or when a manager style principal follows an initiator style principal. One can speculate about the different scenarios as these different style transitions occur; yet, there is no systematic study to date of what happens during these transitions. Again, longitudinal research designs will be needed. Given the emphasis on instructional leadership and the practice of moving leadership personnel for various reasons, more research-based information and recommendations should be developed about transitions in change facilitator styles and what they mean for school improvement and change process success.

DEVELOPMENTALISM AS A SHARED PARADIGM. Clearly, Stages of Concern and Levels of Use are in some ways learning models. The Levels of Use knowledge category and the acquiring information category are direct indicators of the accumulation of knowledge and the learning that occurs during a change process. The Stages of Concern dimension also has a learning characteristic (as an individual moves from self to task to impact concern focus). In the not too distant future, there should be a more systematic examination of the various developmental models of learning, the change process, lifelong growth, and so on. In time, a common set of stages and phases might be identified that relate to these phenomena. When this research and theory are aggregated, there will be greater understanding of how to work with adults and with children, and of how to facilitate not only the change process but teaching and learning as well.

One of the insights from the learning dynamic reflected in the Stages of Concern and Levels of Use work is that the change process is not one way. Clearly, people "regress," shift directions and emphases, and move back and forth across the dimensions. Understanding this movement is closely linked to the earlier suggested research on the arousal and resolution of concerns. When more is known about how to make the change process more successful, teaching and learning will be more successful too.

CBAM in Other Contexts. One of the most exciting aspects of CBAM work in recent years has been its application in the private sector. The change process in industry is very similar to what occurs in schools and colleges. Translating CBAM concepts and measures to the private sector has been easy, and in many instances personnel in the private sector have been quicker to use those concepts and procedures than have been those in the public sector.

The CBAM tools are being tested in a number of other contexts as well. For example, Kolb (1983) has applied Stages of Concern to the training of nurses, Barucky (1984) has tested Stages of Concern on the development of leadership in Air Force cadets and officers, and Jordon-Marsh (1984) has examined concerns about health behavior changes. CBAM concepts are being considered by diabetes health practitioners as a model for working with clients as they learn to manage their health needs (Hord and Huling-Austin, 1985), and the concepts have been used by one textbook publisher to create a national service department with a concerns-based sales and service orientation. Managers of new companies have been using CBAM strategies to manage and monitor geometric growth.

CBAM concepts and procedures have been tested in other countries too. The most extensive cross-national applications have been made by Vandenberghe in Belgium and Van Den Berg in the

Netherlands. They have translated the concepts into Flemish and replicated the verification studies (Van Den Berg and Vandenberghe 1981), coming up with nearly identical results. The concepts and procedures have been tested in Australia and several other countries, also with similar results. Apparently, the CBAM model is applicable to a wide range of innovations and contexts.

The reader is encouraged to continue studying the change process and to apply the concepts and procedures that have been described in this volume. We hope to continue our research and are most interested in corresponding with others who are conducting studies and experimenting with practice. In this way, we will find more effective and personalized means to facilitate the change process. We believe the concerns-based perspective can contribute successfully to the enterprise.

Appendix A
Certified Trainers—The CBAM Cadre International

Merv Bond, Curriculum Officer, Western Australia Dept. of Education, 151 Royal Street, East Perth, Western Australia 6154 AUSTRALIA.

Richard Brickley, RISE, 725 Caley, King of Prussia, PA 19406.

Madalyn Cooke, 4214 Tallwood, Austin, TX 78731.

Jim Cox, Anaheim Union High School District, 501 Crescent Way, Anaheim, CA 92803.

Leslie R. Eastcott, Director, Goulburn Campus, Riverina College of Advanced Education, McDermott Drive, Goulburn, N.S.W. 2580, AUSTRALIA.

Gene E. Hall, Department of Educational Leadership, College of Education, Norman Hall, University of Florida, Gainesville, FL 32611.

Shirley M. Hord, Senior Development Associate, Southwest Educational Development Laboratory, 211 E. Seventh Street, Austin, TX 78701.

Leslie Huling-Austin, 11804 Broad Oaks, Austin, TX 78759.

Bob James, Educational Curriculum and Instruction, College of Education, Texas A&M University, College Station, TX 77843-4232.

Jim Leary, Northland School Division, Box 1440, Peace River, Alberta T0H 2X0, CANADA.

Lucille Leisner, 7223 Minter Place, Takoma Park, MD 20912.

David Lidstrom, Iowa Department of Public Instruction, Grimes State Office Building, Des Moines, IA 50319.

Susan Loucks-Horsley, The NETWORK, 290 S. Main St., Andover, MA 01810.

James W. MacKay, Executive Assistant, Staff Development Services, Prince Edward Island Teachers' Federation, P.O. Box 6000, Charlottetown, P.E.I. C0A 8B4, CANADA.

Colin Marsh, School of Education, Murdoch University, Murdoch, Western Australia 6150, AUSTRALIA.

David Marsh, University of Southern California, 702 Philips Hall, Los Angeles, CA 90007.

Robin Matthews, Victoria College—Rusden Campus, 662 Blackburn Road, Clayton North, 3168, Victoria, AUSTRALIA.

Carolyn McNally, 31 Fernwood Drive, Guilford, CT 06437.

Merrill Meehan, Appalachia Educational Laboratory, P.O. Box 1348, Charleston, WV 25325.

Marge Melle, Jefferson County Public Schools, 1209 Quail St., Lakewood, CO 80215.

Jim Metzdorf, Jefferson County Public Schools, 1209 Quail St., Lakewood, CO 80215.

Joyce Murphy, Elizabeth's Landing, 1007 Cutler Harbour, Pasadena, MD 21122.

Beaulah W. Newlove, Consultant, 4100 Jackson Avenue, Austin, TX 78731.

Jeff Northfield, Faculty of Education, Monash University, Clayton, Victoria 3168, AUSTRALIA.

Raymond Pelland, 1142 Soloy St., Sudbury, Ontario, P3A 5M7, CANADA.

Cyril Poster, University of Bristol, School of Education, 35, Berkeley Square, Clifton, Bristol B58 1JA, UNITED KINGDOM.

Harold Pratt, Jefferson County Public Schools, 1209 Quail St., Lakewood, CO 80215.

Judith Richardson, Des Moines Technical High School, 1800 Grand Ave., Des Moines, IA 50309.

Richard Roberts, Department of Teacher Education, Western Kentucky University, Bowling Green, KY 42101.

William Rutherford, College of Education, The University of Texas at Austin, Austin, TX 78712-1288.

Hank Schaafsma, The Institute of Technical and Adult Education (ITATE), Sydney College of Advanced Education, P.O. Box K-12, Haymarket, N.S.W. 2000, AUSTRALIA.

Larry Schaefer, ACES/Mill Road School, 295 Mill Road, North Haven, CT 06473.

Suzane Stiegelbauer, 628 Christie #1 Toronto, Ontario, M6G 3E5, CANADA.

John C. Thurber, Palm Beach County Schools, 3323 Belvedere, West Palm Beach, FL 33402.

Carolyn Trohoski, Phoenixville Area School District, 1120 Gay Street, Phoenixville, PA 19460.

Roland Vandenberghe, Katholieke Universiteit Leuven, Dept. Didaktiek en Psycho-pedagogiek, Vesuliusstraat 2, B-3000 Leuven, BELGIUM.

Rudolph van den Berg, Catholic Pedagogic Centre, P.O. B. 482, 5201 AL 's-Hertogenbosch, NETHERLANDS.

Susan Williams, Eaton School, 34th & Lowell St., N.W. Washington, DC 20008.

Lee Wolf, Iowa Department of Public Instruction, Grimes State Office Building, Des Moines, IA 50319.

Appendix B
Example Interventions for Each Stage of Concern

Interventions, SoC 0. At this Stage of Concern, the types of interventions that may be appropriate certainly depend upon the context surrounding the individual and upon policies about whether or not use of the innovation is required or even desirable. The following interventions might be relevant:

a. Acknowledge that little concern about the innovation is legitimate and appropriate.

b. Share some information about the innovation in hopes of arousing some interest in it.

c. Tie the innovation to an area that the teacher is concerned about.

d. Decree that use of the innovation is required.

e. Encourage the person to talk with others about the innovation.

Interventions, SoC 1. For pesons with high informational concerns, interventions should be designed to provide very general descriptive information. The following types of interventions might be effective:

a. Share general descriptive information about the innovation through conversation, mailed brochures, or short media presentation.

b. Provide information contrasting what the individual is presently doing with what use of the innovation would entail.

c. Provide an opportunity to visit a nearby site, classroom, or school where the innovation is being used.

d. Express a great deal of enthusiasm and involve others who are excited about what they have been doing with the innovation.

e. State realistic expectations about the benefits and costs associated with use.

Interventions, SoC 2. Change facilitators need to be careful in working with persons who have intense personal concerns—misuses can lead to increased concern. In a case where the personal concerns are clearly innovation related, the following types of interventions might be useful:

a. Establish rapport and show signs of encouragement and assurance of personal adequacy through conversations and notes.

b. Encourage innovation use gingerly; do not push unnecessarily.

c. Clarify how the innovation relates to other priorities that potentially conflict in terms of energy and time demands.

d. Show how the innovation can be used via gradual introduction rather than with a major, all-encompassing leap (set reasonable, easy-to-meet expectations).

e. Provide personal support through easy access to the change facilitator or others who can be supportive and of assistance in use of the innovation.

f. Legitimize the expression of personal concerns.

Interventions, SoC 3. Interventions at this time should focus on the "how-to-do-its." Full group demonstrations may not be the most effective method, since many of the concerns are idiosyncratic.

At one research site, the curriculum coordinators and staff developers establish informal, after school "comfort and caring sessions," where teachers experienced with use of the innovation provided advice and assistance to those with specific management concerns (Loucks and Pratt 1979).

Other types of interventions that might be useful include:

a. Acknowledge the appropriateness of management concerns; offer assurance that they can be resolved.

b. Provide answers in ways that easily address the small, specific "how-to" issues that are the cause of concern.

c. Show how the innovation can be coordinated with other aspects of the teacher's day, so that it can be perceived as fitting in, rather than being added on.

d. Have other users share information about their successful and unsuccessful practices.

e. Demonstrate or provide a model for effective use of the innovation, or provide "hands on" materials to practice with.

f. Do planning on one specific task and than have a mail-back in a certain number of weeks.

g. Establish a buddy system/consulting pair or support group.

h. Set a time line for accomplishments of relatively simple and specific tasks.

Interventions, SoC 4. A person with Stage 4 concerns is one with whom all change facilitators want to work. This person's concerns are targeted toward students and quality of use of the innovation. However, change facilitators should not become preoccupied with attending to persons with impact concerns, since their time can be more effectively spent working with those in more need of assistance. A person with impact concerns probably needs little direct assistance, yet they do appreciate recognition and encouragement. Some interventions that might be appropriate are:

a. Encourage and reinforce regularly. An end of the day visit would be beneficial in that the change facilitator can be cheered up, in addition to being of assistance to the teacher.

b. Send written information about topics that might be of interest.

c. Advertise the teacher's potential for sharing skills with others.

d. Send the person to a conference or workshop to refine their use.

Interventions, SoC 5. In many cases, individuals with Stage 5 concerns, by self-nomination or natural selection, end up being leaders of a change effort. Specific types of interventions that can be done to facilitate and encourage Stage 5 concerns include the following:

a. Arrange a meeting between the interested individuals for idea exchange.

b. Use Stage 5 concerned teachers as school-based teacher educators for technical assistance to others.

c. Encourage advocacy and promotion of collaborative concerns by the unit manager (principal or team leader). They can provide verbal encouragement, materials, and/or linkages toward the development of a "collaborative" awareness.

d. Bring in an organizational development expert to work on a regular basis to facilitate development of group process skills and resources.

e. Create opportunities for them to circulate outside their present situation and work with others who may be less knowledgeable.

Interventions, SoC 6. Stage 6 concerned individuals are self-starters and certainly have their own goals. They will have ideas about ways to move the change process further. If the institutional change effort is moving in a direction antagonistic to their opinions and concerns, some fairly directive actions may be necessary to outline the limits within which he or she can deviate from the mainstream. The following interventions might be useful:

a. Help the individuals focus energy into a productive direction for themselves and others.

b. Involve these individuals as trainers of other teachers (although some of our experiences suggest that these individuals may be too divergent to be the most "loyal" trainers).

c. Encourage the individuals to take action with respect to their concerns.

    d.   Provide them with resources to access the other materials they think may help and encourage them to pilot test these to find out if, in fact, they would be of use to others.

Adapted from: Hall, G. E. (1979). The concerns-based approach to facilitating change. *Educational Horizons, 57*(4), 202–208.

References

Note: Papers published by the Research and Development Center for Teacher Education, The University of Texas at Austin, are available from Southwest Educational Development Laboratory, 211 East Seventh Street, Austin, TX, 78701.

Babb, C. W. (1971). *Some selected relationships between the concerns of elementary school teachers and their verbal behavior in the classroom.* Unpublished doctoral dissertation, The University of Texas at Austin.

Baldridge, J. V., and Deal, T. E. (1975). *Managing change in educational organizations.* Berkeley, California: McCutchan Publishing Corporation.

Bandura, A. (1981). Cultivating competence, self-efficacy, and intrinsic interest through proximal self-motivation. *Journal of Personality and Social Psychology, 41*(3), 586–598.

Barucky, J. M. (1984). *Identification and measurement of the personal leadership development concerns of air force officers, cadets, and trainers participating in air force professional military education programs.* Unpublished doctoral dissertation, The University of Texas at Austin.

Bass, B. M. (1960). *Leadership, psychology and organizational behavior.* New York: Harper.

Bass, B. M. (1981). *Stogdill's handbook of leadership, a survey of theory and research* (rev. and expanded ed.). New York: The Free Press.

Bass, B. M., Farrow, D. L., Valenzi, E. R., and Solomon, R. J. (1975). Management styles associated with organizational, task, personal and inter-personal contingencies. *Journal of Applied Psychology, 60*, 720–729.

Bass, B. M., and Valenzi, E. R. (1974). Contingent aspects of effective management styles. In J. G. Hunt and L. L. Larson (eds.), *Contingency approaches to leadership* (pp. 130–155). Carbondale: Southern Illinois University Press.

Bellman, R. (1961). *Adaptive control processes and a guided tour.* Princeton: University Press.

Bellman, R., and Kalba, R. (1958). *On communication process involving learning and random duration.* Santa Monica: The RAND Corporation.

Bellman, R., and Kalba, R. (1959). *On adaptive control processes* (rev. ed.), Santa Monica: The RAND Corporation.

Bernard, L. L. (1926). *An introduction to social psychology.* New York: Holt.

Blake, R. R., and Mouton, J. S. (1964). *The managerial grid.* Houston: Gulf Publishing.

Blake, R. R., and Mouton, J. S. (1976). *Consultation.* Reading, MA: Addison-Wesley Publishing Co.

Blumberg, A., and Greenfield, W. (1980). *The effective principal: Perspectives in school leadership.* Boston: Allyn & Bacon.

Brickell, H. (1961). *Organizing New York State for change.* Albany: State Education Department.

Brickley, S. (1982). *SoCQ and CFSoCQ questionnaire scoring and profile drawing for the Apple micro-computer, program disk and instruction manual.* Available from Stephen Brickley, 305 Anthony Road, King of Prussia, PA, 19406.

Brophy, J. E., and Evertson, C. M. (1978). Context variables in research on teaching. *Educational Psychologist, 12,* 310–316.

Brown, M. B. (1974). *Identification of the source of significance in two-way contingency tables. Applied Statistics Journal of the Royal Statistical Society, 23*(3), 405–413.

Brown, M. B. (1979). *Two-way frequency tables—empty cells and departures from independence.* Los Angeles: University of California Press.

Calder, B. J. (1977). An attribution theory of leadership. In B. M. Straw and G. R. Salancik (eds.), *New directions in organizational behavior.* Chicago: St. Clair Press.

Cohen, M. (1982). Effective schools: Accumulating research findings. *American Education, 18*(1), 13–16.

Corbett, H. D. (1982, November). Principals' contributions to maintaining change. *Phi Delta Kappan, 63*(3), 190–192.

Cotton, K., and Savard, W. G. (1980). *The principal as instructional leader.* Portland, OR: Northwest Regional Educational Laboratory.

Crandall, D. P. (1977). Training and supporting linking agents. In N. Nash and J. Culbertson (eds.), *Linking processes in educational improvement, concepts and applications.* Columbus, OH: University Council for Educational Administration.

Crandall, D. P. (1982). *A study of dissemination efforts supporting school improvement* (vols. 1–10). Andover, MA: The Network.

Cronbach, L. J., and Meehl, P. E. (1955). Construct validity and the psychological testing. *Psychological Bulletin, 52*(4), 281–302.

Cruickshank, D. (1981). What we know about teachers' problems. *Educational Leadership, 38*, 402–405.

Datta, L. (1980). Changing times: The study of federal programs supporting educational change and the case for local problem solving. *Teachers College Record, 82*(1).

Edmonds, R. (1979, October). Effective schools for the urban poor. *Educational Leadership, 37*, 15–27.

Emrick, J. A., and Peterson, S. M. (1978, June). *A synthesis of findings across five recent studies in educational dissemination and change.* San Francisco: Far West Laboratory.

Fege, A. (1980, June). Recovering from the cult of innovation: Reflections on change and improvement. *School Administrator, 37*(6).

Fiedler, F. E. (1967). *A theory of leadership effectiveness.* New York: McGraw-Hill.

Fiedler, F. E. (1978). The contingency model and the dynamics of the leadership process. In L. Berkowitz (ed.), *Advances in experimental social psychology* (pp. 59–112). New York: Academic Press.

Foster, L., and Nixon, M. (1975). The interview reassessed. *The Alberta Journal of Educational Research, 21*(1), 18–22.

Fullan, M. (1982). *The meaning of educational change.* New York: Teachers College Press, Columbia University.

Fullan, M., Miles, M. B., and Taylor, G. (1981, February). *Organizational development in schools: The state of the art.* Washington, DC: National Institute of Education.

Fullan, M., and Pomfret, A. (1977). Research on curriculum and instruction implementation. *Review of Educational Research, 4*(2), 335–393.

Fuller, F. F. (1969). Concerns of teachers: A developmental conceptualization. *American Educational Research Journal, 6*(2), 207–226.

Fuller, F. F. (1973). *Teacher education and the psychology of behavior change: A conceptualization of the process of affective change of preservice teachers* (Report No. 2324). Austin: The University of Texas at Austin, Research and Development Center for Teacher Education.

Fuller, F. F., and Bown, O. H. (1975). Becoming a teacher. In *Teacher education 1975, 74th yearbook of the National Society for the Study of Education.* Chicago: National Society for the Study of Education.

Fuller, F. F., Bown, O. H., and Peck, R. F. (1967). *Creating climates for growth* (Report No. 0002). Austin: The University of Texas at Austin, Research and Development Center for Teacher Education.

Fuller, F. F., and Case, C. (1972). *A manual for scoring the teacher concerns statement* (Report No. 0003). Austin: The University of Texas at Austin, Research and Development Center for Teacher Education. (ERIC Document Reproduction Service No. ED 079 361)

Gabriel, J. (1957). *An analysis of the emotional problems of the teacher in the classroom.* Melbourne, Australia: F. W. Cheshire.

Gallagher, J. J. (1967). Teacher variation in concept presentation in BSCS curriculum programs. *BSCS Newsletter, 30.*

Gardner, J. (1964). *Self renewal: The individual and the innovative society.* New York: Harper & Row.

George, A. A. (1978). *Measuring self, task and impact concerns: A manual for use of the teacher concerns questionnaire* (Report No. 3067). Austin: The University of Texas at Austin, Research and Development Center for Teacher Education. (ERIC Document Reproduction Service No. ED 175 845)

Ginn Reading Program. (1984). *Implementation checklist.* Lexington, MA: Ginn & Company.

Glasser, W. (1969). *Schools without failure*. New York: Harper & Row.

Goldstein, M. L., and Rutherford, W. L. (1982). *Methodologies for documenting interventions: Strengths of a hybrid/multi-informant approach* (Report No. 3136). Austin: The University of Texas at Austin, Research and Development Center for Teacher Education. (ERIC Document Reproduction Service No. 221 598)

Guba, E., and Clark, D. C. (1976). *Research on institutions of teacher education. Vol. III: An institutional self-report on knowledge production and utilization activities in schools, colleges and departments of education.* Bloomington, IN: RITE Project.

Hall, G. E., George, A., Griffin, T., Hord, S., Loucks, S. F., Melle, M., Metzdorf, J., Pratt, H., and Winters, S. (1980). *Making change happen: A case study of school district implementation* (Report No. 3103). Austin: The University of Texas at Austin, Research and Development Center for Teacher Education. (ERIC Document Reproduction Service No. ED 250 162)

Hall, G. E., George, A., and Rutherford, W. L. (1979). *Measuring stages of concern about the innovation: A manual for use of the SoC questionnaire.* (Report No. 3032). Austin: The University of Texas at Austin, Research and Development Center for Teacher Education. (ERIC Document Reproduction Service No. ED 147 342)

Hall, G. E., and Griffin, T. H. (1982). *Analysis of the context/climate in school settings—Which is which?* (Report No. 3139). Austin: The University of Texas at Austin, Research and Development Center for Teacher Education. (ERIC Document Reproduction Service No. ED 222 513)

Hall, G. E., and Hord, S. M. (1984, March). A framework for analyzing what change facilitators do: The intervention taxonomy. *Knowledge: Creation, Diffusion, Utilization, 5*(3), 275–307.

Hall, G. E., Hord, S. M., and Griffin, T. H. (1980). *Implementation at the school building level: The development and analysis of nine mini-case studies* (Report No. 3098). Austin: The University of Texas at Austin, Research and Development Center for Teacher Education. (ERIC Document Reproduction Service No. ED 207 170)

Hall, G. E., Hord, S. M., Guzman, F., Huling-Austin, L., Rutherford, W. L. and Stiegelbauer, S. M. (1984). *The improvement process in high schools: form function and a few surprises.* Austin: The University of Texas at Austin Research and Development Center for Teacher Education.

Hall, G. E., Hord, S. M., Huling, L. L., Rutherford, W. L., and Stiegelbauer, S. (1983). *Leadership variables associated with successful school improvement* (Report No. 3164). Austin: The University of Texas at Austin, Research and Development Center for Teacher Education.

Hall, G. E., and Loucks, S. F. (1977 Summer). A developmental model for determining whether the treatment is actually implemented. *American Educational Research Journal, 14*,(3), 263–276.

Hall, G. E., and Loucks, S. F. (1978). *Innovation configurations: Analyzing the adaptations of innovations* (Report No. 3049). Austin: The University of Texas at Austin, Research and Development Center for Teacher Education.

Hall, G. E., and Loucks, S. F. (1981 Winter). Program definition and adaptation: Implications for inservice. *Journal of Research and Development in Education, 14*,(2), 46–58.

Hall, G. E., Loucks, S. F., Rutherford, W. L., and Newlove, B. W. (1975). Levels of use of the innovation: A framework for analyzing innovation adoption. *Journal of Teacher Education, 26*(1), 52–56.

Hall, G. E., and Pratt, H. (1984 April). *There really can be a symbiotic relationship between researchers and practitioners: The marriage of a national r&d center and a large school district* (Report No. 3189; award winning paper in the "Contributions to Relating Research to Practice: Professional Service" category, presented at the Annual American Educational Research Association at New Orleans, LA). Austin: The University of Texas at Austin, Research and Development Center for Teacher Education. (ERIC Document Reproduction Service No. ED 250 816)

Hall, G. E., and Rutherford, W. L. (1976). concerns of teachers about implementing team teaching. *Educational Leadership, 34*(3), 227–233.

Hall, G. E., and Rutherford, W. L. (1983). *Three change facilitator styles: How principals affect improvement efforts* (Report No. 3155). Austin: The University of Texas at Austin, Research and Development Center for Teacher Education.

Hall, G. E., Rutherford, W. L., and Griffin, T. H. (1982). *Three change facilitator styles: Some indicators and a proposed framework* (Report No. 3134). Austin: The University of Texas at Austin, Research and Development Center for Teacher Education. (ERIC Document Reproduction Service No. ED 220 961)

Hall, G. E., Rutherford, W. L., Hord, S. M., and Huling-Austin, L. L. (1984 February). Effects of three principal styles on school improvement. *Educational Leadership, 41*(5), 22–29.

Hall, G. E., Wallace, R. C., and Dossett, W. A. (1973). *A developmental conceptualization of the adoption process within educational institutions* (Report No. 3006). Austin: The University of Texas at Austin, Research and Development Center for Teacher Education. (ERIC Document Reproduction Service No. ED 095 126)

Halpin, A. W. (1957). Manual for the leader behavior description questionnaire. Columbus: Ohio State University, Bureau of Business Research.

Halpin, A. W., and Winer, B. J. (1957). A factorial study of the leader behavior descriptions. In R. M. Stogdill and A. E. Coons (eds.), *Leader behavior: Its description and measurement.* Columbus, OH: Ohio State University, Bureau of Business Research.

Hardy, G. (1977). *The impact the concerns of cooperating teachers have on the concerns of student teachers.* Unpublished doctoral dissertation, The University of Houston, Texas.

Hardy, G. (1978). *The cooperating teacher: A most critical factor in teacher education.* Paper presented at the annual meeting of the American Educational Research Association, Toronto, Canada.

Havelock, R. G. (1971). *Planning for innovation through dissemination and utilization of knowledge.* Ann Arbor: University of Michigan, Institute for Social Research.

Havelock, R. G. (1973a). *The change agent's guide to innovation in education.* Englewood Cliffs, NJ: Educational Technology Publications.

Havelock, R. G. (1973b). *Training for change agents.* Ann Arbor: University of Michigan, Institute for Social Research.

Heck, S., Stiegelbauer, S. M., Hall, G. E., and Loucks, S. F. (1981). *Measuring innovation configurations: Procedures and applications* (Report

No. 3108). Austin: The University of Texas at Austin, Research and Development Center for Teacher Education. (ERIC Document Reproduction Service No. ED 204 147)

Hersey, P., and Blanchard, K. H. (1977). *Management of organizational behavior: Utilizing human resources* (3d ed.). Englewood Cliffs, NJ: Prentice-Hall.

Hill, T. E., and Schmitt, N. (1977). Individual differences in leadership decision making. *Organizational behavior and human performance, 19*, 353–367.

Hill, W. A. (1973). Leadership style: Rigid or flexible? *Organizational Behavior and Human Performance, 9*, 35–47.

Hill, W. A., and Hughes, D. (1974). Variations in leader behavior in a function of task type. *Organizational Behavior and Human Performance, 11*, 83–96.

Hord, S. M. (1981). *Analyzing administrator intervention behaviors* (Report No. 3127). Austin: The University of Texas at Austin, Research and Development Center for Teacher Education. (ERIC Document Reproduction Service No. ED 231 060)

Hord, S. M., and Goldstein, M. (1982). *What does the principal do to facilitate change: Their interventions* (Report No. 3132). Austin: The University of Texas at Austin, Research and Development Center for Teacher Education. (ERIC Document Reproduction Service No. ED 220 962)

Hord, S. M., and Hall, G. E. (1982). *Procedures for quantitative analysis of change facilitator interventions* (Report No. 3138). Austin: The University of Texas at Austin, Research and Development Center for Teacher Education. (ERIC Document Reproduction Service No. ED 224 807)

Hord, S. M., Hall, G. E., and Zigarmi, P. (1980). *Anatomy of incident and tactic interventions* (Report No. 3138). Austin: The University of Texas at Austin, Research and Development Center for Teacher Education. (ERIC Document Reproduction Service No. ED 206 108)

Hord, S. M., Huling, L. L., and Stiegelbauer, S. M. (1983). *An analysis of interventions in school improvement efforts* (Report No. 3156). Austin: The University of Texas at Austin, Research and Development Center for Teacher Education.

Hord, S. M. and Huling-Austin, L. L. (1985, Summer). Preparing administrators to be effective facilitators of school improvement. *Inservice.* New York: National Council of States on Inservice Education, Syracuse University.

Hord, S. M. and Huling-Austin, L. (1985, December). Acquiring expertise. *The Diabetes Educator. 11* (Special issue), 13–20.

Hord, S. M., and Huling-Austin, L. (October, 1986). Effective curriculum implementation: Some promising new insights. *Elementary School Journal,* 87(1), 97–115.

Hord, S. M. and Murphy, S. C. (1985). *The high school department head: Powerful or powerless in guiding change?* (Report No. 3210). Austin: The University of Texas at Austin, Research and Development Center for Teacher Education.

Hord, S. M. and Rutherford, W. L. (1985, October-November). Dogs can't sing? Good news, a dash of optimism and high school change. *The High School Journal, 69* (1), 16–20.

Hord, S. M., Stiegelbauer, S. M., and Hall, G. E. (1984, November). How principals work with other change facilitators. *Education and Urban Society, 17,*(1), 89–109.

Hord, S. M. and Thurber, J. C. (forthcoming). Helping principals use tools to support leadership roles in school improvement. In K. Leithwood, W. Rutherford, and R. Van der Vegt (eds.) *Preparing Principals for School Improvement: An International Perspective.* London: Croom-Helm.

House, E. R. (1974). *The politics of educational innovation.* Berkeley: McCutchen.

House, R. J. (1971). A path-goal theory of leader effectiveness. *Administrative Science Quarterly, 16,* 321–338.

Howell, B. (1981, January). Profile of the principalship. *Educational Leadership, 38,*(4), 333–336.

Hrebar, C., and Pratt, H. (1983). Elementry science program. In J. Penick (ed.), *Focus on excellence: Elementary science.* Washington, DC: National Science Teachers Association.

Huberman, M. (1981). *ECRI, Masepa, North Plans: A case study.* Andover, MA: The Network.

Huling, L. L., Hall, G. E., Hord, S. M., and Rutherford, W. L. (1983). *A multi-dimensional approach for assessing implementation success* (Report No. 3157). Austin: The University of Texas at Austin, Research and Development Center for Teacher Education. (ERIC Document Reproduction Service No. ED 250 328)

Isherwood, E. G. (1973, March). The principal and his authority: An empirical study. *High School Journal, 56,* 291–303.

Jago, A. G. (1982, March). Leadership: Perspectives in theory and research. *Management Science, 28,* 315–336.

Jago, A. G., and Vroom, V. H. (1977). Hierarchical level and leadership style. *Organizational Behavior and Human Performance, 18,* 131–145.

James, L. R., and Jones, A. P. (1974). Organizational climate: A review of theory and research. *Psychological Bulletin, 81*(12), 1096–1112.

Janis, I. L., and Mann, L. (1976). Coping with decisional conflict: An analysis of how stress affects decision-making and suggests interventions to improve the process. *American Scientist, 64,* 657–666.

Johnson, D. W., and Johnson, R. T. (1975). *Learning together and alone: Cooperation, competition and individualization.* Englewood Cliffs, NJ: Prentice-Hall.

Jones, A. P., James, L. R., Bruni, J. R., Hornick, C. W., and Sells, S. B. (1979). Psychological climate: Dimensions and relationships of individual and aggregated work environment perceptions. *Organizational Behavior and Human Performance, 23,* 201–259.

Jordan-Marsh, M. (1984). *Development of a tool for diagnosing changes in levels of concern about exercise: A means of enhancing compliance.* Los Angeles: School of Nursing, University of California at Los Angeles.

Kolb, S. E. (1983). *Development and application of a questionnaire for assessing stages of concern among nurses.* Unpublished doctoral dissertation, The University of Texas at Austin.

Leithwood, K. A., and Montgomery, D. (1982). The role of the elementary school principal in program improvement. *Review of Educational Research, 52*(3), 309–339.

Leithwood, K. J., Ross, J., Montgomery, D. and Maynes, F. (1978). *An empirical investigation of teacher's curriculum decision making processes and strategies used by curriculum decision managers to influence such decision making.* Toronto, Canada: Ontario Institute for Studies in Education.

Lieberman, A., and Miller, L. (1981). Synthesis of research on improving schools. *Educational Leadership, 38*(7), 583–586.

Lipham, J. M. (1981). *Effective principal, effective school.* Reston, VA: National Association of Elementary School Principals.

Little, J. (1981). *School success and staff development in urban segregated schools.* Paper presented at the annual meeting of the Southwest Educational Research Association, Dallas.

Loucks, S. F. (1975). *A study of the relationship between teacher level of use of the innovation of individualized instruction and student achievement.* Unpublished doctoral dissertation, The University of Texas at Austin.

Loucks, S. F., and Melle, M. (1980, April). *Implementation of a district-wide science curriculum: The effects of a three year effort.* Paper presented at the annual meeting of the American Educational Research Association, Boston.

Loucks, S. F., Newlove, B. H., and Hall, G. E. (1975). *Measuring levels of use of the innovation: A manual for trainers, interviewers and raters* (Report No. 3013). Austin: The University of Texas at Austin, Research and Development Center for Teacher Education.

Loucks, S. F., and Pratt, H. (1979). A concerns-based approach to curriculum change. *Educational Leadership, 37*(3), 212–215.

Louis, K. S., and Rosenblum, S. (1981, July). *Designing and managing interorganizational networks.* Washington, DC: U.S. Department of Education, National Institute of Education.

Marsh, D. D., and Jordan-Marsh, M. (1985, April). *Addressing teachers' personal concerns in staff development efforts.* Paper presented at the annual meeting of the American Educational Research Association, Chicago.

Martin, W. J. (1980). *The managerial behavior of high school principals.* Unpublished doctoral dissertation, Pennsylvania State University.

McCall, M. W., and Lombardo, M. M. (eds.). (1978). *Leadership: Where else can we go?* Durham, NC: Duke University Press.

McNally, H. J. (1974, September-October). National elementary principal. *Summing Up, 74*(1), 56–65.

Melle, M., and Pratt, H. (1981, April). *documenting program adaptation in a district-wide implementation effort: The three-year evolution from evaluation to an instructional improvement plan.* Paper presented at the annual meeting of the American Educational Research Association at Los Angeles.

Miles, M. B. (ed.). (1971). *Innovation in education.* New York: Columbia University.

Morris, V. C. (1981). *The urban principal: Discretionary decision-making in a large educational organization.* Chicago: University of Illinois.

Mort, P. R. (1953). Educational adaptability. *The School Executive, 71,* 1–23.

Murphy, S. C. and Hord, S. M. (1985). A pathway to instructional improvement: Priming the territory. In E. Ducharme and D. Fleming (eds.), *Rural and Small School Principalship.* Chelmsford, Massachusetts: Northeast Regional Exchange.

Nash, N., and Culbertson, J. (1977). Introduction. In N. Nash and J. Culbertson (eds.), *Linking processes in educational improvement* (pp. 1–5). Columbus, OH: University Council for Educational Administration.

National Diffusion Network, (NDN), Department of Education. (1980). *Educational programs that work.* San Francisco: Far West Laboratory of Educational Research.

Newlove, B. W. (1978). *The use of training tapes, supplementary to the manual: Measuring levels of use of the innovation.* Austin: The University of Texas at Austin, Research and Development Center for Teacher Education.

Newlove, B. W., and Hall, G. E. (1976). *A manual for assessing open-ended statements of concern about an innovation* (Report No. 3029). Austin: The University of Texas at Austin, Research and Development Center for Teacher Education. (ERIC Document Reproduction Service No. ED 144 207)

Paul, D. A. (1977). Change processes at the elementary, secondary, and post-secondary levels of education. In N. Nash and J. Culbertson (eds.) *Linking processes in educational improvements: Concepts and applications.* Columbus, Ohio: University Council for Educational Administration.

Parker, E. W., and Griffin, T. H. (1979). *A quick scoring device for the Stages of Concern questionnaire* (Report No. 3079). Austin: The University of Texas at Austin, Research and Development Center for Teacher Education.

Parker, J. C., and Rubin, L. J. (1966). *Process as content curriculum design and the application of knowledge.* Chicago: Rand McNally.

Patinka, P. G. (1979). One more time: Are leaders born or made? In J. G. Hunt and L. L. Larson (eds.), *Crosscurrents in leadership* (pp. 33–39). Carbondale: Southern Illinois University Press.

Pedulla, J. J., and Reidy, E. F., Jr. (1980). *Evidence of effectiveness of the skills achievement monitoring program.* Fitchburg, MA: Fitchburg Public Schools.

Persell, C. H., and Cookson, P. W., Jr. (1982). The effective prncipal in action. In *The effective principal; A research summary* (pp. 22–29). Reston, VA: National Association of Secondary School Principals.

Phillips, M. (1932). Some problems of adjustment in the early years of a teachers life. *British Journal of Educational Psychology, 2,* 237–256.

Pratt, H., Winters, S., and George, A. (1980, April). *Effects of a concerns-based implementation plan on the achievement of elementary science students.* Paper presented at the Annual Meeting of the American Educational Research Association at Boston.

Rand Change Agent Study—Federal Programs Supporting Educational Change:
    Vol. I, Berman, P., and McLaughlin, M. W. (1974, September). *A model of educational change.* R-158911-HEW.
    Vol. II, Berman, P., and Pauly, E. W. (1975a, April). *Factors affecting change agent projects.* R-158912-HEW.
    Vol. III, Greenwood, P. W., Mann, D., and McLaughlin, M. W. (1975b, April). *The process of change.* R-158913-HEW.
    Vol. IV, Berman, P., and McLaughlin, M. W. (1975c, April). *The findings in review.* R-158914-HEW.
    Vol. V, Berman, P., Greenwood, P. W., McLaughlin, M. W., and Pincus, J. (1975, April). *Executive summary,* R-158915-HEW.
    Vol. VI, Sumner, G., and Zellman, G. (1977, January). *Implementing and sustaining Title VII bilingual projects.* Title VII, R-158916-HEW.

Vol. VII, Berman, P., and McLaughlin, M. W. (1977, April). *Factors affecting implementation and continuation.* R-158917-HEW.

Vol. VIII, Berman, P., and McLaughlin, M. W. (1978, May). *Implementing and sustaining innovations.* R-158918-HEW.

Reid, E. R. (1980). Exemplary Center for Reading Instruction (ECRI). *Educational programs that work.* San Francisco: Far West Laboratory for Educational Research and Development.

Reidy, E. F., Jr., and Hord, S. M. (1979). *Utilizing implementation data in the evaluation of a mathematics skills achievement monitoring program.* Austin: The University of Texas at Austin, Research and Development Center for Teacher Education.

Reinhard, D. L., Arends, R. A., Kutz, W., Lovell, K., and Wyant, S. (1980). *Great expectations: The principal's role and inservice needs in supporting change projects.* Paper presented at the annual meeting of the American Educational Research Association, Boston.

Roecks, A. L., and Andrews, J. H. (1980). *Levels of use interviews: A successful formative evaluation tool.* San Antonio, TX: Education Service Center, Region 20.

Roecks, A. L., and Noonan, A. J. (1981). *Research and evaluation in regional education agencies: A Texas perspective.* San Antonio, TX: Education Service Center, Region 20.

Rogers, E. M., and Shoemaker, F. F. (1971). *Communication of innovations: A cross cultural approach* (2nd ed.). New York: Free Press.

Ross, D. H. (ed.). (1951). *Administration for adaptability: A source book drawing together the results of twelve years' study of the adoption process in education and of the adaptability of school systems.* New York: Columbia University.

Rutherford, W. L. (1981, April). *Team teaching—How do teachers use it?* (Report No. 3017). Austin: The University of Texas at Austin, Research and Development Center for Teacher Education. (ERIC Document Reproduction Service No. ED 251 427)

Rutherford, W. L. (1985, September). School principals as effective leaders. *Phi Delta Kappan, 69*(1), 31–34.

Rutherford, W. L., Hall, G. E., and George, A. S. (1982). *An instrument for measuring the concerns change facilitators have about their role in guiding change* (Report No. 3144). Austin: The University of Texas at Austin, Research and Development Center for Teacher Education (ERIC Document Reprotuction Service No. ED 221 600)

Rutherford, W. L., Hall, G. E., and Newlove, B. W. (1982). *Describing the concerns principals have about facilitating change* (Report No. 3131). Austin: The University of Texas at Austin, Research and Development Center for Teacher Education. (ERIC Document Reproduction Service No. ED 220 960)

Rutherford, W. L., Hord, S. M., Huling, L. L., and Hall, G. E. (1983). *Change facilitators: In search of understanding their role* (Report No. 3159). Austin: The University of Texas at Austin, Research and Development Center for Teacher Education. (ERIC Document Reproduction Service No. ED 250 801)

Rutter, M., Maughan, B., Mortimore, P., and Ouston, J. (1979). *Fifteen thousand hours: Secondary schools and their effects on children.* CA: McCutchan.

Salley, C., McPherson, R. B., and Baehr, M. E. (1979). What principals do: A preliminary occupational analysis. In D. A. Erickson and T. L. Reller (eds.), *The principal in metropolitan schools.* Berkeley, CA: McCutchan.

Sarason, B. (1971). *The culture of the school and the problem of change.* Boston: Allyn and Bacon.

Schmuck, R. A., and Miles, M. B. (1971). *Organization development in schools.* La Jolla, CA: University Associates.

Schmuck, R. A., Runkel, P. J., Arends, J. H., and Arends, R. I. (1977). *The second handbook of organizational development in schools.* Eugene, OR: Center for Educational Policy and Management.

Simon, S. B., Howe, L. W., Kirschenbaum, H. (1972). *Values clarification: A handbook of practical strategies for teachers and students.* New York: Hart Publishing Co.

Sproull, L. S. (1977). *Management attention in new education programs: A micro-behavioral study of program implementation.* Unpublished doctoral dissertation, Stanford University.

Sproull, L. S. (1981). Managing education programs: A micro-behavioral analysis. *Human Organization, 40*(2), 113–122.

Stallings, J. (1982). *How does the principal's leadership style and school policy enhance effective basic skills schooling?* Paper presented at the annual meeting of the Southwest Educational Development Laboratory, Austin, Texas.

Stallings, J., and Mohlman, G. (1981). *School policy, leadership style, teacher change and student behavior in eight secondary schools.*

Report prepared for the National Institute of Education. Mountain View, CA: Stallings Teaching and Learning Institute.

Stewart, R. (1982). the relevance of some studies of managerial work and behavior to leadership research. In J. G. Hunt, U. Sekaran, and C. A. Schriesheim (eds.), *Leadership beyond establishment views* (pp. 11–30). Carbondale: Southern Illinois University Press.

Tannenbaum, R., and Schmidt, W. H. (1958). How to choose a leadership pattern. *Harvard Business Review, 36,* 95–101.

Tead, O. (1929). The technique of creative leadership. In O. Tead (ed.), *Human nature and management.* New York: McGraw-Hill.

Thomas, M. A. (1978). *a study of alternatives in American education.* Vol. II: *The role of the principal.* Santa Monica, CA: Rand Corp.

Thompson, M. L. (1963). Identifying anxieties experienced by student teacher. *Journal of Teacher Education, 114,* 435–439.

Travers, R. M. W., Rabinowitz, W., and Nemovicher, E. (1952). The anxieties of a group of student teachers. *Educational Administration and Supervision, 38,* 368–375.

Treadway, Peter G. (1980). *Functional analysis of educational programs.* Paper prepared for the annual meeting of the American Educational Research Association, Boston.

Tye, K. A. (1972). The school principal: Key man in educational change. *National Association of Secondary School Principals Bulletin, 56,* 77–84.

Van den Berg, R., and Vandenberghe, R. (1981). *Onderwijsinnovatie in verschuivend perspectief.* Amsterdam: Uitgeverij Zwijsen.

Van der Perre. (1984). *Principals as change facilitators: The role of the elementary school principal in Belgium.* Leuven, Belgium: The Catholic University.

Venezky, R., and Winfield, L. (1979). *Schools that succeed beyond expectations in teaching reading.* Newark, DE: University of Delaware.

Vroom, V. H., and Yetton, P. W. (1973). *Leadership and decision-making.* Pittsburgh, PA: University of Pittsburg Press.

Watkins, J. E., and Holley, F. M. (1975). *Technical report: Individually guided education (IGE) program* (Pub. No. 106.56). Austin, TX: Office of Research and Evaluation, Austin Independent School District.

Wolcott, H. F. (1973). *The man in the principal's office: An ethnography.* New York: Holt, Rinehart and Winston.

Zigarmi, P., and Goldstein, M. L. (1979). *A mapping technique for analysis of ethnographic data and its contribution to the development of a theory of innovation implementation* (Report No. 3083). Austin: The University of Texas at Austin, Research and Development Center for Teacher Education. (ERIC Document Reproduction Service No. ED 190 630)

Index